THE NEW AMERICAN SONGSTER

Traditional Ballads and Songs of North America

Compiled and edited by

Charles W. Darling

Youngstown State University

UNIVERSITY
PRESS OF
AMERICA

LANHAM • NEW YORK • LONDON

Copyright © 1983 by

University Press of America,™ Inc.

4720 Boston Way
Lanham, MD 20706

3 Henrietta Street
London WC2E 8LU England

Printed in the United States of America

ISBN (Perfect): 0-8191-3397-3
ISBN (Cloth): 0-8191-3396-5

Library of Congress Catalog Card Number: 83-14584

Dedicated to Anne for putting
up with me and to the late Paul
Clayton for putting me in touch
with the music of the people.

ACKNOWLEDGEMENTS

The editor expresses his hearty thanks to all those who have contributed to this work. From the Youngstown State University History Department they include: Dr. Saul Friedman for his initial encouragement and advice, Mr. John Axe for his generous editorial assistance, and Mrs. Susan Fogaras for her expert secretarial skills in preparing the final camera-ready manuscript. Appreciation is extended to Mr. William Beil and the staff of the Media Center at Youngstown State University for the camera-ready preparation of all photographs, and to Mr. James E. Lyons and Ms. Helen Hudson of University Press of America for their efforts.

The proprietors of two recording companies deserve special recognition. Sandy and Caroline Paton of Folk-Legacy Records permitted the reprinting of numerous song lyrics from their fascinating and significant output of folk albums. They also supplied many of the photographs. The pioneering genius of Folkways Records, Moses Asch, who has preserved much of our folk music heritage for the enjoyment of both current and future generations, authorized the use of lyrics from various albums in his extensive catalogue.

Kind thanks are extended to Ms. Hedy West for permission to reprint many of her songs, and to Mrs. Ruth Barron of Youngstown for authorization to include two ballads learned from her mother and grandmother. Finally, to Molly Jackson, Paul Clayton, Logan English, Pete Seeger, Alan Lomax and those thousands of unnamed, or unknown, composers, singers and collectors who have made life more beneficial, meaningful and enjoyable for many of us, I thank them one and all!

A concerted effort was made to acknowledge the authors, or collectors, of the lyrics printed in this anthology. If anyone was overlooked, I assure them it was inadvertent and offer my sincere apologies.

C. W. D.
Youngstown, Ohio
June, 1983

C O N T E N T S

ILLUSTRATIONS

CHAPTER ONE

FOLK MUSIC AND THE FOLK PROCESS

There are various ways of studying the history of a nation or region. One can concentrate on political events, examine economic episodes, survey social and cultural phenomena, but in most cases these efforts fail to reach the so-called "common men and women," people who may not be so common. This book is about these people: those who endure war, depression, inflation and personal tragedy. They are the people who Walt Whitman eulogized in Leaves of Grass, Carl Sandburg described in Chicago Poems, John Steinbeck wrote about in The Grapes of Wrath, Woody Guthrie knew in "Dust Bowl Refugees" and Studs Terkel interviewed for Working.

The method used to study these people is indirect. It is a collection of some of the ballads and songs they sang, composed and enjoyed--a stirring of the folk juices of North America. These songs reveal a great deal about their owners--their loves, their hates, their faith, their integrity and even their humor.

The music is limited to the Anglo-Scots-Irish-African tradition, the source of practically all North American folk music in English. The separate musical heritages of the Indian, Eskimo, French and Spanish cultures need study as well, but are not addressed within the confines of this survey. Additional volumes will be required.

DEFINITIONS AND EXPLANATIONS

The novice may ask: what exactly is folk music? Definitions vary. There is the vague explanation attributed to the bluesman Big Bill Broonzy: "All the songs I ever heard in my life was folksongs. I never heard horses sing none of them, yet."[1] An unknown traditional singer from the Southern Appalachians put it this way: "These songs are so full of the way we live

---

[1] See Pete Seeger, The Incompleat Folksinger (New York: Simon and Shuster, 1972), p. 62 for a similar quotation attributed to Broonzy. Others cite Louis Armstrong as the author.

1

and the way we think and speak, that it don't take no
fancy mind work to make it come out right."[1] The International Folk Music Council offered a more explicit definition:

> Folk music is the product of a musical
> tradition that has been evolved through the
> process of oral transmission. The factors
> that shape the tradition are: (i) continuity
> which links the present with the past; (ii)
> variation which springs from the creative
> impulse of the individual or the group; and
> (iii) selection by the community which deter-
> mines the form or forms in which the music
> survives.
>
> The term can be applied to music that has
> been evolved from rudimentary beginnings by
> a community uninfluenced by popular and art
> music and it can likewise be applied to music
> which has originated with an individual composer
> and has subsequently been absorbed into the
> unwritten living tradition of a community.
>
> The term does not cover composed popular
> music that has been taken over ready-made by
> a community and remains unchanged, for it is
> the re-fashioning and re-creation of the music
> by the community that gives it its folk
> character.[2]

British folk collector and singer A. L. Lloyd en-
dorsed the Council's position, but stressed variation
within the tradition:

> A song may be born into a tradition that
> fits a certain society; but as that society
> changes, as the folk change, the song may
> change too. A folk song tradition is not a
> fixed and immutable affair, and the word
> "authenticity," favourite among amateurs of
> folk music, is one to use with caution. Tra-
> ditionalists are always disturbed by the appear-

---

[1]Source unknown.

[2]Journal of the International Folk Music Council
(London), VII (1955), p. 23.

ance of novelties on the folklore scene, but
in any living tradition novelties are con-
stantly emerging, often in tiny almost imper-
ceptible details that accumulate over long
periods of time and suddenly, when the social
moment is ripe, come together to result in a
change that may be drastic.[1]

There are dozens of other definitions and explana-
tions, but the essential ingredient seems to be the re-
shaping and restructuring of the music by the folk.
This is the heart of the folk process of continuity and
change.

"Ballad" is another term requiring clarification.
A ballad is simply a folksong that tells a story. The
problem here is not the definition, but the point at
which the song begins to tell a story. Even before the
late nineteenth century when the Harvard scholar Francis
James Child established such rigorous standards that
only 305 English and Scottish ballads were admitted to
his canon, experts had been squabbling over the exact
point at which a folksong becomes a story-song.
MacEdward Leach in The Ballad Book believed that, in
addition to story telling, a ballad must be dramatic
with special concentration paid to the climax of the
story. Other distinguishing features include the use of
first person dialogue and an objective and impersonal
approach.

Another compiler, G. Malcolm Laws, relaxed Child's
standards, especially in the area of subjectivity so
that 314 British broadside ballads found in North American tradition, but not in Child, could be included in
American Balladry from British Broadsides. Laws used
similar criteria in his other major work, Native American Balladry.

Both the compilations by Child and Laws have flaws.
For example, several of the so-called native American
ballads in Laws have close connections with earlier
British broadsides. And again, arbitrary editing by
both scholars excluded some ballads and included others
for no apparent reason except the whim of the respective
editor. For those interested in pursuing further the
criticism of ballad classification, read Anglo-American

---

[1]A. L. Lloyd, Folk Song In England (New York:
International Publishers, 1967), pp. 69-70.

3

Folksong Scholarship Since 1898 by D. K. Wilgus. In spite of these objections, this book follows in general the Child system in Chapter Two and the Laws classification in Chapters Three and Four. This enables the reader to refer to these standard works for further information if desired. As for the songs in Chapters Five and Six, they are organized along my own guide lines.

Folk music--ballad or song--is not popular music, although a popular song may become a folksong in time. Thus the songs of such folk-oriented composers as Bob Dylan, Don McLean, Gordon Lightfoot, Hazel Dickens and Arlo Guthrie are not folksongs, at least not yet. They may become folk music in the future, but only if the folk accept them into their tradition. Folk music was not necessarily the popular music of past generations, neither was folk music separate from it. Ray B. Browne, in his introduction to Folksongs and Their Makers, explains:

> The folklore that lasts is the creative acts of single individuals and the recreative acts of many persons--the mass of the folk. Larry Gorman, Woody Guthrie, and others of their kind, were creative geniuses who were of the folk. The material they created was from and of the folk, contained characteristics easily taken up and possessed by the folk. But these individuals were active creators. The mass of the folk, on the other hand, are passive recreators. The material they accept and recreate must be their kind of lore. They do not simply absorb indiscriminately the popular culture and recreate it in their own image. To a certain extent popular culture becomes so much a part of society at large and therefore so cliched that unwittingly the folk absorb it--through the pores, as it were. But such lore is once removed from popular culture. Generally, therefore, although much of the stimulus for the creation of folklore might come from popular culture or from the same sources popular culture comes from, folklore and popular culture are born through similar but separate channels.[1]

---

[1]Henry Glassie, Edward D. Ives, John F. Szwed, Folksongs and Their Makers (Bowling Green, Ohio: Bowling Green University Popular Press, 1971), vii.

However, Browne cautions that these two channels are not isolated, but have an indefinite connection to each other.

There is one final question that is continually asked: when did folk music die? Folk music was dead in the eighteenth century, in the nineteenth and again in the twentieth--at least in the estimation of contemporary collectors. It is all nonsense! Today, in spite of all obstacles--books, motion pictures, radio, television, computer games--folk music is alive and well.

The purpose of this book is not to examine dead specimens, but to encourage the exploration of the living music of the people. This concept of a living and developing folk process is the reason this book features musical examples from recent recordings where possible. It may be true that "purer" and more "poetic" texts are available, but by printing works from current recordings along with the necessary discography the reader can obtain the music and hear it. This is vital, for folk music is not meant to be read, but heard, enjoyed and sung! If this book accomplishes that end then it has served its purpose.

THE FOLK PROCESS ILLUSTRATED

The folk process is the key to understanding the songs that follow. It involves the transmission of a song from person to person, removing frills or adding new ones, changing words and word patterns, revitalizing the song for a new generation, until there emerges a song similar to, but unlike, the original.

One way to explain the folk process is to take one group of songs and trace the family tree from tap root to branches. One of the most famous ballads to undergo such scrutiny is "The Unfortunate Rake" listed as Q-26 in G. Malcolm Laws, American Balladry from British Broadsides, under the title "The Bad Girl's Lament," and B-1, "The Cowboy's Lament," in Laws, Native American Balladry. The ballad goes back in print to at least 1848 when a folklorist collected it from an Irish singer who had learned it in Dublin, Ireland, in 1790. The earliest complete texts were printed as broadsides in England and Ireland during the nineteenth century. (A broadside was a sheet of paper, printed on one side, containing the words to a song or songs and sold to the public for a penny or half-penny apiece.) It is probable that even earlier antecendents of the ballad describe the "hero" as a member of the armed forces since the request for a military funeral is a feature of most variants.

The following nineteenth century broadside probably is close enough to the original ballad to qualify it as the source of "The Unfortunate Rake" cycle. A. L. Lloyd sings it on the informative Folkways album The Unfortunate Rake, FS 3805, edited by Kenneth S. Goldstein (used by permission of Folkways Records).

THE UNFORTUNATE RAKE

1 As I was a-walking down by St. James' Hospital,
I was a-walking down by there one day,
What should I spy but one of my comrades
All wrapped up in flannel though warm was the day.

2 I asked him what ailed him, I asked him what failed him,
I asked him the cause of all his complaint.
"It's all on account of some handsome young woman,
'Tis she that has caused me to weep and lament.

3 "And had she but told me before she disordered me,
Had she but told me of it in time,
I might have got pills and salts of white mercury,
But now I'm cut down in the height of my prime.

4 "Get six young soldiers to carry my coffin,
Six young girls to sing me a song,
And each of them carry a bunch of green laurel
So they don't smell me as they bear me along.

5 "Don't muffle your drums and play your fifes merrily,
Play a quick march as you carry me along,
And fire your bright muskets all over my coffin,
Saying: "There goes an unfortunate lad to his home'."

The "salts of white mercury" referred to in the song was the basic treatment for venereal disease in those days. Another variant, "The Trooper Cut Down In His Prime," was popular among members of the British army and dates to the Boer War, 1899-1902. The "flash girls" mentioned are street girls or prostitutes. Sung by Ewan MacColl on The Unfortunate Rake, Folkways FA 3805 (used by permission of Folkways Records.

THE FOLK PROCESS - A BALLAD'S FAMILY TREE

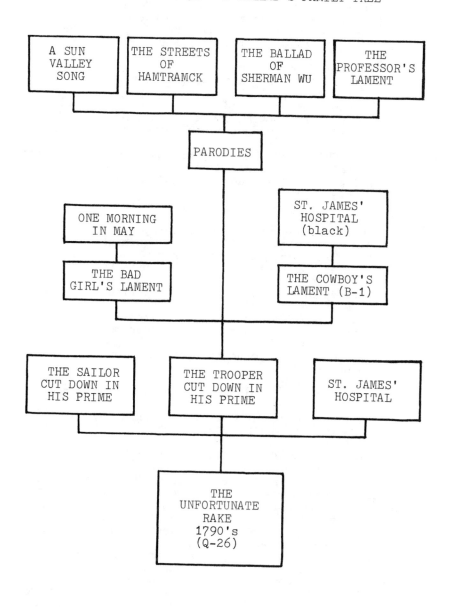

THE TROOPER CUT DOWN IN HIS PRIME

1 As I was a-walkin' down by the Royal Arsenal,
  Early the morning though warm was the day,
  When who should I see but one of my comrades
  All wrapped up in flannel, and cold as the clay.

   chorus:
       Then beat the drum lowly and play your fife
           slowly,
       And sound the dead march as you carry me along;
       And fire your bundooks right over my coffin,
       For I'm a young trooper cut down in my prime.

2 The bugles were playin'; his mates were a-prayin';
  The chaplain was kneelin' down by his bed;
  His poor head was achin'; his poor heart was
       breakin',
  This poor young trooper cut down in his prime.

3 "Get six of my comrades to carry my coffin,
  Six of my comrades to carry me on high;
  And six young maidens to carry white roses,
  So they won't smell me as they pass by."

4 Outside of the barracks you will find two girls
       standin',
  And one to the other she whispered and said:
  "Here comes the young swaddy whose money we
       squandered,
  Here comes the young trooper cut down in his
       prime."

5 On the cross by his grave you will find these
       words written:
  "All you young troopers take warnin' by me;
  Keep away from them flash-girls who walk in the
       city,
  Flash-girls of the city have quite ruined me."

"The Unfortunate Rake" crossed the Atlantic Ocean
to North America where it underwent considerable revi-
sion. Most new world texts change the sex from a male
"rake" to a "bad girl" (except for the cowboy adapt-
ations). In 1941, Alan and Elizabeth Lomax collected
the song "One Morning In May" from Mrs. Texas Gladden
of Salem, Virginia. Hally Wood learned it from the
Library of Congress recording that Gladden had made;
Caroline Paton learned it from the Wood recording; and
I heard it from Caroline in 1973. The folk process was
at work again, only this time updated by the phonograph.

"One Morning In May" is the Paton version (courtesy of Caroline Paton). Incidentally, the phrase "my body's salivated" refers to the effects of mercury treatment for venereal disease.

ONE MORNING IN MAY

1 When I was a young girl I used to see pleasure,
  When I was a young girl I used to drink ale;
  Right out of the alehouse and into the jail house,
  Right out of a bar room and down to my grave.

2 Come Mama, come Papa, and sit you down by me,
  Come Mama, come Papa, and pity my case;
  My poor head is aching, my poor heart is breaking,
  My body's salivated and I'm bound to die.

3 Go send for the preacher to come and pray for me;
  Go send for the doctor to heal up my wounds;
  My poor head is aching, my poor heart is breaking,
  My body's salivated, but Hell is my doom.

4 I want four young ladies to bear up my coffin,
  I want four young maidens to carry me on,
  And each of them carry a bunch of wild roses,
  To lay on my body as I pass along.

5 One mornin', one mornin', one mornin' in May,
  I saw this young lady all wrapped in white linen,
  All wrapped in white linen and cold as the clay.

Western cowboys easily adapted the "Rake" ballads to fit the conditions of frontier life. Lead poisoning replaced syphillis as the cause of death. In 1919, Vance Randolph collected "The Cowboy's Lament" (or "The Streets of Loredo") from Jim Fitzhugh of Sylamore, Arkansas. Bruce Buckley sings a similar version on The Unfortunate Rake, Folkways FA 3805 (used by permission of Folkways Records).

THE COWBOY'S LAMENT

1 As I rode out in the streets of Loredo,
  As I rode in the streets of Loredo one day,
  I seen a poor cowboy in Tom Sherman's dance hall,
  All dressed in his buckskins and fit for his grave.

2 "Oh, once in the saddle I used to go dashing,
  Once in the saddle I used to go gay,

But I first took to drinking and then to card
        playing,
And then I got shot so I'm dying today.

3 "I once had a mother, gray-haired old mother,
   She rocked me to sleep and she sung me this song,
   And there was another more dear than a mother,
   She never will know where her cowboy has gone.

4 "Go gather around me a bunch of young cowboys,
   And tell 'em the tale of a cowboy's sad fate,
   And warn them all gently to quit their wild roving,
   To quit their wild roving before it's too late.

5 "My friends and relations they live in the Nation,
   They never will know where their cowboy has gone,
   I first went to Texas and hired to a ranchman,
   I'm just a poor cowboy, I know I've done wrong.

6 "Then beat your drums slowly and play your fife
        lowly,
   Get six of them gamblers to carry me along,
   And in the grave throw me and roll some rocks
        o'er me,
   I'm just a poor cowboy, I know I've done wrong."

Black Americans were quick to identify with the
central character in the "Rake" ballads. Following the
Civil War a number of ex-slaves became cowboys herding
cattle northward from Texas to the various railheads in
Kansas. The harsh and lonely life depicted in "The Cowboy's Lament" was familiar enough to them, but they also
identified with elements in the older British broadsides. One of the highlights of the 1973 Ann Arbor
Blues and Jazz Festival was bluesman Roosevelt Sykes
performing an amalgamation of both the cowboy and British versions. Dave Van Ronk sings a close copy,
"Gambler's Blues," on The Unfortunate Rake, Folkways FA
3805 (used by permission of Folkways Records). This
variant is considered by some experts to be separate
from the other "Rake" ballads; nevertheless, there is an
apparent connection.

GAMBLER'S BLUES

1 It was down by old Joe's barroom
  On the corner by the square;
  They were serving drinks as usual,
  And the usual crowd was there.

2 On my left stood Big Joe McKennedy,
  And his eyes were bloodshot red;
  Well, he turned to the crowd around him,
  These are the very words he said.

3 "I went down to that St. James Infirmary,
  I saw my baby there,
  Stretched out on a long white table,
  So sweet, so cold, so fair.

  chorus:
    "Let her go, let her go, God bless her,
    Wherever she may be;
    She may search this wide world over,
    Never find a sweet man like me.

4 "When I die please bury me
  In my high topped Stetson hat,
  Put a twenty dollar gold piece on my watch chain,
  My gang will know I died standing pat.

5 "I want six crap shooters for pall bearers,
  A chorus girl to sing me a song;
  Put a jazz band on my hearse wagon,
  Raise hell as I stroll along.

6 "Well, now that I've told my story,
  I'll take another shot of booze,
  And if anyone should happen to ask you
  Well, I've got those gambler's blues."

Parodies of the "Rake" cycle are numerous. This is a good indication of the popularity and extent of the original forms. A college student at the University of Denver, and a skiing enthusiast as well, composed this parody, "A Sun Valley Song." Jan Brunvand sings it on The Unfortunate Rake (used by permission of Folkways Records).

A SUN VALLEY SONG

1 When I was a-skiing the hills of Sun Valley,
  As I was a-skiing old Baldy one day,
  I spied a young skier all wrapped in alpaca,
  All wrapped in alpaca, and cold as der Schnee.

2 "I see by your suntan that you are a skier,"
  These words he did say as I boldly schussed by;
  "Come fall down beside me, and hear my sad story,
  I caught a right edge and I'm dying today.

3 "It was once upon Baldy I used to ski gaily,
  It was once upon Baldy I used to ski by;
  It was first down the canyon, and then through the
       narrows,
  I caught a right edge and I know I must die.

4 "Get six from the ski school to carry my coffin,
  Get six little bunnies to sing me a song;
  Oh, lower me gently and sprinkle Schnee o'er me,
  For I was a skier, my life was not long."

The Dodge Pension Strike of 1949 was the inspiration for "The Streets of Hamtramck." Written by United Auto Workers Union member Kuppy Scott, the title refers to a Polish community in Detroit. Text: The Unfortunate Rake, Folkways FA 3805 (used by permission of Folkways Records).

THE STREETS OF HAMTRAMCK

1 As I walked out in the streets of the city,
  As I walked out in the city one day,
  I spied an old worker all wrinkled and weary,
  All wrinkled and weary with a head that was grey.

2 "I see by your outfit that you are a worker,"
  This old fellow cried as I boldly stepped by;
  "Come sit down beside me and hear my sad story,
  For I'm too old to work and I'm too young to die.

3 "It was once in the factory I used to go daily,
  Once in the factory I worked for my pay;
  Twenty long years for the same corporation,
  Now I'm too old to work and I'm starving today.

4 "For when I reached sixty the line was too speedy
  And I couldn't keep up at my usual rate;
  The boss was hard-hearted and that's when we
       parted,
  The company kicked me right out of the gate.

5 "Now who's going to hire a man who's past sixty,
  Who will believe that he's willing to try,
  Who's going to feed him and keep the roof o'er him
  When he's too old to work and he's too young to
       die?

6 "Now listen young fellows and learn from this
       story
  So you won't meet my fate as the years pass on by;

12

Fight for those pensions so you can retire
When you're too old to work and you're too young
    to die."

"The Ballad of Sherman Wu" apparently was composed
communally by University of Chicago students in 1956
following an actual discrimination case at Northwestern
University. Pete Seeger sings it on The Unfortunate
Rake, Folkways FA 3805 (used by permission of Folkways
Records).

THE BALLAD OF SHERMAN WU

1 As I was out walking the streets of Northwestern,
  I spied a young freshman dejected and blue,
  And so when I asked him, "Why are you dejected?"
  He said, "I'm Chinese and I can't join Psi U.

2 "I see by your frat pin that you are a Psi U,
  If I had a frat pin I'd be one too,
  If I had a frat pin then I'd be a Psi U,
  I can't have a frat pin 'cause I'm Sherman Wu."

3 The dean said, "Now, Sherman, don't make a com-
        motion,
  It's wrong to wash laundry in public you know;
  The SGB soon will make a motion
  Condemning the action that bothers you so."

4 Now they still haven't made a Psi U out of Sherman,
  'Cause Jack said Wu had to go;
  If he were just Jewish or Spanish or German,
  But he's so damn Chinese the whole campus would
        know.

5 As I was out walking the streets of Northwestern,
  I spied a young freshman dejected and blue;
  And so when I asked him, "Why are you dejected?"
  He said, "I'm Chinese and can't join Psi U."

The final parody is "The Professor's Lament,"
written by Nanette Morrison and Oma Louise Miller, two
students in a 1957 folklore class of Professor Holger
Nygard. The text was printed in Western Folklore, XVII,
3 (July, 1958), pp. 204-205, and is sung by Roger
Abrahams on The Unfortunate Rake album (used by permission of Folkways Records).

THE PROFESSOR'S LAMENT

1 As I walked out in the streets of West L. A.,
As I walked out in West L. A. one day,
I spied a professor wrapped up in white linen,
Wrapped up in white linen as cold as the clay.

chorus:
   "Oh, beat the drum slowly and play the fife
      lowly,
   Play the death march as you carry me along;
   Take me back to fair Kansas, there lay the
      sod o'er me,
   For I'm a professor and know I've done wrong.

2 "Let sixteen students come handle my coffin,
Let sixteen teachers come sing me a song;
Take me to the graveyard and lay the sod o'er me,
For I'm a professor and know I've done wrong.

3 "It was once on the campus I used to go dashing,
Once on the campus I used to go gay;
First to the Co-op and then to the rest room,
Got shot in the breast and I'm dying today.

4 "Get six happy colleagues to carry my coffin,
Get six pretty coeds: short, medium and tall;
Put acres of bluebooks all over my coffin,
Bluebooks to deaden the sods as they fall.

5 "Oh, read the books slowly and toll the chimes
      lowly,
Bring 'Lady I and the Elf Knight' along;[1]
And in the grave throw me and roll the sod o'er me,
For I'm a professor and know I've done wrong.

6 "Oh, bury beside me my pen and portfolio,
My cap on my head, and my gown wrapped around me;
And on top of my coffin put a bottle of likker,
That my colleagues may drink and thus have one on
      me."

7 We read his books slowly and tolled the chimes
      lowly,
Bitterly wept as we bore him along;

---

[1] A reference to Child ballad number 4, "Lady Isabel
and the Elf-Knight."

14

For we'll miss our dear teacher, so brave, young
    and handsome,
We all loved our teacher although he'd done wrong.

Variants and parodies of "The Unfortunate Rake"
illustrate the folk process of creation and recreation,
of continuity and change. The next three chapters offer
additional examples of this key element in folk music.
These chapters divide the ballads arbitrarily into three
parts: (1) the pre-industrial classic ballads mainly
from the Child collection, (2) the British broadsides
which travelled with their owners across the Atlantic
Ocean, and (3) the native ballads of North America.
Chapters Five and Six select examples of folksongs--not
ballads--from the hundreds that have entered the folk
tradition. Chapter Six also contains protest songs,
both traditional and otherwise. They have been included
because they further define and sharpen the image of the
men and women who are the underlying heroes of this
book. Join this exploration into the roots of North
American music as together we discover the music of the
people.

PAUL CLAYTON
Photo courtesy Folkways Records

FRANCIS JAMES CHILD

CHAPTER II

THE CLASSIC BALLADS

In the late nineteenth century, Harvard English professor Francis James Child catalogued 305 ballads in his definitive five volume work, The English and Scottish Popular Ballads. In spite of references to lords and ladies, milk-white steeds and pen knives, castles and elves, many of the Child ballads have remained a part of the folk tradition of both the British Isles and North America down to the present time. This continuing popularity is aided by the intense sexual and criminal content of the ballads, but of greater importance is their honesty, objectivity and integrity--ideals the folk still cherish.

These ballads, and a handful more not in the Child canon, can be designated "classic" since they are among the oldest surviving folk music in the English-speaking world and pre-date the changes brought about by the Industrial Revolution during the eighteenth century. They are organized by the editor around seven major topics common to the classic ballads--from supernatural to protest. The examples which follow include the numbers assigned to them by Child; the few non-Child works are so noted.

SUPERNATURAL

Supernatural themes dominate the ballads listed in the first volume of Child. Number 1, "Riddles Wisely Expounded," which dates from the fifteenth century Rawlinson manuscript, was originally a question and answer battle-of-wits between the devil and an innocent young girl. Later variants demoted satan in rank and power to either a knight or a lusty male. Confusion with Child 46, "Captain Wedderburn's Courtship," is common as well as with the song "I Will Give My Love an Apple" (or "Cherry"). This a result of "floating verses" which move in and out of various songs. Helen Hartness Flanders printed a Vermont version "There Was a Man Lived in the West" and Alfreda Peel discovered a Virginia variant with the more familar title "The Devil's Nine Questions." Most American texts begin something like this:

> If you can't answer my questions nine
> Sing ninety nine and ninety;

Oh, you're not God's, you're one of mine
And the crow flies over the white oak tree.

The text is Child D from <u>Motherwell's</u> <u>Manuscript</u>,
1825 and after, p. 142.

RIDDLES WISELY EXPOUNDED

1 "O what is higher than the trees?
     Gar lay the bent to the bonny broom;
 And what is deeper than the seas?
     And you may begile a fair maid soon.

  [similarly]

2 "O what is whiter than the milk?
 Or what is softer than the silk?

3 "O what is sharper than the thorn?
 O what is louder than the horn?

4 "O what is longer than the way?
 And what is colder than the clay?

5 "O what is greener than the grass?
 Or what is worse than woman was?"

6 "O heaven's higher than the trees,
 And hell is deeper than the seas.

7 "And snow is whiter than the milk,
 And love is softer than the silk.

8 "O hunger's sharper than the thorn,
 And thunder's louder than the horn.

9 "O wind is longer than the way,
 And death is colder than the clay.

10 "O poison's greener than the grass,
 And the Devil's worse than eer woman was."

A Vermont variant concludes:

"Snow is whiter than the milk,
Down is softer than the silk,
The Devil's meaner than womankind."

A ballad with wider currency in North America is
Child number 2, "The Elfin Knight." Its popularity was
aided by the publication of sixteenth century broadsides
in Britain. The ballad relates to British courtship

18

customs and contains vestigial remains of ancient ferti-
lity rites. The herbs rosemary and thyme were part of
those rites and were placed on either side of a woman's
bed so that she might dream of her lover. North American texts generally have lost this ancient symbolism as
the Sara Cleveland variant shows with its corruptive
phrase "every rose grows merry in time." Version A is
a broadside from about 1670 (Child A text); B was sent
to Child by the Rev. F. D. Huntington, who learned it
from his father in Hadley, Massachusetts, in 1828; C is
the Cleveland version, learned from her mother and recorded on Ballads and Songs of the Upper Hudson Valley,
Folk-Legacy FSA-33; D is from the singing of Lawrence
Older recorded on Adirondack Songs, Ballads and Fiddle
Tunes, Folk-Legacy FSA-15 (both C and D are used by permission of Folk-Legacy Records, Sharon, Conn.). The
Simon and Garfunkel number "Scarborough Fair," from the
motion picture The Graduate, was simply another triumph
for an ancient best seller.

A - THE ELFIN KNIGHT

My plaid awa, my plaid awa,
And ore the hill and far awa,
And far awa to Norrowa,
My plaid shall not be blown awa.

1 The elphin knight sits on yon hill,
    Ba, ba, ba, lilli ba
He blaws his horn both lowd and shril.
    The wind hath blown my plaid awa.

[similarly]

2 He blowes it east, he blowes it west
He blowes it where he lyketh best.

3 "I wish that horn were in my kist,
Yea, and the knight in my armes two."

4 She had no sooner these words said
When that the knight came to her bed.

5 "Thou art over young a maid," quoth he,
"Married with me thou il wouldst be."

6 "I have a sister younger than I,
And she was married yesterday."

7 "Married with me if thou wouldst be,
A courtesie thou must do to me.

19

8 "For thou must shape a sark to me,
. Without any cut or heme," quoth he.

9 "Thou must shape it knife-and-sheerlesse,
And also sue it needle-threedlesse."

10 "If that piece of courtesie I do to thee,
Another thou must do to me.

11 "I have an aiker of good ley-land,
Which lyeth low by yon sea-strand.

12 "For thou must eare it with thy horn,
So thou must sow it with thy corn.

13 "And bigg a cart of stone and lyme,
Robin Redbreast he must trail it hame.

14 "Thou must barn it in a mouse-holl,
And thrash it into thy shoes soll.

15 "And thou must winnow it in thy looff,
And also seck it in thy glove.

16 "For thou must bring it over the sea,
And thou must bring it dry home to me.

17 "When thou hast gotten thy turns well done,
Then come to me and get thy sark then."

18 "I'l not quite my plaid for my life;
It haps my seven bairns and my wife."
    The wind shall not blow my plaid awa.

19 "My maidenhead I'l then keep still,
Let the elphin knight do what he will."
    The wind's not blown my plaid awa.

B - THE ELFIN KNIGHT

1 Now you are a-going to Cape Ann,
    Followmingkathellomeday
Remember me to the self-made man.
    Ummatiddle, ummatiddle, ummatallyho, tallyho,
        followmingkathellomeday.

2 Tell him to buy me an acre of land
Between the salt-water and the sea-sand.

3 Tell him to plough it with a ram's horn
 Tell him to sow it with one peppercorn.

4 Tell him to reap it with a penknife,
 And tell him to cart it with two mice.

5 Tell him to cart it to yonder new barn
 That never was built since Adam was born.

6 Tell him to thrash it with a goose quill,
 Tell him to fan it with an egg-shell.

7 Tell the fool, when he's done his work,
 To come to me, and he shall have his shirt.

C - EVERY ROSE GROWS MERRY IN TIME

1 As I was a-walking down by the seashore,
 Every rose grows merry in time,
 I met there a maiden I'd ne'er seen before,
 And I said, "Will you be a true lover of mine?
 If you are to be a true lover of mine,
 Every rose grows merry in time,
 You must make me a shirt without needle or twine,
 And then you will be a true lover of mine.

2 "You must wash it in an old dry well,
 Every rose grows merry in time,
 Where never a drop of water e'er fell,
 And then you will be a true lover of mine.
 You must dry it on an old buckthorn,
 Every rose grows merry in time,
 That never has blossomed since Adam was born,
 And then you will be a true lover of mine.

3 "You must iron it with an old flat rock,
 Every rose grows merry in time,
 One ne'er cold nor one ne'er hot,
 And then you will be a true lover of mine."
 "Now, you have asked me questions three,
 Every rose grows merry in time,
 Now, you must do the same thing for me,
 And then I will be a true lover of thine.

4 "You must buy me an acre of dry land,
 Every rose grows merry in time,
 Between the sea shore and the sea sand,
 And then you will be a true lover of mine.
 You must plow it with an old cow's horn,
 Every rose grows merry in time,

And sow it all over with one grain of corn,
And then you will be a true lover of mine.

5 "You must reap it with a strap of leather,
Every rose grows merry in time,
And bind it all up with a peacock feather,
And then you will be a true lover of mine.
You must stack it up against the wall,
Every rose grows merry in time,
And pick it all up with a cobbler's awl,
And then you will be a true lover of mine.

6 "And when you have done and finished your work,
Every rose grows merry in time,
Then come to me and I'll make your darn shirt,
And then I will be a true lover of thine."

D - FLIM-A-LIM-A-LEE

1 Where are you going? I am going to the fair;
   Flim-a-lim-a-lee castle-o Mollee
If you see my girl, tell her I'll be there;
   To my tassel-o, fa-lassel-o,
   Flim-a-lim-a-lassel castle-o Mollee.

2 Tell her to make me a cambric shirt,
Without one stitch of needle work.

3 Tell her to wash it in yonder dry well,
Where never one drop of water has fell.

4 Tell her to hang it on yonder thorn,
Where the sun ain't shone since Adam was born.

5 Where are you going? I am going to the fair.
If you see my love tell him I'll be there.

6 Tell him to buy me an acre of land,
Between the salt sea and the salt sea sand.

7 Tell him to plow it with a ram's horn,
And sow it with a pepper-corn.

8 Tell him to reap it with a pen-knife,
And haul it in with a yoke of mice.

9 Tell him to reap it with a goose-quill,
And thresh it in an old egg shell.

10 When the fool has done his work,
Tell him to come and get his shirt.

"Lady Isabel and the Elf-Knight," number 4, is a story of a scoundrel who decoys maidens to their death until he is outwitted by a sharp female who knows a few tricks of her own. Version A is from the Roxburghe Ballads (listed in Child as F); B is a fragment learned by Mrs. Ruth Barron of Youngstown, Ohio, from the singing of her mother (used by permission). It is in the half-spoken, half-singing style of Nathan Hatt of Nova Scotia, whose variant is sung by Alan Mills on the Folkways album, Alan Mills and Jean Carignan, FG 3532.

A - LADY ISABEL AND THE ELF-KNIGHT

1 "Go fetch me some of your father's gold,
  And some of your mother's fee;
 And I'll carry you into the north land,
  And there I'll marry thee."

2 She fetchd him some of her father's gold,
  And some of her mother's fee;
 She carried him into the stable,
  Where horses stood thirty and three.

3 She leapd on a milk-white steed,
  And he on a dapple-grey;
 They rode til they cam to a fair river's side,
  Three hours before it was day.

4 "O light, O light, you lady gay,
  O light with speed, I say,
 For six knight's daughters have I drowned here,
  And you the seventh must be."

5 "Go fetch the sickle, to crop the nettle
  That grows so near the brim,
 For fear it should tangle my golden locks,
  Or freckle my milk-white skin."

6 He fetchd the sickle, to crop the nettle,
  That grows so near the brim,
 And with all the strength that pretty Polly had
  She pushd the false knight in.

7 "Swim on, swim on, thou false knight,
  And there bewail thy doom,
 For I don't think thy cloathing too good
  To lie in a watry tomb."

8 She leaped on her milk-white steed,
  She led the dapple grey;

She rid till she came to her father's house,
      Three hours before it was day.

9 "Who knocked so loudly at the ring?"
      The parrot he did say;
  "O where have you been, my pretty Polly,
      All this long summer's day?"

10 "O hold your tongue, parrot,
      Tell you no tales of me;
   Your cage shall be made of beaten gold,
      Which is now made of a tree."

11 O then bespoke her father dear,
      As he on his bed did lay:
   "O what is the matter, my parrot,
      That you speak before it is day?"

12 "The cat's at my cage, master,
      And sorely frighted me,
   And I calld down my Polly
      To take the cat away."

B - LADY ISABEL AND THE ELF KNIGHT

[spoken] There was a handsome young man who
asked a young girl to run away with him to get
married and to be sure to bring all her jewels
and possessions. This she did.

[sung] Oh, they rode and they rode unto the
      seashore
Three hours before it was day-a-ay
Three hours before it was day.

[spoken] They got to the sea shore and he
demanded the jewels and possessions from her and
tormented her, singing:

[sung] "Six pretty maidens I've drownded here
And you'll the seventh shall be-ee-ee
And you the seventh shall be."

[spoken] Well, the girl was not dumb and she decided to trick him. She asked him: "Surely you'd
like to have my fine clothes, wouldn't you? they're
worth money and if you turn your back, I'll un-
dress." He did this, stupidly believing her and
very sure of himself as well. [parts missing]

[sung] . . . And she bundled him into the sea-ee-ee
And she bundled him into the sea.

[parts missing]

[sung] She rode and she rode back from the
    seashore
One hour before it was day-a-ay
One hour before it was day.

[spoken] She was afraid her poll parrot would
awaken the family, but she told it to not tell
on her and she was safe.

The earliest known text of Child number 26, "The
Three Ravens,"dates back to Ravenscroft's Melismata,
1611. In that text the function of the ravens is limited to introducing the story which tells how the body of
a slain knight is guarded by his faithful hounds and
hawks until his mistress (a "fallow doe") can give him
a decent burial. If it is true that the "Corpus
Christi" ballad (text later) is an adaptation of an
earlier variant, then "The Three Ravens" could have
originated in the fifteenth century. Scottish versions
are usually cynical in nature, such as B from Walter
Scott, Minstrelsy of the Scottish Border, 1803. North
American variants are generally from the Scottish tradition as is the case with C from the singing of Fred
Terry, Joplin, Missouri, as printed in Vance Randolph,
Ozark Folksongs, Vol. I, p. 75. It is recorded by Peggy
Seeger on The Long Harvest, Record 7, Argo ZDA-72. The
A text is from Melismata, via Ritson, Ancient Songs,
1790.

A - THE THREE RAVENS (or, "RAUENS")

1 There were three rauens sat on a tree,
    Downe a downe, hay downe, hay downe
There were three rauens sat on a tree,
    With a downe
There were three rauens sat on a tree,
They were as blacke as they might be,
    With a downe derrie, derrie, derrie, downe,
    downe.

[similarly]

2 The one of them said to his mate,
"Where shall we our breakfast take?"

3 "Downe in yonder green field,
   There lies a knight slain vnder his shield.

4 "His hounds they lie downe at his feete,
   So well they can their master keepe.

5 "His haukes they flie so eagerly,
   There's no fowle dare him come nie."

6 Downe there comes a fallow doe,
   As great with young as might goe.

7 She lift vp his bloudy hed,
   And kist his wounds that were so red.

8 She got him vp vpon her backe,
   And carried him to earthen lake.

9 She buried him before the prime,
   She was dead herselfe ere euen-song time.

10 God send euery gentleman
   Such haukes, such hounds, and such a leman.

B - THE TWA CORBIES

1 As I was walking all alane,
   I heard twa corbies making a mane;
   The tane unto t'other say,
   "Where sall we gang and dine to-day?"

2 "In behint yon auld fail dyke
   I wot there lies a new slain knight;
   And naebody kens that he lies there,
   But his hawk, his hound, and lady fair.

3 "His hound is to the hunting gane,
   His hawk to fetch the wild-fowl hame,
   His lady's ta'en another mate,
   So we may mak our dinner sweet.

4 "Ye'll sit on his white hause-bane,
   And I'll pike out his bonny blue een;
   Wi ae lock o his gowden hair
   We'll theek our nest when it grows bare.

5 "Mony a one for him makes mane,
   But nane sall ken where is gane;
   Oer his white banes, when they are bare,
   The wind sall blaw for evermair."

C - THE THREE CROWS

1 There was three crows set on a tree,
  Billy Magee MaGaw,
  There was three crows set on a tree,
  They was as black as black could be,
  Billy Magee MaGaw, MaGaw,
  Billy Magee MaGaw.

  [similarly]

2 The old crow said to his mate, (2X)
  "What shall we do for meat to eat?"

3 There lies a horse in Yonder's Town, (2X)
  That by the butcher has been slain.

4 We'll all set ourselves on his backbone, (2X)
  And pick his eyes out one by one.

"Tam Lin," Child number 39, is an ancient ballad
which traces back in print to 1769, but it is clear that
similar tales were sung as early as 1549. Tam Lin is a
young man kidnapped by elves. They are planning to
sacrifice him in order to appease the devil, but he out-
wits them with the help of another mortal--Janet, his
mistress. As far as is known, the ballad is not traditional in North America, but it did gain recognition
with the release of the folk-rock interpretation by
Fairport Convention in the early 1970's. Rick and
Lorraine Lee sing an abridged version of "Tam Lin" on
their Front Hall album. The text is Child A from James
Johnson, Scots Musical Museum, 1787-1803, as communi-
cated by Robert Burns.

TAM LIN

1 O I forbid you, maidens a',
    That wear gowd on your hair,
  To come or gae by Carterhaugh,
    For young Tam Lin is there.

2 There's nane that gaes by Carterhaugh
    But they leave him a wad,
  Either their rings, or green mantles,
    Or else their maidenhead.

3 Janet has kilted her green kirtle
    A little aboon her knee,
  And she has broded her yellow hair
    A little aboon her bree,

27

And she's awa to Carterhaugh,
 As fast as she can hie.

4 When she came to Carterhaugh
 Tam Lin was at the well,
And there she fand his steed standing,
 But away was himsel.

5 She had na pu'd a double rose,
 A rose but only twa,
Til up then started young Tam Lin,
 Says, "Lady, thou's pu nae mae.

6 "Why pu's thou the rose, Janet,
 And why breaks thou the wand?
Or why comes thou to Carterhaugh
 Withoutten my command?"

7 "Carterhaugh, it is my ain,
 My daddie gave it me;
I'll come and gang by Carterhaugh,
 And ask nae leave at thee."

8 Janet has kilted her green kirtle
 A little aboon her knee,
And she has snooded her yellow hair
 A little aboon her bree,
And she is to her father's ha,
 As fast as she can hie.

9 Four and twenty ladies fair
 Were playing at the ba,
And out then cam the fair Janet,
 Ance the flower amang them a'.

10 Four and twenty ladies fair
 Were playing at the chess,
And out then cam the fair Janet,
 As green as onie glass.

11 Out then spak an auld grey knight,
 Lay oer the castle wa,
And says, "Alas, fair Janet, for thee
 But we'll be blamed a'."

12 "Haud your tongue, ye auld fac'd knight,
 Some ill death may ye die!
Father my bairn on whom I will,
 I'll father nane on thee."

13 Out then spak her father dear,
     And he spak meek and mild;
   "And ever alas, sweet Janet," he says
     "I think thou gaes wi child."

14 "If that I gae wi child, father,
     Mysel maun bear the blame;
   There's neer a laird about your ha
     Shall get the bairn's name.

15 "If my love were an earthly knight,
     As he's an elfin grey,
   I wad na gie my ain true-love
     For nae lord that ye hae.

16 "The steed that my true-love rides on
     Is lighter than the wind;
   Wi siller he is shod before,
     Wi burning gowd behind."

17 Janet has kilted her green kirtle
     A little aboon her knee,
   And she has snooded her yellow hair
     A little aboon her her bree,
   And she's awa to Carterhaugh,
     As fast as she can hie.

18 When she cam to Carterhaugh
     Tam Lin was at the well,
   And there she fand his steed standing,
     But away was himsel.

19 She had na pu'd a double rose,
     A rose but only twa,
   Till up then started young Tam Lin,
     Says "Lady, thou pu's nae mae.

20 "Why pu's thou the rose, Janet
     Amang the groves sae green,
   And a' to kill the bonie babe
     That we gat us between?"

21 "O tell me, tell me, Tam Lin," she says,
     "For's sake that died on tree,
   If eer ye was in holy chapel,
     Or christendom did see?"

22 "Roxbrugh he was my grandfather,
     Took me with him to bide,
   And ance it fell upon a day
     That wae did me betide.

23 "And ance it fell upon a day,
    A cauld day and a snell,
When we were frae the hunting come,
    That frae my horse I fell;
The Queen o Fairies she caught me,
    In yon green hill to dwell.

24 "And pleasant is the fairy land,
    But, an eerie tale to tell,
Ay at the end of seven years
    We pay a tiend to hell;
I am sae fair and fu o flesh,
    I'm feard it be mysel.

25 "But the night is Halloween, lady,
    The morn is Hallowday;
Then win me, win me, and ye will,
    For weel I wat ye may.

26 "Just at the mirk and midnight hour
    The fairy folk will ride,
And they that wad their true-love win,
    At Miles Cross they maun bide."

27 "But how shall I thee ken, Tam Lin,
    Or how my true-love know,
Amang sae mony unco knights
    The like I never saw?"

28 "O first let pass the black, lady,
    And syne let pass the brown,
But quickly run to the milk-white steed,
    Pu ye his rider down.

29 "For I'll ride on the milk-white steed,
    And ay nearest the town;
Because I was an earthly knight
    They gie me that renown.

30 "My right hand will be glovd, lady
    My left hand will be bare,
Cockt up shall my bonnet be,
    And kaimd down shall my hair,
And thae's the takens I gie thee,
    Nae doubt I will be there.

31 "They'll turn me in your arms, lady,
    Into an esk and adder;
But hold me fast, and fear me not,
    I am your bairn's father.

32 "They'll turn me to a bear sae grim,
    And then a lion bold;
But hold me fast, and fear me not,
    As ye shall love your child.

33 "Again they'll turn me in your arms
    To a red het gaud of airn;
But hold me fast, and fear me not,
    I'll do to you nae harm.

34 "And last they'll turn me in your arms
    Into the burning gleed;
Then throw me into well water,
    O throw me in wi speed.

35 "And then I'll be your ain true-love,
    I'll turn a naked knight;
Then cover me wi your green mantle,
    And cover me out of sight."

36 Gloomy, gloomy was the night,
    And eerie was the way,
As fair Jenny in her green mantle
    To Miles Cross she did gae.

37 About the middle o the night
    She heard the bridles ring;
This lady was as glad at that
    As any earthly thing.

38 First she let the black pass by,
    And syne she let the brown;
But quickly she ran to the milk-white steed,
    And pu'd the rider down.

39 Sae weel she minded whae he did say,
    And young Tam Lin did win;
Syne coverd him wi her green mantle,
    As blythe's a bird in spring.

40 Out then spak the Queen o Fairies,
    Out of a bush o broom;
"Them that has gotten young Tam Lin
    Has gotten a stately groom."

41 Out then spak the Queen o Fairies,
    And an angry woman was she:
"Shame betide her ill-far'd face,
    And an ill death may she die,
For she's taen awa the boniest knight
    In a' my companie.

31

42 "But had I kend, Tam Lin," she says,
     "What now this night I see,
   I wad hae taen out thy twa grey een,
     And put in twa een o tree."

"The Unquiet Grave," number 78, deals with the folk belief that excessive grieving for the dead disturbs their rest. The fine lyrical style of the ballad is demonstrated by Sandy Paton on the Folk-Legacy album _Sandy and Caroline Paton_, EGO-30. His source is Mrs. Lily M. Delorme of Cadyville, New York. (Used by permission of Folk-Legacy Records, Sharon, Conn.)

THE UNQUIET GRAVE

1 Cold blows the wintry wind, sweetheart;
    Cold are the drops of rain.
  I never had but one sweetheart,
    And in the greenwood she lies slain.

2 I'll do as much for my sweetheart
    As any young man may.
  I'll sit and mourn all at her grave
    A twelve-month and a day.

3 The twelve-month and a day being past,
    The dead began to speak.
  "Who sits all on my grave and mourns,
    And will not let me sleep?

4 "What do you want of me, sweetheart?
    What do you want of me?"
  "One kiss from your clay-cold lips,
    And that is all I want of thee."

5 "My lips are colder than the clay;
    My breath is earthy strong.
  If one kiss of these lips you have,
    Your time on earth will not be long."

Another revenant ballad is "The Wife of Usher's Well," number 79. Pagan superstitions found in early versions of the ballad, such as the wearing of birch hats to protect the spirits from the living, have been emasculated by Christian coloration in more recent examples. The A text makes the visit just a dream eliminating the supernatural completely (Child D from Emma Backus of North Carolina, 1896). The B version by Hedy West is collated from several sources, including her grandmother, and recorded on _Old Times and Hard Times_, Folk-Legacy FSA-32 (used by permission of Hedy West).

A - THE WIFE OF USHER'S WELL

1 There was a lady fair and gay,
    And children she had three;
  She sent them away to some northern land,
    For to learn their grammeree.

2 They hadn't been gone but a very short time,
    About three months to a day,
  When sickness came to that land
    And swept those babes away.

3 There is a king in the heavens above
    That wears a golden crown;
  She prayed that he would send her babies home
    To-night or in the morning soon.

4 It was about one Christmas time,
    When the nights were long and cool,
  She dreamed of her three little lonely babes
    Come running in their mother's room.

5 The table was fixed and the cloth was spread,
    And on it put bread and wine:
  "Come sit you down, my three little babes,
    And eat and drink of mine."

6 "We will neither eat your bread, dear mother,
    Nor we'll neither drink your wine;
  For to our Saviour we must return
    To-night or in the morning soon."

7 The bed was fixed in the back room;
    On it was some clean white sheet,
  And on the top was a golden cloth,
    To make those little babies sleep.

8 "Wake up! wake up!" says the oldest one,
    "Wake up! it's almost day.
  And to our Saviour we must return
    To-night or in the morning soon.

9 "Green grass grows at our head, dear mother,
    Green moss grows at our feet;
  The tears that you shed for us three babes
    Won't wet our winding sheet."

B - THE WIFE OF USHER'S WELL

1 There was a woman and she lived alone
  And babies she had three.

She sent them away to the north country
To learn their grammarie.

2 They'd not been gone but a very short time,
Scarcely six weeks to the day,
When death, cold death spread through the land
And swept them babes away.

3 She prayed to the Lord in Heaven above,
Wearing a starry crown.
"Oh, send to me my three little babes,
Tonight, or in the morning soon."

4 It was very close to Christmas time;
The nights were long and cold.
And the very next morning at the break of day
Them babes come a-running home.

5 She set the table for them to eat,
Upon it spread bread and wine.
"Come eat, come drink, my three little babes;
Come eat, come drink of mine."

6 "Oh, mother, we cannot eat your bread,
Neither can we drink your wine,
For tomorrow morning at the break of day,
Our Saviour must we join."

7 She made the bed in the back-most room,
Upon it she spread a sheet,
Upon the top a golden spread
For to help them babes asleep.

8 "Rise up, rise up," said the eldest one,
"Rise up, rise up," said she,
"For tomorrow morning, at the break of day,
Our Saviour must we see.

9 "Cold clods of clay roll o'er our heads,
Green grass grows on our feet,
And thy sweet tears, my mother dear,
Will wet our winding sheet."

"The Great Silkie of Sule Skerry," Child number
113, is a fine example of the folklore found among the
seafaring people of the Hebrides and Orkney islands
north of Scotland. There is no known example of this
ballad in North America, but Gordon Bok's Maine saga of
"Peter Kagin and the Wind" has a setting as supernatural
as this story of a silkie, or seal, and his human mistress. Text: R. M. Fergusson, Rambling Sketches in the

Far North, 1883, p. 140.

THE GREAT SILKIE OF SULE SKERRY

1 In Norway lands there lived a maid,
  "Balloo my babe," this maid began;
 "I know not where your father is,
  Or if land or sea he travels in."

2 It happened on a certain day,
  When this fair lady fell fast asleep,
 That in cam' a good grey selchie,
  And set him doon at her bed feet,

3 Saying, "Awak', awak' my pretty fair maid,
  For oh! how sound as thou dost sleep!
 An' I'll tell thee where thy baby's father is;
  He's sittin' close at thy bed feet."

4 "I pray, come tell me thy name,
  Oh! tell me where they dwelling be?"
 "My name is good Hein Mailer,
  An' I earn my livin' oot o' the sea.

5 "I am a man upon the land;
  I am a selchie in the sea;
 An' whin I'm far frae every strand,
  My dwellin' is in Shool Skerrie."

6 "Alas! alas! this woeful fate!
  This weary fate that's been laid for me!
 That a man should come frae the Wast o' Hoy,
  To the Norway lands to have a bairn wi' me."

7 "My dear, I'll wed thee with a ring,
  With a ring, my dear, I'll wed wi' thee."
 "Thoo may go wed thee weddens wi' whom thou wilt;
  For I'm sure thoo'll never wed none wi' me."

8 "Thoo will nurse my little wee son
  For seven long years upo' thy knee,
 An' at the end o' seven long years
  I'll come back an' pay the norish fee."

9 She's nursed her little wee son
  For seven long years upo' her knee,
 An' at the end o' seven long years
  He cam' back wi' gold an' white monie.

10 He says, "My dear, I'll wed thee wi' a ring,
  With a ring, my dear, I'll wed wi' thee."

"Thoo may go wed thee weddens wi' whom thoo will;
    For I'm sure thoo'll never wed none wi' me.

11 "But I'll put a gold chain around his neck,
    An' a grey good gold chain it'll be,
That if ever he comes to the Norway lands,
    Thoo may hae a gey good guess on hi'.

12 "An' thoo will get a gunner good,
    An' a gey good gunner it will be,
An' he'll gae oot on a May mornin'
    An' shoot the son an' the grey selchie."

13 Oh! she has got a gunner good,
    An' a gey good gunner it was he,
An' he gaed oot on a May mornin',
    An' he shot the son and the grey selchie.

14 "Alas! alas! this woeful fate!
    This weary fate that's been laid for me!"
An' ance or twice she sobbed and sighed,
    An' her tender heart did brak in three.

The final example of a supernatural ballad "James Harris," number 243, is more commonly known as "The House Carpenter." Dating back in print to the Pepys broadside of about 1675, it details a most unusual love triangle featuring married couple number one, Jane and James. Then James dies at sea and Jane marries an unnamed carpenter. The second couple enjoy four years of bliss and several children, when Jane is visited by an apparition who claims he is James. The ghost lures Jane to sea, where she dies; meanwhile, the carpenter hangs himself. The following two North American texts eliminate the supernatural element thereby turning the ballad into a morality play stressing the consequences of infidelty. Version A is by Paul Clayton on Cumberland Mountain Folksongs, Folkways FP 2007; B is similar to Clarence Ashley's 1930 recording reissued on Anthology of American Folk Music, Volume One: Ballads, Folkways FA 2951 (A used by permission of Folkways Records).

A - THE HOUSE CARPENTER

1 Well met, well met, said an old true love,
    I've long been searching for thee;
    I've lately crossed on the salt, salt sea,
And it's all for the sake of thee.

2 I could have married a king's daughter there,
    In vain she would have had me,

But now I refused that rich crown of gold,
And it's all for the sake of thee.

3 If you could have married a king's daughter there,
I'm sure you are to blame;
Now I am married to a house carpenter
And I think he's a nice young man.

4 If you will leave your house carpenter
And come go along with me,
I'll take you to the salt, salt sea
And there I'll marry thee.

5 She picked up her darlin' little babe,
Kisses gave it one, two three;
Lay there, lay there, my darling little babe,
To keep poppa company.

6 They had not been sailing more days than one or
      two,
I'm sure it wasn't three,
Till she knelt down on her true lover's knee
And wept most bitterly.

7 What are you weeping about, my darling little girl,
What are you weeping about, said he.
I'm weeping for my darling little babe
That I never anymore can see.

8 Straight news, straight news, to the house
      carpenter,
Straight news, straight news, back to land.
The ship that your wife is sailing on
Is sinking under the sand.

B - THE HOUSE CARPENTER

1 "Well met, well met," said an old true love,
"Well met, well met," said he;
"I'm just returning from the salt, salt sea,
And it's all for the love of thee."

2 "Come in, come in, my old true love,
And have a seat with me.
It's been three-fourths of a long, long year
Since together we have been."

3 "Well I can't come in or I can't sit down,
For I haven't but a moment's time.
They say you're married to a house carpenter,
And your heart will never be mine.

4 "Now it's I could have married a king's daughter
      dear,
   I'm sure she'd a married me;
   But I've forsaken her crowns of gold,
   And it's all for the love of thee.

5 "Now will you forsaken your house carpenter
   And go along with me?
   I'll take you where the grass grows green
   On the banks of the deep blue sea."

6 She picked up her little babe,
   And kisses gave it three.
   Says, "Stay right here, my darling little babe,
   And keep your poppa company."

7 Well he hadn't been on ship but about two weeks,
   I'm sure it was not three,
    Till his true love begin to weep and mourn
   And to weep most bitterly.

8 Says, "Are you weeping for my silver or my gold?"
   Says, "Are you weeping for my store?
   Are you weeping for that house carpenter
   Whose face you'll never see any more?"

9 "No, it's I'm not a-weeping for your silver or
      your gold,
   Or neither for your store;
   I am weeping for my darling little babe
   Whose face I'll never see any more."

10 Well he hadn't been on ship but about three weeks,
   I'm sure it was not four,
   Till they sprung a leak in the bottom of the ship
   And it sunk for to rise no more.

RELIGIOUS THEMES

   If medieval drama contained many Biblical stories,
why do so few of the classic ballads include religious
themes? The answer may be that the folk were more interested in keeping alive their local and rural secular
traditions and not those of the Church. However, the
few ballads with religious themes that were preserved
are special. For example, "Judas," number 23, is the
oldest printed ballad in Child, dating from the
thirteenth century; "The Cherry Tree Carol," number 54,
is one of the most popular in the collection; and "Sir
Hugh, or The Jew's Daughter," number 155, is perhaps the

most controversial and certainly the most intolerant. In his introduction to "Sir Hugh," professor Child condemned the anti-Jewish sentiment of the ballad. He wrote:

> Murders like that of Hugh of Lincoln have been imputed to the Jews for at least seven hundred and fifty years, and the charge, which there is reason to suppose may still from time to time be renewed, has brought upon the accused every calamity that the hand of man can inflict, pillage, confiscation, banishment, torture, and death, and this in huge proportions. The process of these murders has often been described as a parody of the crucifixion of Jesus. The motive most commonly alleged, in addition to the expression of contempt for Christianity, has been the obtaining of blood for use in the Paschal rites,--a most unhappily devised slander, in stark contradiction with Jewish precept and practice. . . . And these pretended child-murders, with their horrible consequences, are only a part of a persecution which, with all moderation, may be rubricated as the most disgraceful chapter in the history of the human race.[1]

Version A is from Jamieson, Popular Ballads, I, p. 151 (Edinburgh, 1806), and tells the full story. Most North American texts take their hostility out on gypsies, jewelers, or rich ladies, as shown in B, from a 1930 recording by Nelstone's Hawaiians titled "The Fatal Flower Garden," reissued on the Anthology series, Folkways FA 2951. C is a children's song from Virginia learned by Peggy Seeger and printed in Arthur Kyle Davis, Traditional Ballads of Virginia (Cambridge, Mass.: Harvard University Press, 1929).

A - SIR HUGH, OR THE JEW'S DAUGHTER

1 Four and twenty bonny boys
  Were playing at the ba,
And by it came him sweet Sir Hugh,
  And he playd oer them a'.

---

[1]Francis James Child, The English and Scottish Popular Ballads (New York: Dover Publications, Inc., 1965), III, pp. 240-241 (reprint of the 1888 volume).

2 He kicked the ba with his right foot,
    And catchd it wi his knee,
And throuch-and thro the Jew's window
    He gard the bonny ba flee.

3 He's doen him to the Jew's castell,
    And walkd it round about;
And there he saw the Jew's daughter,
    At the window looking out.

4 "Throw down the ba, ye Jew's daughter,
    Throw down the ba to me!"
"Never a bit," says the Jew's daughter,
    "Till up to me come ye."

5 "How will I come up? How can I come up?
    How can I come to thee?
For as ye did to my auld father,
    The same ye'll do to me."

6 She's gane till her father's garden,
    And pu'd an apple red and green;
'Twas a' to wyle him sweet Sir Hugh,
    And to entice him in.

7 She's led him in through ae dark door,
    And sae has she thro nine;
She's laid him on a dressing-table,
    And stickit him like a swine.

8 And first came out the thick, thick blood,
    And syne came out the thin,
And syne came out the bonny heart's blood;
    There was nae mair within.

9 She's rowd him in a cake of lead,
    Bade him lie still and sleep;
She's thrown him in Our Lady's draw-well,
    Was fifty fathom deep.

10 When bells were rung, and mass was sung,
    And a' the bairns came hame,
When every lady gat hame her son,
    The Lady Maisry gat nane.

11 She's taen her mantle her about,
    Her coffer by the hand,
And she's gane out to seek her son,
    And wandered oer the land.

12 She's doen her to the Jew's castell,
   Where a' were fast asleep:
"Gin ye be there, my sweet Sir Hugh,
   I pray you to me speak."

13 She's doen her to the Jew's garden,
   Thought he had been gathering fruit:
"Gin ye be there, my sweet Sir Hugh,
   I pray you to me speak."

14 She neard Our Lady's deep draw-well,
   Was fifty fathom deep:
"Whareer ye be, my sweet Sir Hugh,
   I pray you to me speak."

15 "Gae hame, gae hame, my mither dear,
   Prepare my winding sheet,
And at the back of merry Lincoln
   The morn I will you meet."

16 Now Lady Maisry is gane hame,
   Made him a winding sheet,
And at the back of merry Lincoln
   The dead corpse did her meet.

17 And a' the bells o merry Lincoln
   Without men's hands were rung,
And a' the books of merry Lincoln
   Were read without man's tongue,
And neer was such a burial
   Sin Adam's days begun.

B - THE FATAL FLOWER GARDEN

1 It rained, it poured, it rained so hard,
   It rained so hard all day,
But all the boys in our school
   Came out to toss and play.

2 They tossed their ball again so high
   Then again so low,
They tossed it into a flower garden
   Where no one was allowed to go.

3 Up stepped this gypsy lady,
   All dressed in yellow and green:
"Come in, come in, my pretty little boy,
   And get your ball again."

4 "I won't come in, I shan't come in,
   Without my playmates all.

41

I'll go t' my father 'n' tell him about it,
That'll cause tears to fall."

5 She first showed him an apple seed [sweet?]
Then again a gold ring,
Then she showed him a diamunt,
That enticed him in.

6 She took him by his lily-white hand,
She led him through the hall,
She put him into an upper room,
Where no one could hear him call.

7 "Oh take these finger-rings off my fingers,
Smoke them with your breath.
If any of my friends should call for me,
Tell them that I'm at rest.

8 "Tether the Bible at my head,
The Testament at my feet
If my dear mother should call for me,
Tell her that I'm fast asleep.

9 "Tether the Bible at my feet,
The Testament at my head.
If my dear father should call for me,
Tell him that I am dead."

C - IT RAINED A MIST

It rained a mist, it rained a mist,
It rained all over the town, town, town,
It rained all over the town.

And all the boys went out to play
A-tossing their ball around, round, round,
A-tossing their ball around.

At first they tossed their ball too low,
And then they tossed it too high, high, high,
And then they tossed it too high.

They tossed it into a lady's garden
Where roses and lilies lie, lie, lie,
Where roses and lilies lie.

"The Cherry-Tree Carol," number 54, based on the
Pseudo-Matthew Gospel, is widespread throughout Europe
with the fruit varying from country to country. The
text is Child A, from Sandys Christmas Carols, London,
1833.

42

THE CHERRY TREE CAROL

1 Joseph was an old man,
    and an old man was he,
When he wedded Mary,
    in the land of Galilee.

2 Joseph and Mary walked
    through an orchard good,
Where was cherries and berries,
    so red as any blood.

3 Joseph and Mary walked
    through an orchard green,
Where was berries and cherries,
    as thick as might be seen.

4 O then bespoke Mary,
    so meek and mild:
"Pluck me one cherry, Joseph,
    for I am with child."

5 O then bespoke Joseph,
    with words most unkind:
"Let him pluck thee a cherry
    that brought thee with child."

6 O then bespoke the babe,
    within his mother's womb:
"Bow down then the tallest tree,
    for my mother to have some."

7 Then bowed down the highest tree
    unto his mother's hand;
Then she cried, "See, Joseph
    I have cherries at command."

8 O then bespake Joseph:
    "I have done Mary wrong;
But cheer up, my dearest,
    and be not cast down."

9 Then Mary plucked a cherry,
    as red as the blood,
Then Mary went home
    with her heavy load.

10 Then Mary took her babe,
    and sat him on her knee,
Saying, "My dear son, tell me
    what this world will be."

11 "O I shall be as dead, mother,
      as the stones in the wall;
   O the stones in the streets, mother,
      shall mourn for me all.

12 "Upon Easter-day, mother
      my uprising shall be;
   O the sun and the moon, mother,
      shall both rise with me."

"Corpus Christi" or "All Bells In Paradise" is not
from the Child collection; indeed most scholars would
classify it as a lyrical song. It is included here because of its dramatic and brooding nature and also because of its possible connection with "The Three
Ravens." The work is filled with symbolism: the bleed-
ing knight, the mysterious hound, an altar stone. No
one has ever quite figured out the meaning of it all,
although references to the Holy Grail legends are apparent. Perhaps no rational explanation is possible.
The text is from Staffordshire, England, 1862, plus the
final stanza from a fifteenth century manuscript.

ALL BELLS IN PARADISE

1 Over yonder's a park which is newly begun,
   All bells in Paradise I hear them ring,
   Which is silver on the outside and gold within,
   And I love sweet Jesus above a thing.
      [repeat lines 2 and 4 in stanzas 2-7]

2 And in that park there stands a hall,
   Which is covered all over with purple and pall.

3 And in that hall there stands a bed,
   Which is hung all round with silk curtains red.

4 And in that bed there lies a knight,
   Whose wounds they do bleed by day and by night.

5 At that bed side there lies a stone,
   Which is our blessed Virgin Mary then kneeling on.

6 At that bed's foot there lies a hound,
   Which is licking the blood as it daily runs down.

7 At that bed's head there grows a thorn,
   Which was never so blossomed since Christ was born.

   And by that bede side there standeth a stone,
   Corpus Christi wreten there on.

FATAL ROMANCE

Many of the prime classic ballads are those which
focus on tragedy. This should not be surprising, for
as the well-written tragic play or book commands attention, so too does the tragic ballad. And when tragedy
and romance are intertwined in a well constructed
ballad, its chance of being passed on generation by
generation increases significantly. It is not acci-
dental that at least three of the best known Child
ballads fall into the "fatal romance" category: "Lord
Randall," "Lord Lovel," and "Barbara Allen."

"Lord Randall," number 12, in one form or another,
is a tale known throughout most of Europe. An Italian
version was printed in Verona in 1629; the story is told
in Gaelic under the title "An Tighearna Randal." Elements in the tale vary: the murderer could be the mistress, the wife, or the grandmother; the poisoned food
could be snake or eel meat, or even cakes. However, the
end result is universal--the death of the hero. The
ballad is an excellent example of incremental repetition, that is, the continued repetition of a line or
stanza but with an important change at some point. This
technique helps build the suspense until the final repetition dramatically concludes the story. Version A,
learned by Ewan MacColl from his mother in Scotland, is
recorded on The English and Scottish Popular Ballads,
Folkways Records FG 3509 (used by permission of Folkways
Records). B, from Lawrence Older of Middle Grove, New
York, apparently traces back to a Celtic source. Older
sings it on Adirondack Songs, Ballads and Fiddle Tunes,
Folk-Legacy Records FSA-15 (used by permission of Folk-
Legacy Records, Sharon, Conn.).

A - LORD RANDALL

1 "O where hae ye been, Lord Randall my son?
  O where hae ye been, my bonnie young man?"
  "I've been tae the wild wood mither, mak' my bed
    soon,
  For I'm weary wi' hunting and fain would lie
    doon."

2 "Whaur gat ye your supper, Lord Randall, my son?
  Whaur gat ye your supper, my bonnie young man?"
  "I dined wi' my true love, mither, mak' my bed
    soon,
  For I'm weary wi' hunting and I fain would lie
    doon."

[similarly]

3 "What happened to your bloodhounds, Lord Randall,
        my son?"
   "O, they swelled and they died, mither, mak' my
        bed soon."

4 "What gat ye to your supper, Lord Randall, my son?"
   "I had eels boiled in bro', mither, mak' my bed
        soon."

5 "O, I fear that ye are poisoned, Lord Randall, my
        son!"
   "O, aye, I am poisoned, mither, mak' my bed soon."

6 "What will ye leave your brither, Lord Randall,
        my son?"
   "The horses and the saddle that hangs in yon
        stable."

7 "What will ye leave your sweetheart, Lord Randall,
        my son?"
   "The tow and the halter that hangs on yon tree,
   And there let her hang for the poisoning of me."

B – JOHNNY RANDALL

1 "What'd you have for your breakfast,
        Johnny Randall, my son?
   What'd you have for your breakfast,
        My beloved sweet one?"
   "A quart of cold poison, mother;
        Make my bed soon,
   I'm sick to my heart and I long to lie down."

[similarly]

2 "What'll you leave your dear mother?"
   "My gold and my silver."

3 "What'll you leave your dear father?"
   "A pair of white horses."

4 "What'll you leave your dear wife?"
   "Hell's gates opened wide."

The plot in "Lord Lovell," number 75, is uncompli-
cated: the lord leaves the country, his wife dies, he
returns, mourns her death, and dies of sorrow. Child
wrote: "It is silly sooth, like the old age. Therefore a gross taste has taken pleasure in parodying it

46

. . .but there are people in this world who are amused
even with a burlesque of Othello."[1] One scholar called
it insipid. But the folk have loved "Lord Lovell," perhaps because it is so simple and because it is an ideal-
istic tale of love and tragedy. Version A is from a
London broadside of 1846 in Dixon's Ancient Poems,
Ballads, and Songs of the Peasantry of England (Child
H). This is probably the source of North American
variants. Frank Proffitt sings a similar one on his
Folk-Legacy Memorial Album. B, "Abe Lincoln Stood At
the White House Gate," is a parody from Mrs. T. C.
Cummins of Rumford, Virginia, in Arthur Kyle Davis,
Traditional Ballads of Virginia (Cambridge, Mass.:
Harvard University Press, 1929), p. 258. C, "The New
Ballad of Lord Lovell," is a Missouri parody satirizing
the Confederate officer Mansfield Lovell who fled Ad-
miral Faragut's guns at New Orleans in 1862. Reprinted
from Ballads and Songs, Collected by the Missouri Folk-
Lore Society, edited by H. M. Belden, by permission of
the University of Missouri Press, University of Missouri
Studies, Volume IX, No. 1, p. 54.

A - LORD LOVELL

1 Lord Lovell he stood at his castle-gate,
    Combing his milk-white steed,
When up came Lady Nancy Belle,
    To wish her lover good speed, speed,
    To wish her lover good speed.

2 "Where are you going, Lord Lovell?" she said,
    "Oh where are you going?" said she;
"I'm going, my Lady Nancy Belle,
    Strange countries for to see."

3 "When will you be back, Lord Lovell?" she said,
    "Oh when will you come back?" said she;
"In a year or two, or three, at the most,
    I'll return to my fair Nancy."

4 But he had not been gone a year and a day,
    Strange countries for to see,
When languishing thoughts came into his head,
    Lady Nancy Belle he would go see.

5 So he rode, and he rode, on his milk-white steed,
    Till he came to London town,

---

[1]Child, English and Scottish Ballads, II, 204.

And there he heard St. Pancras bells,
  And the people all mourning round.

6 "O what is the matter?" Lord Lovel he said,
  "O what is the matter?" said he.
"A lord's lady is dead," a woman replied,
  "And some call her Lady Nancy."

7 So he ordered the grave to be opened wide,
  And the shroud he turned down,
And there he kissed her clay-cold lips,
  Till the tears came trickling down.

8 Lady Nancy she died, as it might be, today,
  Lord Lovel he died as tomorrow;
Lady Nancy she died out of pure, pure grief,
  Lord Lovell he died out of sorrow.

9 Lady Nancy was laid in St. Pancras church,
  Lord Lovel was laid in the choir;
And out of her bosom there grew a red rose,
  And out of her lover's a briar.

10 They grew, and they grew, to the church-steeple
    too,
  And then they could grow no higher;
So there they entwined in a true-lover's knot,
  For all lovers true to admire.

    B - ABE LINCOLN STOOD AT THE WHITE HOUSE GATE

1 Abe Lincoln stood at the White House Gate
  Combing his milk-white steed,
When along came Lady Lizzie Tod,
  Wishing her lover good speed, speed, speed,
    Wishing her lover good speed.

2 "Where are you going, Abe Lincoln?" she said,
  "Where are you going?" said she.
"I'm going, my dearest Lizzie Tod,
  O'er Richmond for to see, see, see," [etc.]

3 "When will you be back, Abe Lincoln?" she said,
  "When will you be back?" said she.
"In sixty or ninety days at the most,
  I'll return to my Lady Lizzie, -zie, -zie," [etc.]

4 He hadn't been gone more than one or two days,
  O'er Richmond for to see,
When back to the White House Gate he came,
  All tattered and torn was he, he, he, [etc.]

48

5 "How do you flourish, Abe Lincoln?" she said,
  "How do you flourish?" said she.
  "The rebels have killed my old Scotch horse,
  And I have skedaddled, -dee, -dee, -dee, -dee,"
      [etc.]

6 Abe Lincoln rode his Burnside horse
  Which started at the rebel's fire,
  He threw the baboon heels over head,
  And there he stuck tight in the mire, -ire, -ire,
      And there he stuck tight in the mire.

C - THE NEW BALLAD OF LORD LOVELL

1 Lord Lovel he sat in St. Charles Hotel,
  In St. Charles Hotel sat he,
  A-cutting as big a rebel swell,
  As ever you'd wish to see, see, see,
      As ever you'd wish to see.

2 He had thirty thousand gallant men,
  Thirty thousand men had he,
  Who'd all sworn with him they'd never surrender
  To any tarnation Yankee, -kee, -kee, [etc.]

3 His thirty thousand gallant men
  Dwindled down to a thousand and six;
  And all of them then and there instanter
  Commenced to cutting their sticks, sticks, sticks,
      [etc.]

4 Lord Lovel he sat in St. Charles Hotel,
  In St. Charles Hotel sat he;
  And gallant old Ben sailed in with his men,
  And captured their great citee, -tee, -tee, [etc.]

Child number 81, "Little Musgrave and Lady
Barnard," commonly known as "Mattie Groves," is mentioned in the 1611 Beaumont and Fletcher play, Knight of the
Burning Pestle. References are found in other seventeenth century plays and a copy of the ballad appeared
in Wit Restored, 1658. In North America the ballad is
over three hundred years old and developed almost exclusively through the oral process since few broadsides
were ever printed. "Mattie Groves" captures a full
range of human emotions set within a love triangle for-
mat that culminates in one of the greatest scenes of re-
tribution in the English language. The intensity of the
drama is heightened by the accompanying music. The result is a ballad unsurpassed by few, if any, others.
Bob Gibson and Joan Baez recorded personalized inter-

pretations. The text, "Lord Darnell," is a composite from the singing of Boyd Bolling and Finlay Adams of Wise County, Virginia, by Paul Clayton on Folksongs and Ballads of Virginia, Folkways FA 2110 (used by permission of Folkways Records).

LORD DARNELL

1 One day, one day, one holiday,
  The very first day of the year,
  Little Mathy Groves to the church did go
  Some holy words to hear.

2 The first came in was lily white,
  The next was pink and blue,
  The next come in was Lord Darnell's wife,
  A flower among the few.

3 She placed her eyes on the little Mathy Groves,
  These words to him did say:
  "You must come home with me this night,
  This livelong night to stay."

4 "I can't go home with you this night,
  I can not for my life,
  For by the rings that's on your fingers
  You are Lord Darnell's wife."

5 "Oh, what if I am Lord Darnell's wife,
  Lord Darnell ain't at home,
  He's off in some foreign country
  A-learning the tailor's [?] trade."

6 She looked at him, he looked at her,
  The like had never been done.
  Lord Darnell's footpage went to tell
  Before the rising sun.

7 He rode till he came to the broad river side,
  He bowed his breast and he swum,
  He swum till he came to the other side
  And he buckled his shoes and he run.

8 He went all to Lord Darnell's hall,
  He tingled at the ring,
  No one came but Darnell himself
  To rise and bid him come in.

9 "What news, what news you bring to me,
  What news you bring to me,

50

Has any of my castle walls fell down
Or any of my work undone?"

10 "Oh, none of your castle walls fell down,
Nor none of your work's undone.
Little Mathy Groves in the North Scotland
In bed with the gayly one."

11 He rode till he came to the broad river side,
He bowed his breast and he swum,
He swum till he came to the other side
And he buckled his shoes and he run.

12 "I must get up, I must get up,
I must get up and go,
Lord Darnell he's a-coming now
I heard his bugle blow."

13 "You shan't get up, you shan't get up,
You shan't get up and go.
It's nothing but my father's boys
A-blowing the shepherd's horn."

14 Then they fell to huggin' and a-kissin',
And then they fell asleep.
When little Mathy wakened up
Lord Darnell was at their feet.

15 "Get up, get up," Lord Darnell said,
"Get up and put on your clothes.
Won't have it to say in North Scotland
I murdered a naked man."

16 "I can't get up, I can't get up,
I cannot for my life,
For you have got two glittering swords
And I have nary a knife."

17 "Well, If I have got two glittering swords,
Which cost me deep in the purse,
You may have the very best one,
And I will take the worst.

18 "And you can strike the first blow,
And strike it like a man.
And I will strike the next blow
And I'll kill you if I can."

19 Little Mathy struck the first lick,
Which hurt Lord Darnell sore;

Lord Darnell struck the next lick
Brought Mathy to the floor.

20 He called his true love to his knee,
These words to her did say,
"Oh, which do you love the best now,
Little Mathy Groves or me?"

21 "Very well I like your red rose cheeks,
Very well I like your chin,
But I like Mathy Groves in his gore of blood
More than you and all your kin."

22 He took her by the lily white hand
And led her through the hall,
And with his sword he cut off her head
And he kicked it against the wall.

And so we come to what many believe is the most
popular ballad in the English-speaking world, "Barbara
Allen," Child number 84. It has remained popular for
centuries. Samuel Pepys recorded in his Diary for
January 2, 1666, that he enjoyed hearing the actress
Mrs. Knipp sing the "little Scotch song of Barbary
Allen." Goldsmith wrote in 1765 that he was moved to
tears by an old dairymaid's version of the ballad. The
editor's own interest in folk music began one evening
in Massachusetts when he heard a fellow teenager by the
name of Paul Clayton singing "Barbara Allen" over a New
Bedford radio station. In the United States the ballad
has the widest geographical spread and overall currency
of any ballad--over ninety-two variants uncovered in
Virginia alone. Version A is the Child B text from the
Roxburghe Ballads. B is the splendid version Hedy West
sings on Hedy West: Old Times and Hard Times, Folk-
Legacy Records FSA-32 (used by permission of Hedy West).

A - BARBARA ALLEN

1 In Scarlet Town, where I was bound,
There was a fair maid dwelling,
Whom I had chosen to be my own,
And her name was Barbara Allen.

2 All in the merry month of May,
When the green leaves they was springing,
This young man on his death-bed lay,
For the love of Barbara Allen.

3 He sent his man unto her then,
To the town where she was dwelling:

"You must come to my master dear,
    If your name be Barbara Allen.

4 "For death is printed in his face,
    And sorrow's in him dwelling,
  And you must come to my master dear,
    If your name be Barbara Allen."

5 "If death be printed in his face,
    And sorrow's in him dwelling,
  Then little better shall he be
    For bonny Barbara Allen."

6 So slowly, slowly she got up,
    And so slowly she came to him,
  And all she said when she came there,
    "Young man, I think you are a dying. "

7 He turned his face unto her then:
    "If you be Barbara Allen,
  My dear," said he, "come pitty me,
    As on my death-bed I am lying."

8 "If on your death-bed you be lying,
    What is that to Barbara Allen?
  I cannot keep you from [your] death;
    So farewell," said Barbara Allen.

9 He turnd his face unto the wall,
    And death came creeping to him:
  "Then adieu, adieu, and adieu to all,
    And adieu to Barbara Allen!"

10 And as she was walking on a day,
    She heard the bell a ringing,
  And it did seem to ring to her
    "Unworthy Barbara Allen."

11 She turnd herself round about,
    And she spy'd the corps a coming:
  "Lay down, lay down the corps of clay,
    That I may look upon him."

12 And all the while she looked on,
    So loudly she lay laughing,
  While all her friends cry'd [out] amain,
    "Unworthy Barbara Allen!"

13 When he was dead, and laid in grave,
    Then death came creeping to she:

"O mother, mother, make my bed,
   For his death hath quite undone me.

14 "A hard-hearted creature that I was,
   To slight one that lovd me so dearly;
  I wish I had been more kinder to him,
   The time of his life when he was near me."

15 So this maid she then did dye,
   And desired to be buried by him,
  And repented her self before she dy'd,
   That ever she did deny him.

B - BARBRO ALLEN

1 In London city where I was born
  And where I got my learning,
  I fell in love with a blue eyed girl
  And her name was Barbro Allen.

2 It was in the month of May,
  When green buds they were swelling,
  Young William come from the western states
  And he courted Barbro Allen.

3 Sometime then a little later on,
  When the buds was blooming,
  Young William on his death bed lay
  For the love of Barbro Allen.

4 He sent his servant to the town,
  To the town where she was dwelling:
  "My master's sick and he bids you come,
  If your name be Barbro Allen."

5 Slowly, slowly she got up,
  And slowly she came nigh him;
  And all she said when she got there,
  "Young man, I think you're dying."

6 "Oh, yes, I'm sick, I'm very sick
  And death is on me dwelling;
  No better, no better I ever shall be
  If I can't have Barbro Allen."

7 "Don't you remember the other day,
  You was in the tavern drinking?
  You gave a health to the ladies all around,
  But you slighted Barbro Allen."

8 "Yes, I remember the other day,
   I was in the tavern drinking;
   I made a health to the ladies all around,
   I gave my love to Barbro Allen."

9 He turned his pale face to the wall,
   For death was drawing nigh him:
   "Farewell, farewell, my dear friends all,
   Be kind to Barbro Allen."

10 As she was walking o'er the hill,
   She heard the death bells knelling,
   And every stroke it seemed to say,
   "Hard hearted Barbro Allen."

11 She looked to the east and looked to the west,
   She saw his cold corpse coming;
   The more she looked the more she wept,
   She busted out a-crying.

12 "Lay down, lay down that corpse," she said,
   "That I may look upon it."
   The more she looked the more she wept,
   She busted out a-weeping.

13 "Oh, mother, go and make my bed,
   And make it long and narrow;
   William died for me today,
   I'll die for him tomorrow.

14 "Oh, father, oh father, go dig my grave,
   And dig it deep and narrow,
   For young William died for me today,
   I'll die for him tomorrow."

15 They buried them both in the old churchyard,
   They buried her beside him;
   From William's grave grew a red, red rose,
   From Barbro's grew a briar.

16 They grew and grew to the old church top,
   Till they could grow no higher;
   They all tied up in a true love's knot,
   The rose run 'round the briar.

In "The Braes O' Yarrow," number 214, a young woman
dreams that her relatives kill her lover. She warns him
of her vision, but he is unafraid. The dream becomes
reality when, at the Yarrow River, he is attacked and
killed by her disapproving relatives. In some endings
the woman commits suicide, in others she dies of a

broken heart. Variations of this basic plot are many including the following text, "The Dewey Dens of Yarrow." Collected by Max Hunter from the singing of Herbert Philbrick of Crocker, Missouri, it is one of the most lyrical of the variants. From: Ozark Folksongs and Ballads sung by Max Hunter, Folk-Legacy FSA-11 (used by permission of Folk-Legacy Records, Sharon, Conn.).

THE DEWEY DENS OF YARROW

1 There were five sons and two were twins,
  There were five sons of Yarrow;
  They all did fight for their own true love
  In the dewy dens of Yarrow.

2 "O mother dear, I had a dream,
  A dream of grief and sorrow;
  I dreamed I was gathering heather bloom
  In the dewy dens of Yarrow."

3 "O daughter dear, I read your dream,
  Your dream of grief and sorrow;
  Your love, your love is lying slain
  In the dewy dens of Yarrow."

4 She sought him up and she sought him down,
  She sought him all through Yarrow;
  And then she found him lying slain
  In the dewy dens of Yarrow.

5 She washed his face and she combed his hair,
  She combed it neat and narrow;
  And then she washed that bloody, bloody wound
  That he got in the Yarrow.

6 Her hair it was three-quarters long,
  The color it was yellow;
  She wound it round his waist so small,
  And took him home from Yarrow.

7 "O mother dear, go make my bed,
  Go make it neat and narrow;
  My love, my love he died for me,
  I'll die for him tomorrow."

8 "O daughter dear, don't be so grieved,
  So grieved with grief and sorrow;
  I'll wed you to a better one
  Than you lost in the Yarrow."

9 She dressed herself in clean white clothes,
  And away to the waters of Yarrow;
  And there she laid her own self down,
  And died on the banks of the Yarrow.

10 The wine that runs through the water deep
  Comes from the sons of Yarrow;
  They all did fight for their own true love
  In the dewy dens of Yarrow.

TRAGEDY

In addition to fatal romance, the classic ballads
have their share of other forms of tragedy. They range
from such an unbelievable episode as the death of the
ship's cabin boy in "The Golden Vanity," to the fratri-
cides in "The Twa Sisters" and "Edward," and to the
grisly tale of horror in "Lamkin."

The first example of tragic themes is one of the
oldest ballads in Child, number 10, "The Twa (or Two)
Sisters." The early texts had an element of the supernatural, but the more recent ones have concentrated on
the crime. Even so, there are considerable plot variations as the following examples show. Text A is by
traditional singer Lee Monroe Presnell from Beech
Mountain, North Carolina, on The Traditional Music of
Beech Mountain, North Carolina, Vol. I, FSA-22 (used by
permission of Folk-Legacy Records. Sharon, Conn.). B
is from the singing of Gerry Armstrong, Howie Mitchell
and friends. They learned it from Bob Coltman as
"Rollin' a-Rollin'" and must be heard to be appreciated
on Golden Ring, Folk-Legacy FSI-16 (used by permission
of Folk-Legacy Records, Sharon, Conn.) C, "Wind and
Rain," by Kilby Snow has different ingredients, the most
significant being the role of the fiddle and bow made
from parts of the dead woman. In Snow's variant we are
hearing echoes of an age in Great Britain dating back
to well before 1656 when the first known broadside of
"The Twa Sisters" was printed. Text: Kilby Snow:
Country Songs and Tunes with Autoharp, Asch Recordings
AH 3902 (used by permission of Folkways Records).

A - THE TWO SISTERS

1 There was two sisters that loved one man,
    Jenny flower genty, rosemary;
  And the youngest of them he loved best,
    And the jury hangs over the rosemary.

57

[repeat lines 2 and 4 in stanzas 2-10]

2 Oh, sister, sister, walk with me;
  Walk with me to the miller's pond.

3 Oh, the oldest pushed the youngest in;
  It was all for the sake that the water was clear.

4 Oh, sister, sister, reach me your hand;
  You may have half of that land.

5 Oh, sister, sister, I won't reach my hand;
  I will have all of that land!

6 Oh, sister, sister, reach me your glove;
  You may have sweet William for your old true love.

7 Oh, sister, sister, I won't reach my glove;
  I will have sweet William for my own true love!

8 Oh, she floated around and she floated down;
  She floated down to the miller's pond.

9 Oh, miller, miller, come and see;
  There is something here a-floating by me.

10 Oh, it is not a fish, nor is it not a swan;
   It is sweet William's old true love.

B - ROLLIN' A-ROLLIN'

1 There lived an old lord by the northern sea,
      Rollin', a-rollin',
  And he had daughters, one, two, and three,
      Down by the waters a-rollin'.

[repeat lines 2 and 4 in stanzas 2-11]

2 Two little sisters, side by side;
  The oldest one for Johnny cried.

3 Now, Johnny brought the old one a beaver hat;
  And the youngest one she thought hard of that.

4 Then Johnny brought the young one a gay, gold ring;
  He didn't bring the old one a single thing.

5 "Oh, sister, oh, sister, let's walk the seashore
  And see the ships as they sail o'er."

6 Two little sisters walking downstream;
  The oldest pushed the young one in.

7 Down she sank and away she swam;
  She floated on down to the miller's dam.

8 The miller he took her by the hand;
  And brought her safely back to the land.

9 The miller took off her gay, gold ring;
  And he pushed her back into the river again.

10 The miller was hung on the gallows so high;
   The oldest sister she was hung close by.

11 Thus endeth my tale of the north countrie;
   It is known as the Berkshire Tragedy.

C - WIND AND RAIN

1 It was early one morning in the month of May,
     Oh, the wind and the rain.
  Two lovers went fishing on a hot summer day,
     Crying the dreadful wind and rain.

  [repeat lines 2 and 4]

2 He said to the lady, "Won't you marry me?
  Then my little wife you'll always be."

3 Then he knocked her down and kicked her around,
  Knocked her down and he kicked her around.

4 And he hit her in the head with a battering ram,
  Hit her in the head with a battering ram.

5 And threw her in the river to drown,
  Threw her in the river to drown.

6 Watched her as she floated on down,
  Watched her as she floated on down.

7 Floated on down to the miller's little farm,
  Floated on down to the miller's little farm.

8 Then the miller fished her out with his long
     fishing line.
  The miller fished her out with his long fishing
     line.

59

9 Made fiddle pegs of her long finger bones,
   Made fiddle pegs of her long finger bones.

10 And made a fiddle bow of her long curly hair,
   And made a fiddle bow of her long curly hair.

11 Only tune that fiddle would play,
   Only tune that fiddle would play
     Was, crying the dreadful wind and rain.

"Edward," number 13, was originally a serious tale of fratricide and later, patricide. Tristram Coffin maintains that incest was the original motive for the murder. In stanza five of the following text, the line "We fell out about a sycamore bush" refers to an argument by the brothers over a woman, while older texts contain the phrase "breaking of the bush" which indicates her mistreatment. Max Hunter learned "How Come that Blood?" from Clyde Johnson of Fayetteville, Arkansas. In spite of its irony, the ballad is a parody of earlier texts, while the tempo and tune make it a humorous children's song. See Max Hunter, FSA-11 (used by permission of Folk-Legacy Records, Sharon, Conn.).

HOW COME THAT BLOOD?

1 "How come that blood on your coat sleeve?
     My son, come tell it to me."
   "It is the blood of the little yellow pony
   That plowed a furr' for me, me, me,
     That plowed a furr' for me."

2 "Oh, it is too red for that;
     My son, come tell it to me."
   "It is the blood of the guinea gay hawk
   That sailed away from me, me, me,
     That sailed away from me."

3 "Oh, it is too red for that;
     My son, come tell it to me."
   "It is the blood of the old gray hound
   That treed a coon for me, me, me,
     That treed a coon for me."

4 "Oh, it is too red for that;
     My son, come tell it to me."
   "It is the blood of my old dear brother
   That rode aside of me, me, me,
     That rode aside of me."

5 "What'd you and your brother fall out about?
      My son, come tell it to me."
   "We fell out about a sycamore bush
   That might have made a tree, tree, tree,
      That might have made a tree."

6 "Oh, what you gonna do when your father comes home?
      My son, come tell it to me."
   "I'll set my foot on yonder ship
   And sail across the sea, sea, sea,
      And sail across the sea."

7 "Oh, what you gonna do with your pretty little
      children?
      My son, come tell it to me."
   "I'll leave them here for my dear old mother
   To keep her company, nee, nee,
      To keep her company."

8 "Oh, what you gonna do with your house and barn?
      My son, come tell it to me."
   "I'll leave them here for my dear old mother
   To raise my children on, on, on,
      To raise my children on."

9 "Oh, what you gonna do with your pretty little
      wife?
      My son, come tell it to me."
   "I'll set her foot on yonder ship
   And sail across the sea, sea, sea,
      And sail across the sea."

10 "Oh, when you coming back?
      My son, come tell it to me."
   "I'm not coming back until the sun and the moon
   Both set in the north.
   And I'm sure it'll never be, be, be,
      And I'm sure it'll never be."

Featuring both rapid transitions and ironical
statements, "Sir Patrick Spens," number 58, is one of
the finest of the Scottish ballads. It may be based on
an actual historical event in 1281. Margaret, daughter
of Scotland's Alexander III, was married to the king of
Norway. On the return voyage the courtiers who accompanied her to Norway were drowned. However, all this is
speculation. The ballad received new life in the early
1970's with the folk-rock treatment by Fairport Convention. The text is from the recitation of Mrs. Notman
in 1826 as found in Motherwell's Manuscript, 493 (Child
C). Note the swift transition in stanza 3, and yet the

lingering in stanzas 8-10 to heighten the tension.

SIR PATRICK SPENS

1 The king sat in Dunfermline toun,
    Drinking the blude red wine:
"Where will I get a bold sailor,
    To sail this ship of mine?"

2 Out then spak an auld auld knicht,
    Was nigh the king akin:
"Sir Patrick Spens is the best sailor
    That ever sailed the main."

3 The king's wrote a large letter,
    Sealed it with his own hand,
And sent to Sir Patrick Spens,
    Was walking on dry land.

4 The first three lines he looked on,
    The tears did blind his ee;
The neist three lines he looked on
    Not one word could he see.

5 "Wha is this," Sir Patrick says,
    "That's tauld the king o me,
To set me out this time o the year
    To sail upon the sea!

6 "Yestreen I saw the new new mune,
    And the auld mune in her arm;
And this is the sign since we were born
    Even of a deadly storm.

7 "Drink about, my merry boys,
    For we maun sail the morn;
Be it wind, or be it weet,
    Or be it deadly storm."

8 We hadna sailed a league, a league,
    A league but only ane,
Till cauld and watry grew the wind,
    And stormy grew the main.

9 We hadna sailed a league, a league,
    A league but only twa,
Till cauld and watry grew the wind,
    Come hailing owre them a'.

10 We hadna sailed a league, a league,
    A league but only three,

Till cold and watry grew the wind,
   And grumly grew the sea.

11 "Wha will come," the captain says,
      "And take my helm in hand?
   Or wha'll gae up to my topmast,
      And look for some dry land?

12 "Mount up, mount up, my pretty boy,
      See what you can spy;
   Mount up, mount up, my pretty boy,
      See if any land we're nigh."

13 "We're fifty miles from shore to shore,
      And fifty banks of sand;
   And we have all that for to sail
      Or we come to dry land."

14 "Come down, come down, my pretty boy,
      I think you tarry lang;
   For the saut sea's in at our coat-neck
      And out at our left arm.

15 "Come down, come down, my pretty boy,
      I fear we here maun die;
   For thro and thro my goodly ship
      I see the green-waved sea."

16 Our Scotch lords were all afraid
      To weet their cork-heeled shoon;
   But land or a' the play was played
      Their hats they swam abune.

17 The first step that the captain stept,
      It took him to the knee,
   And the next step that the captain stepped
      They were a' drowned in the sea.

18 Half owre, half owre to Aberdour
      It's fifty fathoms deep,
   And their lay good Sir Patrick Spens,
      And the Scotch lords at his feet.

19 Lang may our Scotch lords' ladies sit,
      And sew their silken seam,
   Before they see their good Scotch lords
      Come sailing owre the main.

20 Lang lang may Sir Patrick's lady
      Sit rocking her auld son,

Before she sees Sir Patrick Spens
     Come sailing owre the main.

"Lamkin," number 93, is perhaps the most gory of
all the Child ballads, although "Prince Heathen," number
104, is a strong competitor for the title of most dis-
gusting. The plot of "Lamkin" remains much the same in
all twenty-six variants in Child. A stone mason murders
a wife and her child because her husband refused to pay
his wages. The weakness of the plot indicates that much
is missing from the original ballad. "Bo Lamkin" is the
title of Frank Proffitt's version which he sings on
Folkways FA 2360, Frank Proffitt Sings Folk Songs (used
by permission of Folkways Records).

BO LAMKIN

1 Bo Lamkin was as fine a mason
   As ever laid a stone,
   He built a fine castle
   And pay he got none,
   He built a fine castle,
   And pay he got none.

   [repeat lines 3 and 4 in all other stanzas]

2 He swore by his Maker
   He'd kill them unknown;
   Beware of Bo Lamkin
   When I'm gone from home.

3 Bo Lamkin he came to the castle
   And he knocked loud and long,
   There was no one as ready as the faultress,
   She arose and let him in.

4 "Oh, where is the landlord,
   Or is he at home?"
   "Oh, no, he's gone to merry England
   For to visit his son."

5 "How will we get her downstairs,
   Such a dark night as it is?"
   "Stick pins and needles
   In the little baby."

6 Bo Lamkin rocked the cradle
   And the faultress she sung,
   While the tears and red blood
   From the cradle did run.

7 The lady, comin' downstairs,
Not thinking no harm,
Bo Lamkin stood ready
He caught her in his arms.

8 "Bo Lamkin, Bo Lamkin,
Spare my life one day,
You can have all the gay gold
Your horse can tote away."

9 "Oh, keep your daughter Betsy,
For to go through the flood,
To scour the silver basin
That catches your heart's blood."

10 Daughter Betsy was a-settin',
In the castle so high,
She saw her dear father
Come a-ridin' hard by.

11 "Dear father, dear father,
Come see what's been done,
Bo Lamkin has been here
And he's killed your dear son.

12 "Bo Lamkin has been here
He's killed your baby,
Bo Lamkin has been here,
And killed your lady."

13 Bo Lamkin was hung
To the scaffold so high,
And the faultress was burned
To a stake standin' by.

"The Sweet Trinity" or "The Golden Vanity," number 286, is a highly popular ballad, especially in the United States. It has many titles including: "The Sweet Kumadee," "The Merry Golden Tree," "The Turkish Revery," and "Sinking in the Lonesome Sea." It can be traced back to a broadside from the 1680's in which the deceitful captain is named Sir Walter Raleigh. The ending of the ballad varies: the boy dies after being hauled on board, the boy receives his promised reward, the boy's ghost sinks the ship, but, in the most frequent ending, the boy drowns after the captain refuses to take him on board. The ballad has been recorded by such diverse singers as Odetta, Pete Seeger, Woody Guthrie, Richard Dyer-Bennett, Burl Ives, Gordon Bok, The Chad Mitchell Trio and a Canadian group, The Friends of Fiddler's Green. Version A is the first stanza from

Pepys' Ballads in which Raleigh is mentioned.   B is by
Horton Barker from his school days in Nashville, Tennessee, as recalled on Horton Barker: Traditional Singer,
Folkways FA 2362 (used by permission of Folkways Records).

A - THE SWEET TRINITY

Sir Walter Rawleigh has built a ship,
   In the Neatherlands
Sir Walter Rawleigh has built a ship,
   In the Neather-lands
And it is called The Sweet Trinity,
And it was taken by the false gallaly.
   Sailing in the Low-lands

B - THE GOLDEN WILLOW TREE

1 There was a little ship that sailed on the sea
And the name of this ship was the Turkish Rebilee;
She sailed on the lonely, lonesome water,
She sailed on the lonesome sea.

2 There was another ship that sailed on the sea
And the name of this ship was the Golden Willow
      Tree;
She sailed on the lonely, lonesome water,
She sailed on the lonesome sea.

3 Up stepped a little sailor, saying: "What'll you
      give to me
If I will sink that ship to the bottom of the sea?
If I'll sink her in the lonely, lonesome water.
If I sink her in the lonesome sea."

4 "I have a house and I have land
And I have a daughter that shall be at your
      command
If you'll sink her in the lonely, lonesome water,
If you'll sink her in the lonesome sea."

5 He bowed on his breast and away swam he;
He swam till he came to the Golden Willow Tree;
He sunk her in the lonely, lonesome water,
He sunk her in the lonesome sea.

6 He had a little auger all fit for to bore;
He bored nine holes in the bottom of the floor;
He sunk her in the lonely, lonesome water,
He sunk her in the lonesome sea.

7 Some had hats and some had caps
   A-trying to stop the salt water gaps
   As she sunk in the lonely, lonesome water,
   As she sunk in the lonesome sea.

8 Some were playing cards and some were shooting dice
   While others stood around a-giving good advice,
   As she sunk in the lonely, lonesome water,
   As she sunk in the lonesome sea.

9 He bowed on his breast and away swam he;
   He swam till he came to the Turkish Rebilee:
   "I've sunk her in the lonely, lonesome water,
   I've sunk her in the lonesome sea.

10 "Now captain, will you be as good as your word,
   Or either will you take me in on board?
   I've sunk her in the lonely, lonesome water,
   I've sunk her in the lonesome sea."

11 "No, I won't be as good as my word
   And neither will I take you in on board,
   Though you've sunk her in the lonely, lonesome
       water,
   Though you've sunk her in the lonesome sea."

12 "If it were not for the love I have for your men,
   I'd do unto you as I've done unto them;
   I'd sink you in the lonely, lonesome water,
   I'd sink you in the lonesome sea."

13 He bowed on his breast and down sunk he,
   A-bidding farewell to the Turkish Rebilee;
   He sunk in the lonely, lonesome water,
   He sunk in the lonesome sea.

LOVE CONQUERS ALL

   Most of the classic ballads concentrate on tragedy,
a theme that has intrigued audiences through the centuries. But there is another theme just as compelling
--true-love (as it is printed in the old texts) with a
happy ending. Here are six of the best.

   "Young Beichan," number 53, was considered by Child
"a favorite ballad, and most deservedly."[1] He printed

---

[1]Child, English and Scottish Ballads, I, 455.

fourteen versions of this saga which also is told in other languages from Icelandic to Italian. "Lord Bateman," the version below, is mainly from the singing of Pleaz Mobley of Manchester, Kentucky, with additions by the group who recorded it on The New Golden Ring: Five Days Singing, Vol. I, FSI-41 (used by permission of Folk-Legacy Records, Sharon, Conn.). It is a superb group performance of a splendid ballad.

LORD BATEMAN

1 Lord Bateman was a noble lord,
He thought himself of high degree;
He could not rest, nor be contented,
Until he'd sailed the old salt sea.

2 He sailed to the east, he sailed to the westward,
He sailed all over to Turkey's shore,
And there the Turks threw him into prison,
No hope of getting free anymore.

3 The Turk he had an only daughter,
The fairest one eye ever did see;
She stole the key to her father's prison
And there she set Lord Bateman free.

4 Then she led him down to the lowest cellar
And gave him a drink of the strongest wine;
Each moment seemed to be an hour:
"Oh, Lord Bateman, if you were mine!

5 "It's seven long years, let's make this bargain;
It's seven long years, give me your hand
That you will wed no other woman
And I will marry no other man."

6 Then she led him down to her father's harbor
And gave to him a ship so fine,
"Farewell to you, farewell Lord Bateman,
Farewell until we meet again."

7 When seven long years had gone and passed over,
It seemed to her like ninety-nine;
She bundled up her fine gold clothing;
Declared Lord Bateman she's go find.

8 She sailed to the east, she sailed to the westward,
She sailed all over to England's shore;
And when she came to Lord Bateman's castle,
Straightway she knocked upon the door.

9 "Oh, now, is this Lord Bateman's castle,
   And is his Lordship here within?"
   "Oh, yes, oh, yes," cried the proud young porter,
   "He's just now taken his new bride in."

10 "Tell him to send me a slice of cake
   And a bottle of the best red wine,
   And not to forget the fair young lady
   Who did release him when close confined."

11 "What news, what news, my proud young porter?
   What news, what news do you bring to me?"
   "There is the fairest of young ladies,
   The fairest one I ever did see.

12 "She's got gold rings on every finger,
   And on her middle finger three!
   She's got as much gold around her middle
   Would buy Northumberland from thee."

13 Lord Bateman rose from where he was sitting,
   His face it looked as white as snow:
   "Oh, if this is the Turkish lady,
   I'm bound with her, love, for to go."

14 And then up spoke the young bride's mother,
   She'd never been known to speak so free:
   "Then what's to become of my young daughter
   Who's just been made a bride to thee?"

15 Lord Bateman spoke to the young bride's mother:
   "She's none the better nor worse by me;
   She came here on a horse and saddle,
   She shall go home in a coach with thee.

16 "Let another wedding be made ready,
   Another wedding there must be;
   I must go marry the Turkish lady
   Who crossed the roaring seas for me."

   Another well-known ballad is "The Maid Freed from
the Gallows" or "The Hangman," number 95. It is a
model folksong with a simple plot, the important
question and answer response, and incremental repetition. The original story probably revolved around a
woman captured by pirates for ransom. After being refused by her relatives and friends, the pirates are
finally paid the ransom by her husband, or lover. The
story has served the folk in many ways: as a play-party
song, a game, a drama and a folktale.

In the United States John Jacob Niles popularized
the ballad on his extensive club and concert tours both
before and after World War II. The related black ballad
"The Gallows Pole" excited another generation, thanks
to recordings by the British pop star Rod Stewart in
1969 and by the rock group Led Zeppelin in 1970.

Practically all variants end happily, although
Harry Jackson concludes his cowboy variant on a cynical
note--the lover brings gold to make sure the hanging
takes place! Version A, from Emma Backus of North
Carolina, is a late addition in Child. The text has
been modernized by this editor. B is Fred Gerlach's
version of the "Gallows Pole" on Folkways FG 3529,
Twelve-String Guitar: Folk Songs and Blues (used by permission of Folkways Records).

A - THE HANGMAN

1 "Hangman, hangman, hold your hand,
        Oh, hold it wide and far!
    For there I see my father coming,
        Riding through the air.

2 "Father, father, have you brought me gold?
        Have you paid my fee?
    Or have you come to see me hung,
        Beneath the hangman's tree?"

3 "I have not brought you gold,
        I have not paid your fee,
    But I have come to see you hung
        Beneath the hangman's tree."

4 "Hangman, hangman, hold your hand,
        Oh, hold it wide and far!
    For there I see my mother coming
        Riding through the air.

5 "Mother, mother, have you brought me gold?
        Have you paid my fee?
    Or have you come to see me hung,
        Beneath the hangman's tree?"

6 "I have not brought you gold,
        I have not paid your fee,
    But I have come to see you hung
        Beneath the hangman's tree."

7 "Hangman, hangman, hold your hand,
        Oh, hold it wide and far!

For there I see my sister coming,
    Riding through the air.

8 "Sister, sister, have you brought me gold?
    Have you paid my fee?
  Or have you come to see me hung,
    Beneath the hangman's tree?"

9 "I have not brought you gold,
    I have not paid your fee,
  But I have come to see you hung
    Beneath the hangman's tree."

10 "Hangman, hangman, hold your hand,
    Oh, hold it wide and far!
  For there I see my sweetheart coming,
    Riding through the air.

11 "Sweetheart, sweetheart, have you brought me gold?
    Have you paid my fee?
  Or have you come to see me hung,
    Beneath the hangman's tree?"

12 "Oh, I have brought you gold,
    And I have paid your fee,
  And I have come to take you from
    Beneath the hangman's tree."

B - GALLOWS POLE

[spoken] In olden times when they put a man in
prison if he couldn't bring up a little money
they'd hang on the gallows pole. They're taking
this man to the gallows--hear death walking alongside shaking his bones. Putting the noose around
his neck. Here's the very last words he said:

1 "Hangman, hangman, hold it a little while,
Think I see my friends a-coming,
Riding a-many a mile.

2 "Friends, you get me some silver, get a little
    gold,
What did you bring me, my dear friends, to keep
    me from the gallows pole?
What did you bring me--keep me from the gallows
    pole?"

3 "Couldn't get you no silver,
Couldn't get you no gold,

You know that we're too damn poor
To keep you from the gallows pole."

4 "Hangman, hangman, hold it a little while,
Think I see my brother a-riding,
Riding a-many mile.

5 "Brother, you get me some silver, get a little
gold,
What did you bring me, my dear brother, to keep
me from the gallows pole?"

6 "Brother, I got some silver,
Brought a little gold,
Brought a little everything to keep you from the
gallows pole;
Yes, I brought you--keep from the gallows pole."

"Willie O Winsbury," number 100, is a classic tale
of an angry father out to punish his daughter's lover
for her pregnancy. However, he relents after meeting
the young man. There is also the theme of youthful re-
bellion: the lover rejects the father's offer of wealth
and rank. The ballad is rare in the United States, but
fairly common in Newfoundland. The text is Child A
from the Campbell Manuscripts, circa 1830.

WILLIE O WINSBURY

1 The king he hath been a prisoner,
A prisoner lang in Spain, O
And Willie a the Winsbury
Has lain lang wi his daughter at hame, O.

2 "What aileth thee, my daughter Janet,
Ye look so pale and wan?
Have ye had any sore sickness,
Or have ye been lying wi a man?
Or is it for me, you father dear,
And biding sae lang in Spain?"

3 "I have not had any sore sickness,
Nor yet been lying wi a man;
But it is for you, my father dear,
In biding sae lang in Spain."

4 "Cast ye off your berry-brown gown,
Stand straight upon the stone,
That I may ken ye by yere shape,
Whether ye be a maiden or none."

5 She's coosten off her berry-brown gown,
   Stooden straight upo yon stone;
Her apron was short, and her haunches were round,
Her face it was pale and wan.

6 "Is it to a man o might, Janet"
   Or is to a man of fame?
Or is it to any of the rank robbers
That's lately come out o Spain?"

7 "It is not to a man of might," she said,
   "Nor is it to a man of fame;
But it is to William of Winsbury;
I could lye nae langer my lane."

8 The king's called on his merry men all,
   By thirty and by three:
"Go fetch me William of Winsbury,
For hanged he shall be."

9 But when he cam the king before,
   He was clad o the red silk;
His hair was like to threeds o gold,
And his skin was as white as milk.

10 "It is nae wonder," said the king,
   "That my daughter's love ye did win;
Had I been a woman, as I am a man,
My bedfellow ye should hae been.

11 "Will ye marry my daughter Janet,
   By the truth of thy right hand?
I'll gie ye gold, I'll gie ye money,
And I'll gie ye an earldom of land."

12 "Yes, I'll marry yere daughter Janet,
   By the truth of my right hand'
But I'll hae nane o yer gold, I'll hae nane o
   yer money,
Nor I winna hae an earldom o land.

13 "For I hae eighteen corn-mills,
   Runs all in water clear,
And there's as much corn in each o them
As they can grind in a year."

   "The Bailiff's Daughter of Islington," number 105,
has the well-worn themes of separated lovers and mistaken identity combined together in a charming story.
Most North American variants appear to be based on the
eighteenth century Brooksly broadside below (from

Child).

THE BAILIFF'S DAUGHTER OF ISLINGTON

1 There was a youth, and a well belovd youth,
    And he was a esquire's son,
He loved the bayliff's daughter dear,
    That lived in Islington.

2 She was coy, and she would not believe
    That he did love her so,
No, nor at any time she would
    Any countenance to him show.

3 But when his friends did understand
    His fond and foolish mind.
They sent him up to fair London,
    An apprentice for to bind.

4 And when he had been seven long years,
    And his love he had not seen,
"Many a tear have I shed for her sake
    When she little thought of me."

5 All the maids of Islington
    Went forth to sport and play;
All but the bayliff's daughter dear;
    She secretly stole away.

6 She put off her gown of gray,
    And put on her puggish attire;
She's up to fair London gone,
    Her true-love to require.

7 As she went along the road,
    The weather being hot and dry,
There was she aware of her true-love,
    At length came riding by.

8 She stept to him, as red as any rose,
    And took him by the bridle-ring:
"I pray you, kind sir, give me one penny,
    To ease my weary limb."

9 "I prithee, sweetheart, canst thou tell me
    Where that thou was born?"
"At Islington, kind sir," said she.
    "Where I have had many a scorn."

10 "I prithee, sweetheart, canst thou tell me
    Whether thou dost know

74

The bayliff's daughter of Islington?"
"She's dead, sir, long ago."

11 "Then I will sell my goodly steed,
    My saddle and my bow'
 I will into some far countrey,
    Where no man doth me know."

12 "O stay, O stay, thou goodly youth!
    She's alive, she is not dead;
 Here she standeth by thy side,
    And is ready to be thy bride."

13 "O farewel grief, and welcome joy,
    Ten thousand times and more!
 For now I have seen my own true-love,
    That I thought I should have seen no more."

"The Gypsy Laddie," number 200, is probably only
second to "Barbara Allen" in long-term popularity.
Friedman, in his book of balladry, lists the ballad
under the category "romantic tragedy," for in the Scottish variants the lord hangs the gypsy and his colleagues, but no North American version ends that way.
Among the democratic folk of this continent, the lady
chooses the rag tag gypsy laddie over her rich husband.
Love does indeed conquer all! The ballad is known by
several other titles: "Black Jack Davy," "Big John
Davy," "Gypsy Lover," "Clayton Boone" (a cowboy variant)
and "Gyps of David" (revealing how oral transmission
can distort words). Version A is from Newton Pepoun
who learned it from a fellow student in Stockbridge,
Massachusetts, about 1845 (Child J). B, "Gyps of
David," is from Frank Proffitt, Folk-Legacy FSA-1 (used
by permission of Folk-Legacy Records, Sharon, Conn.).
C is an incomplete version from Lawrence Older, Folk-
Legacy FSA-15 (used by permission of Folk-Legacy
Records, Sharon, Conn.). D is the first stanza, utili-
zing the well known "Spanish leather" phrase, from Mrs.
Helena Titus Brown of New York, circa 1820 (Child K).

A - THE GYPSY LADDIE

1 There was a gip came oer the land,
    He sung so sweet and gaily;
 He sung with glee, neath the wild wood tree,
    He charmed the great lord's lady.

        Ring a ding a ding go ding go da,
          Ring a ding a ding go ding go da,

Ring a ding a ding go ding go da,
    She's gone with the gipsey Davy.

2 The lord he came home late that night;
    Enquiring for his lady,
"She's gone, she's gone," said his old servant-man,
    "She's gone with the gipsey Davy."

3 "Go saddle me my best black mare;
    The grey is neer so speedy;
For I'll ride all night, and I'll ride all day,
    Till I overtake my lady."

4 Riding by the river-side,
    The grass was wet and dewy;
Seated with her gipsey lad,
    It's there he spied his lady.

5 "Would you forsake your house and home?
    Would you forsake your baby?
Would you forsake your own true love,
    And go with the gipsey Davy?"

6 "Yes, I'll forsake my house and home,
    Yes, I'll forsake my baby;
What care I for my true love?
    I love the gipsey Davy."

7 The great lord he rode home that night,
    He took good care of his baby,
And ere six months had passed away
    He married another lady.

B - GYPS OF DAVID

1 Who's that galloping on the king's highway,
    Singing so gay and haley?
It's that dark and handsome lad
Known as the Gyps of David,
Known as the Gyps of David.

2 "Where may the good man be," said he,
    "My own true fair lady?"
"He's gone a-searching far and wide,
A-searching for the Gyps of David,
A-searching for the Gyps of David.

3 "Will you come away with me
And give up all you've saved,
And give up all the ones you love

To go with the Gyps of David
To go with the Gyps of David?"

4 "I'll leave the good man of the house,
   The baby in the cradle,
   And all the gold that's stored away,
   To go with the Gyps of David,
   To go with the Gyps of David."

5 So away they rode for many a day,
   Across the mirey heather;
   They didn't stop for vine nor briar,
   Or any sort of weather,
   Or any sort of weather.

6 The good man, when he returned,
   Inquiring for his lady:
   "She sped away awhile ago,
   In the arms of the Gyps of David,
   In the arms of the Gyps of David."

7 "Go saddle me up the fleetest steed
   And don't fool time a-dawdling;
   I'll have his head on the end of my sword,
   The head of the Gyps of David,
   The head of the Gyps of David."

8 He rode till he come to the waters wide
   And he couldn't go any farther;
   On the other side he spied his bride
   In the arms of the Gyps of David,
   In the arms of the Gyps of David.

9 "Will you return to the gold I have,
   Will you return to your baby?"
   "No, never will I leave the arms,
   The arms of the Gyps of David,
   The arms of the Gyps of David."

10 He jumped in the waters wide,
   In madness he was raving,
   And floated off down to the sea,
   Because of the Gyps of David,
   Because of the Gyps of David.

C - GYPSY DAVY

1 He came walking o'er the hills,
   Singing loud and gaily;
   Made the aisles of the green woods ring
   And he charmed the heart of a lady.

77

Rattle lattle lingo lingo ling,
Rattle lattle lingo Davy;
Rattle lattle lingo ling,
She's gone with the Gypsy Davy.

2 "Go harness up the old grey mare,
The black is not so speedy;
I'll ride all day and I'll ride all night,
Till I overtake my lady."

3 Last night she slept on a warm feather bed
And on her arm a baby;
Tonight she sleeps on the cold, cold ground,
Beside the Gypsy Davy.

D - THE GYPSY LADDIE

"Go bring me down my high-heeled shoes,
Made of the Spanish leather,
And I'll take off my low-heeled shoes,
And away we'll go together.

"Lizzie Lindsay," number 226, is a fine example of a Scottish love ballad. The folk in North America have confused it with another ballad, "The Blaeberry Court-ship," Laws N-19, and have even turned it into a lyrical song. The text is a late addition in Child, from traditional sources.

LIZZIE LINDSAY

1 "Will ye gang to the Highlands, Lizzie Lindsay?
Will ye gang to the Highlands wi me?
Will ye gang to the Highlands, Lizzie Lindsay,
My bride an my darling to be?"

2 She turned her round on her heel,
And a very loud laugh gaed she:
"I'd like to ken whaur I'm ganging,
An wha I am gaun to gang wi."

3 "My name is Donald Macdonald,
I'll never think shame nor deny;
My father he is an old shepard,
My mither she is an old dey.

4 "Will ye gang to the Highlands, bonnie Lizzie?
Will ye gang to the Highlands wi me?
For ye shall get a bed o green rashes,
A pillow on a covering of grey."

5 Upraise then the bonny young lady,
    An drew till her stockings an sheen,
  An packd up her claise in fine bundles,
    An away wi young Donald she's gaen.

6 When they cam near the end o their journey,
    To the house o his father's milk-dey,
  He said, "Stay still there, Lizzie Lindsay,
    Till I tell my mither o thee.

7 "Now mak us a supper, dear mither,
    The best of yer curds and green whey,
  An mak up a bed o green rashes,
    A pillow and covering o grey.

8 "Rise up, rise up, Lizzie Lindsay,
    Ye have lain oer lang i the day;
  Ye should hae been helping my mither
    To milk her ewes an her kye."

9 Out then spak the bonnie young lady,
    As the saut tears drapt frae her ee,
  "I wish I had bidden at hame;
    I can neither milk ewes or kye."

10 "Rise up, rise up, Lizzie Lindsay
    There is mair ferlies to spy;
  For yonder's the castle o Kingussie,
    An it stands high an dry."

11 "Ye are welcome here, Lizzie Lindsay,
    The flower o all your kin
  For ye shall be lady o Kingussie,
    An ye shall get Donald my son."

HUMOR

With the exception of the later parodies, humor plays a minor role in the classic ballads--drama and humor are difficult to mix. Nevertheless, there are a few ballads that contain some chuckles. "Our Goodman," number 274, exhibits some of the best characteristics of the more serious ballads including the question and answer technique. Version A, "Five Nights Drunk," is from the singing of Hattie Presnell as recorded on The Traditional Music of Beech Mountain, North Carolina, Volume 1, FSA-22 (used by permission of Folk-Legacy Records, Sharon, Conn.). Since version A omits the final stanzas which are bawdy in some variants, B supplies the last four verses from the Child B text and offers the drunken husband some sobering thoughts.

A - FIVE NIGHTS DRUNK

1 One night I come home,
  Drunk as I could be;
  I found a head upon the pillow
  Where my head ought to be.
  "Come here, my little wife, baby,
  Explain this thing to me.
  How come a head on the pillow
  Where my head ought to be?"

2 "You old fool, you blind fool,
  Can't you never see?
  It's nothing but a cabbage head
  My mama sent to me."
  "I've travelled this wide world over
  Ten thousand miles or more;
  A moustache on a cabbage head
  I never have seen before."

3 Next night I come home,
  Drunk as I could be;
  Found a coat a-hanging on a rack
  Where my coat ought to be.
  "Come here, my little wife, baby,
  Explain this thing to me.
  How come a coat a-hanging on a rack
  Where my coat ought to be?"

4 "You old fool, you blind fool,
  Can't you never see?
  It's nothing but a bed quilt
  My mama sent to me."
  "I've travelled this wide world over
  Ten thousand miles or more;
  Pockets on a bed quilt
  I never did see before."

5 Next night I come home,
  Drunk as I could be;
  I found a hat on the table
  Where my hat ought to be.
  "Come here, my little wife, baby,
  Explain this thing to me.
  How come a hat on the table
  Where my hat ought to be?"

6 "You old fool, you blind fool,
  Can't you never see?

It's nothing but a butter-dish
My mama sent to me."
"I've travelled this wide world over
Ten thousand miles or more,
But a band around a butter-dish
I never did see before."

7 Next night I come home,
   Drunk as I could be;
   Found a pair of boots a-setting in the corner
   Where my boots ought to be.
   "Come here, my little wife, baby,
   Explain this thing to me.
   How come a pair of boots in the corner
   Where my boots ought to be?"

8 "You old fool, you blind fool,
   Can't you never see?
   It's nothing but a churn
   My mama sent to me."
   "I've travelled this wide world over
   Ten thousand miles or more;
   Heel-irons upon a churn
   I never did see before."

9 Next night I come home,
   Drunk as I could be;
   Found a horse in the stable
   Where my horse ought to be.
   "Come here, my little wife, baby,
   Explain this thing to me
   How come a horse in the stable
   Where my horse ought to be?"

10 "You old fool, you blind fool,
   Can't you never see?
   It's nothing but a milk cow
   My mama sent to me."
   "I've travelled this wide world over
   Ten thousand times or more;
   Saddle upon a milk cow's back
   I never did see before."

B - OUR GOODMAN

1 I went into the chamber,
      and there for to see,
   And there I saw three men in bed lie,
      by one, by two, and by three.

2 I called to my loving wife,
    and "Anon, kind sir!" quoth she:
"O what do these three men in bed,
    without the leave of me?"

3 "Why, you old cuckold, blind cuckold,
    don't you very well see?
They are three milking-maids,
    my mother sent to me."

4 "Heyday! Godzounds! Milking-maids with beards on!
    the like was never known!"
Old Wichet a cuckold went out,
    and a cuckold he came home.

At one time "The Wife Wrapt In Wether's Skin,"
number 277, was very popular in Scotland. It tells of
a too proud wife who refused to bake, wash, or spin.
The husband strips off a wether's skin (a sheep's skin),
lays it on her back and beats the skin. This is done
so that the wife can not complain to her relatives that
her husband abused her. Today, such an over-reaction is
hardly humorous, but the original version of the tale
may have prescribed a beating in order to drive out evil
spirits in possession of the wife. Many North American
variants are called "The Wee Cooper of Fife," but the
following retains the traditional title. It was handed
down in Hedy West's family from her great-grandmother
and is recorded on Old Times and Hard Times, Folk-Legacy
FSA-32 (used by permission of Hedy West).

THE WIFE WRAPT IN WETHER'S SKIN

1 A little old man he lived a way out west,
    Dandoo, dandoo,
A little old man he lived a way out west,
    Clash to my clingo,
A little old man he lived a way out west,
He had a wife, she was none of the best,
    Splat-ta-ma-lat-ma-lingo.

[similarly]

2 The little old man went whistling to his plow,
Said, "Old woman, any bread baked now?"

3 "There's a little piece of crust a-laying on the
    shelf,
If that ain't enough, you can make it yourself."

4 He went out to his sheepfold
   And got him a wether, tough and old.

5 He hung it up on two little pins,
   About two jerks fetched its skin.

6 He threw it across his old wife's back
   And got him a stick and made it go whack.

7 "You can go tell your people and all your kin,
   I'll do as I please with my old sheepskin."

"The Farmer's Curst Wife," number 278, is summarized succintly by Child: "The devil comes for a
farmer's wife and is made welcome to her by the husband.
The woman proves to be no more controllable in hell than
she had been at home; she kicks the imps about, and even
brains a set of them with her pattens or maul. For
safety's sake, the devil is constrained to take her back
to her husband."[1] Version A is by Paul Clayton from the
singing of Miss Burma Bowie of Culpepper County, Virginia. Hear it on Folksongs and Ballads of Virginia,
Folkways FA 2110 (used by permission of Folkways Records). B is from the Adirondacks by Lawrence Older
who learned it from his father. Recorded on Folk-Legacy
FSA-15, Lawrence Older (used by permission of Folk-
Legacy Records, Sharon, Conn.). For other interesting
variants listen to Lena Armstrong and Etta Jones on
Beech Mountain, North Carolina, Volume I, Folk-Legacy
FSA-22 and Bill and Belle Reed's 1928 recording re-
issued on Anthology of American Folk Music, Volume I,
Folkways, FP 251.

A - THE FARMER'S CURST WIFE

1 There was an old farmer and he had a little farm,
      [whistle]
   And he had no horse to carry it on,
      Sing fol de rol dol de rol di do.

[repeat lines 2 and 4 in remaining stanzas]

2 So he hitched up his oxen and went out to plow,
   Along came the Devil a-crossing his brow.

3 "Oh, now, Mr. Devil, what is it you'll have?"
   "Your darned old scolding wife I'll have."

---

[1]Child, English and Scottish Ballads, V, 107.

4 "Oh, now, Mr. Devil, I'll tell you apart,
   You may have her with all of my heart."

5 So he threw the old woman over his back,
   And away he went ta-clickety-clack.

6 When he arrived at his hall door,
   He threw the old woman upon the floor.

7 One little devil came dragging a chain,
   She up with her foot and she kicked out his brains.

8 And one little devil, he called her a liar,
   She up with her foot and she kicked nine in the
        fire.

9 One little devil peeped over the wall,
   Cried, "Take her back, pap, or she'll kill us all."

10 The Devil he bundled her up in a sack,
   And like an old fool he came lugging her back.

11 Said he, "Old woman, did you fare very well?"
   Says she, "Old man I flattened all Hell."

12 What will become of the women?
   Won't have them in Hell and they can't get to
        Heaven.

B - RANDY RILEY

1 There was an old man, he lived in a barn,
        Twice fee and a high lily ho dum;
   He had an odd team to plow up his farm,
        With a twice fie lee fie lay fie lily ho dum.

   [repeat lines 2 and 4 in remaining stanzas]

2 He hadn't plowed o'er a furrow or two;
   Down come the Devil, right on a flue.

3 "Now," said old Randy, "I am undone;
   Here comes the Devil for my oldest son."

4 "No," said the Devil, "I don't want your son;
   Your scolding wife is the only one."

5 "Then," said old Randy, "with all my heart,
   Oh, how I hope that you never do part."

84

6 He grabbed the old woman, slung her on his back;
Started for hell with a clickety-clack.

7 He set her down at the gates of Hell;
Said, "I'll leave you there 'cause you look pretty
well."

8 A little young devil came up with his ire;
She up with her rake and knocked him in the fire.

9 Another young devil peeked over the wall;
Said, "Take her 'way, Daddy, or she'll kill us
all."

10 The Devil come out, slung her on his back;
He says, "I'm a fool, but I'll take her back."

11 As she went tumbling over the hills;
"The devil won't have me, I wonder who will."

12 To prove that women are worse than men;
One went to hell and got kicked out again.

PROTEST

Very few of the classic ballads deal with protest
per se, although an element of protest appears in many.
There are a few, however, where it is clear that the
message is protest--political, economic, or social.
"Johnie Cock," number 114, is one. Child called it a
"precious specimen of the unspoiled traditional
ballad,"[1] but the plot reveals it is more than that.
Johnie (Johny, Johnny, etc.) Cock, or "Johnie o
Breadislee," goes out to hunt deer, disregarding the law
prohibiting such an activity. He kills a deer and, together with his hounds, feasts on the remains. Later,
he falls asleep and is spotted by an old man who informs
the king's game wardens, or foresters. They confront
Johnie, wound him, but in the following fierce fight he
kills all of them but one. Badly wounded, the remaining forester is allowed to escape to spread the word of
Johnie's exploits.

The love of the Scots for this ballad reveals
their admiration for the outlaw-hero who breaks the law
and then destroys those who have come to enforce the

---

[1]Child, English and Scottish Ballads, III, p. 1.

85

law. Notice that Johnie's action is an individual act
of aggression against the establishment. Individualism
is praised by the folk, revolution is not! In North
American folklore, the outlaw Jesse James is treated
in much the same way. The text is Child A, from Percy,
1780.

JOHNIE COCK

1 Johny he has risen up i the mourn,
    Calls for water to wash his hands;
  But little knew he that his bloody hounds
    Were bound in iron bands,
    Were bound in iron bands.

2 Johny's mother has gotten word o that,
    And care-bed she has taen:
  "O Johny, for my benison,
    I beg you'l stay at hame;
  For the wine so red, and the well baken bread,
    My Johny shall want nane.

3 "There are seven forsters at Pickeram Side,
    At Pickeram where they dwell,
  And for a drop of thy heart's bluid
    They wad ride the fords of hell."

4 Johny he's gotten word of that,
    And he's turnd wondrous keen;
  He's put off the red scarlett,
    And he's put on the Lincoln green.

5 With a sheaf of arrows by his side,
    And a bent bow in his hand,
  He's mounted on a prancing steed,
    And he has ridden fast oer the strand.

6 He's up i Braidhouplee, and down in Bradyslee,
    And under a buss o broom,
  And there he found a good dun deer,
    Feeding in a buss of ling.

7 Johny shot, and the dun deer lap,
    And she lap wondrous wide,
  Until they came to the wan water,
    And he stemd her of her pride.

8 He 'as taen out the little pen-knife,
    'Twas full three quarters long,
  And he has taen out of that dun deer
    The liver bot and the tongue.

86

9 They eat of the flesh, and they drank of the blood,
    And the blood it was so sweet,
Which caused Johny and his bloody hounds
    To fall in a deep sleep.

10 By then came an old palmer,
    And an ill death may he die!
For he's away to Pickram Side,
    As fast as he can drie.

11 "What news, what news?" says the Seven Forsters,
    "What news have ye brought to me?"
"I have noe news," the palmer said,
    "But what I saw with my eye.

12 "High up i Bradyslee, low down i Bradisslee,
    And under a buss of scroggs,
O there I spied a well-wight man,
    Sleeping among his dogs.

13 "His coat it was of light Lincolm,
    And his breeches of the same,
His shoes of the American leather,
    And gold buckles tying them."

14 Up bespake the Seven Forsters,
    Up bespake they ane and a':
"O that is John o Cockleys Well,
    And near him we will draw."

15 O the first y stroke that they gae him,
    They struck him off by the knee;
Then up bespake his sister's son:
    "O the next'll gar him die!"

16 "O some they count ye well-wight men,
    But I do count ye nane;
For you might well ha wakend me,
    And askd gin I wad be taen.

17 "The wildest wolf in aw ths wood
    Wad not ha done so by me;
She'd ha wet her foot ith wan water,
    And sprinkled it oer my brae,
And if that wad not ha wakend me,
    She wad ha gone and let me be.

18 "O bows of yew, if ye be true,
    In London where ye were bought,
Fingers five, get up belive,
    Manhuid shall fail me nought."

19 He has killd the Seven Forsters,
   He has killd them all but ane,
And that wan scarce to Pickeram Side,
   To carry the bode-words hame.

20 "Is there never a boy in a' this wood
   That will tell what I can say;
That will go to Cockleys Well,
   Tell my mither to fetch me away?"

21 There was a boy into that wood,
   That carried the tidings away,
And many ae was the well-wight man
   At the fetching o Johny away.

Child catalogued thirty-eight separate Robin Hood ballads. A few of them he judged to be among the best in the ballad world, a few among the worst. The ballads trace the adventures of Robin Hood literally from birth to death. But was Robin's birth legitimate, that is, was he a historical character or an invention of fiction? After extensive research, Child reached an inescapable conclusion:

> Robin Hood is absolutely a creation of the
> ballad-muse. The earliest mention we have of
> him is as the subject of ballads. The only two
> historians who speak of him as a ballad-hero,
> pretend to have no information about him except
> what they derive from ballads, and show that
> they have none other by the the description
> they give of him; this description being in
> entire conformity with ballads in our possession,
> one of which is found in a MS. as old as the
> older of these two writers.[1]

Child raised a second question: what did this fictional character stand for that endeared him to so many generations of the folk? He supplied the answer:

> Robin Hood is a yeoman, outlawed for reasons
> not given but easily surmised, "courteous and
> free," religious in sentiment, and above all

---

[1]Child, English and Scottish Ballads, III, p. 42.
However, J. W. Walker in The True History of Robin Hood
and P. Valentine Harris in The Truth about Robin Hood
present evidence of a real fourteenth century Robin Hood
around whom the legends may have developed.

reverent of the Virgin, for the love of whom
he is respectful to all women. He lives by
the king's deer (though he loves no man in the
world so much as his king) and by levies on the
superfluity of the higher orders, secular and
spiritual, bishops and archbishops, abbots,
bold barons, and knights, but harms no husband-
man or yeoman, and is friendly to poor men
generally, imparting to them of what he takes
from the rich. Courtesy, good temper, liber-
ality, and manliness are his chief marks: for
courtesy and good temper he is a popular Gawain.
Yeoman as he is, he has a kind of royal dignity,
a princely grace, and a gentleman-like refine-
ment of humor. This is the Robin Hood of the
Gest especially; the late ballads debase this
primary conception in various ways and degrees.

This is what Robin Hood is, and it is
equally important to observe what he is not.
He has no sort of political character, in the
Gest or any other ballad. This takes the
ground from under the feet of those who seek
to assign him a place in history.[1]

So, as with Johnie Cock, Robin Hood is not a revolution-
ist, but an individualist protesting governmental in-
justice.

Less than a dozen Robin Hood ballads survive in
oral tradition, seven of them in North America including
number 140, "Robin Hood Rescuing Three Squires." It is
an excellent example of folk resentment toward authori-
ty. Three squires are about to be hanged for poaching.
Robin Hood devises a plan to free the three and hang the
sheriff instead! The text is from the singing of
Charles Finnemore listed as A[2] in Helen Hartness
Flanders, Ancient Ballads Traditionally Sung in New England (Philadelphia: University of Pennsylvania Press,
1963), III, pp. 112-115 (used by permission of the
Flanders Ballad Collection, Middlebury College, Middlebury, Vermont). An abridged version is sung by Wallace
House on Robin Hood Ballads, Folkways FW 6839.

ROBIN HOOD RESCUING THREE SQUIRES

1 Bold Robin Hood marched along the highway
  Along the highway marched he,

---

[1]Ibid., pp. 42-43.

Until he met with a lady fair
A-weeping along the highway.

2 "Oh, do you mourn for gold," he says
"Or do you mourn for fee,
Or do you mourn for any high knight
That's deserted your company?"

3 "No, I don't mourn for gold," she sayed,
"Nor I don't mourn for fee,
Nor I don't mourn for any high knight
That's deserted my company.

4 "But I do mourn for my three sons;
Today they're condemned to die;
In Nottingham town so fast they lie bound,
In Nottingham prison they lie."

5 "Oh, have they sat any temple on fire
Or any high knight have they slain
Or have they enticed fair maidens to sin
Or with married men's wives have they lain?"

6 "No, the've not sat any temple on fire
Nor any high knight have they slain
Nor they've not enticed fair maidens to sin
Nor with married men's wives they've not lain.

7 "But they have killed the King's fallow deer.
Today they're condemned to die.
In Nottingham town so fast they lie bound,
In Nottingham prison they lie."

8 "Go home, go home," said bold Robin Hood,
"And weep no more today
And I will stand hangman this livelong day
To hang the squires all three."

9 Then Robin Hood called on his merry men all,
By one, by two, and by three,
"When you hear three blasts on my bugle horn
You must hasten most speedily."

10 Bold Robin Hood marched along the highway,
Along the highway marched he,
Until he met with an old beggarman
A-begging along the highway.

11 "Good morning, good morning, my old beggarman,
What news do you bring to me?"

"There is weeping and wailing in all Nottingham
For the loss of the squires all three."

12 "Come change your clothing," said bold Robin Hood,
"Come change your clothing for mine.
Here's fifty bright guineas I'll give in exchange.
'Twill buy you cake and wine."

13 Robin Hood put on the beggarman's clothes.
They were made of hemp and tow.
"They will cause me to scrub," said bold Robin
    Hood,
"But further today I must go."

14 Bold Robin Hood marched along the highway,
Along the highway marched he,
Until he met with the master high sheriff,
And with him the squires three.

15 "Good morning, good morning, my old beggarman,
What can I do for thee?"
"I want to stand hangman this livelong day
To hang the squires three."

16 "Yes, you can have all of their gay clothing,
And all of their bright monee,
And you may stand hangman this livelong day
To hang the squires three."

17 "I don't want none of their gay clothing
Nor none of their bright monee,
But I want three blasts on my bugle horn
That their souls in heaven might be."

18 Bold Robin Hood marched to the gallus so high,
To the gallus so high marched he,
And by his side was the master high sheriff
And with him the squires three.

19 He put the bugle horn to his mouth.
He blew it loud and shrill.
A hundred and ten of bold Robin Hood's men
Come trippeling over the hill.

20 "Whose men, whose men?" O cried the high sheriff,
"Whose men? I pray, tell me."
"They are mine and not thine," said bold Robin
    Hood,
"Come to borrow three squires of thee."

21 "O take them, O take them," then cried the high
        sheriff,
    "O take them, O take them," cried he;
    "But there's not another beggar in all Nottingham
    Could borrow three more from me."

The Maine text fails to complete the story, however,
Child B, circa 1786, does:

    They took the gallows from the slack,
        They set it in the glen,
    They hangd the proud sheriff on that,
        Released their own three men.

"Lilliburlero," a non-Child propaganda piece, was
credited with the overthrow of James II during Britain's
Glorious Revolution of 1688. This was probably an ex-
aggeration. More likely, the song served as a symbol
for the anti-James forces as "We Shall Overcome" did for
the civil rights movement of the 1960's and Country Joe
McDonald's "I-Feel-Like-I'm-Fixin'-to-Die-Rag" did for
the anti-Vietnam War movement. Text: Chappel, <u>Popular
Music</u>, II, p. 572.

LILLIBURLERO

1 Ho! broder Teague, dost hear de decree?
        Lilli burlero, bullen a-la.
    Dat we shall have a new deputie,
        Lilli burlero burlen a-la.
        Lero lero, lilli burlero, lero lero, bullen
            a-la,
        Lero lero, lilli burlero, lero lero, bullen
            a-la.

    [similarly]

2 Ho! by shaint Tyburn, it is de Talbote:
    And he will cut de Englishmen's troate.

3 Dough by my shoul de English do praat,
    De law's on dare side, and Creish knows what.

4 But if dispence do come from de pope
    We'll hang Magna Charta, and dem in a rope.

5 For de good Talbot is made a lord,
    And with brave lads is coming abroad.

6 Who all in France have taken a sware,
    Dat dey will have no protestant heir.

7 Ara! but why does he stay behind?
  Ho! by my shoul 'tis a protestant wind.

8 But see de Tyrconnel is now come ashore,
  And we shall have commissions gillore.

9 And he dat will not go to de mass,
  Shall be turn out, and look like an ass.

10 Now, now de hereticks will go down,
   By Chrish and shaint Patrick, de nation's our own.

11 Dare was an old prophesy found in a bog,
   "Ireland shall be rul'd by an ass, and a dog."

12 And now dis prophesy is come to pass,
   For Talbot's de dog, and James is de ass.

A final specimen of early protest music is "The Cutty Wren." Today it is regarded as a children's song, but in England during the fourteenth century it was sung at pagan midwinter rituals in spite of opposition by religious and civil authorities. The song thus became a symbol of defiance with the wren representing the peasant--oppressed, but resistant. The text is similar to the John Roberts and Tony Barrand version on The Second Nowell, Volume 2, Front Hall Records FHR-026.

THE CUTTY WREN

1 O where are you going? said Milder to Malder,
  O we may not tell you, said Festle to Fose.
  We're off to the woods, said John the Red Nose,
  We're off to the woods, said John the Red Nose.

[repeat line 3 in remaining stanzas]

2 What will you do there? said Milder to Malder,
  O we may not tell you, said Festle to Fose.
  We'll shoot the Cutty Wren, said John the Red Nose.

3 How will you shoot her? said Milder to Malder,
  O we may not tell you, said Festle to Fose.
  With bows and arrows, said John the Red Nose.

4 That will not do, said Milder to Malder,
  O what will we do then? said Festle to Fose.
  Big guns and big cannons, said John the Red Nose.

5 How will you bring her home? said Milder to Malder,
  O we may not tell you, said Festle to Fose.

On four strong men's shoulders, said John the Red
    Nose.

6 That will not do, said Milder to Malder,
O what will we do then? said Festle to Fose.
Big carts and big waggons, said John the Red Nose.

7 How will you cut her up? said Milder to Malder,
O we may not tell you, said Festle to Fose.
With knives and with forks, said John the Red Nose.

8 That will not do, said Milder to Malder,
O what will we do then? said Festle to Fose.
Big hatchets and cleavers, said John the Red Nose.

9 Who'll get the spare ribs? said Milder to Malder.
O we may not tell you, said Festle to Fose.
We'll give it all to the poor, said John the Red
    Nose.

SARAH CLEVELAND
Photo by Suzanne Szasz Courtesy Folk-Legacy Records

LAWRENCE OLDER
Photo by Sandy Paton Courtesy Folk-Legacy Records

FRANK PROFFITT
Photo by Sandy Paton   Courtesy Folk-Legacy Records

HEDY WEST
Berkeley Folk Music Festival Photo   Courtesy Folk-Legacy Records

CHAPTER THREE

AMERICAN BALLADS FROM BRITISH BROADSIDES

In the mid-twentieth century the American scholar
G. Malcolm Laws classified a total of 314 then current
traditional North American ballads based on British
broadsides (or printed texts) not included in the Child
collection. Previously, many collectors had treated the
broadsides with contempt calling them literarily inferi-
or--"trashy," said one--to the classic ballads, as well
as being "impure" since they were not a part of the oral
process. But the research of Laws pointed to a surprising conclusion: the broadsides dominated the re-
pertoires of most traditional singers, surpassing in
number not only the Child ballads, but the native American variety as well. The folk, it seemed, were unim-
pressed by the critics.

Several factors account for the popularity of the
broadsides. First, the music received continual rein-
forcement from the stream of British immigrants crossing the Atlantic Ocean. Secondly, the nineteenth century public school movement in the United States created
a literate citizenry who demanded song books in quanti-
ties unparalleled in contemporary Europe. Also, the
broadsides were more meaningful and vital than most
Child ballads and their themes were less parochial and
more universal than most native American ballads.

But why would the folk reject so many Child ballads
with their higher literary quality and objectivity in
favor of lowly broadsides? The answer relates to time
and the historical framework. As the feudal world of a
stable village economy and culture, in which the classic
ballads thrived, gave way to the new and unsettling
nature of capitalist agriculture and the Industrial Revolution, there arose a need for a new kind of story-
telling to fit the need of the new civilization. The
broadsides replaced medieval romances and intrigues with
more ordinary stories about merchants, farmers, poach-
ers, sailors, and criminals. This fact, combined with
the usage of good tunes, made them popular with the
folk.

The ballads are listed according to the framework
devised by G. Malcolm Laws in American Balladry from
British Broadsides, but with some deviations to suit the
content of this work. The Laws letter-number system
identifying the ballads is retained so that the reader

can refer to Laws for texts and sources. Under the Laws'
system, each ballad is assigned the letter of the category it is arbitrarily placed in (J for War Ballads, K
for Ballads of Sailors and the Sea, etc.), and then a
number identifying it within the category.

WAR

        Among the twenty-three war ballads listed in Laws,
"The Chesapeake and the Shannon," I, J-20, is well-known
in Nova Scotia. The broadside commemorates the victory
of the British frigate HMS Shannon over the USS Chesa-
peake during the War of 1812 and within the sight of
Boston harbor. The text is from W. Roy Mackenzie,
Ballads and Sea Songs from Nova Scotia, (Cambridge,
Mass.: Harvard University Press, 1928), p. 208.

                THE CHESAPEAKE AND THE SHANNON

    1 The Chesapeake so bold
        Out of Boston as we're told,
        Came to take the British frigate neat and handy O.
        The people all in port
        They came out to see the sport,
        And their music played up Yankee Doodle Dandy O.

    2 Before this action it begun
        The Yankees made much fun
        Saying, "We'll tow her up to Boston neat and handy
            O."
        And after that we'll dine,
        Treat our sweethearts all with wine,
        And we'll dance a jig of Yankee Doodle Dandy O."

    3 Our British frigate's name,
        All for the purpose came
        In so cooling Yankee's courage neat and handy O,
        Was the Shannon, Captain Brookes,
        And his crew all hearts of oaks,
        And in fighting they were allowed to be the dandy
            O.

    4 The action scarce begun
        When they flinched from their guns,
        They thought they had worked us neat and handy O;
        But Brookes he wove his sword,
        Saying, "Come, my boys, we'll board,
        And we'll stop this playing up Yankee Doodle Dandy
            O."

5 When Britons heard this word
  They all sprang on board;
  They hauled down the Yankee's ensign neat and handy
     O.
  Notwithstanding all their brags,
  The British raised their flags
  On the Yankee's mizzen-peak was quite the dandy O.

6 Brookes and all his crew
  In courage stout and true,
  They worked the Yankee frigate neat and handy O.
  O may they ever prove
  In fighting or in love
  That the bold British tars will be the dandy O!

SAILORS AND THE SEA

   When collector Sandy Paton visited the Beech Mountain region of North Carolina in the 1960's, "Sweet
Soldier Boy" was the favorite ballad among the local
singers. A variant of "The Sailor Boy," I, K-12, it is
found traditionally from Quebec to Texas. Monroe Presnell's version is recorded on The Traditional Music of
Beech Mountain, North Carolina, I, FSA-22 (used by permission of Folk-Legacy Records, Sharon, Conn.). Lines
1 and 2 in stanza 1 and the entire stanza 7 are examples
of "wandering" lyrics that move in and out of many folksongs.

                   SWEET SOLDIER BOY

  1 Dark is the color of my true lover's hair;
    His cheeks is like some lily fair.
    If he'd return, it would give me great joy,
    For I never loved any like my sweet soldier boy.
         Oh, if he'd return, it would give me great joy,
         For I never loved any like my sweet soldier
            boy.

  2 "Father, father, go build me a boat
    And over the ocean I will float;
    And every ship that I pass by,
    There I'll inquire for my sweet soldier boy.
         Oh, it's every ship that I pass by,
         Oh, it's there I'll inquire for my sweet
            soldier boy."

  3 She rowed her boat into the plain;
    She saw three ships a-coming from Spain.

She halted each ship as it drew nigh;
Oh, there she inquired for her sweet soldier boy.

4 "Captain, captain, tell me true,
Does my sweet William sail with you?
Answer me, oh, answer me; you'll give me great joy,
For I never loved any like my sweet soldier boy."

5 "Oh, no, lady, he's not here;
Got drownded in the gulf, my dear.
At the head of Rocky Island, as we passed by,
There we let your true lover lie.
    At the head of Rocky Island, as we passed by,
    There we let your true lover lie."

6 She rowed her boat unto a rock.
I thought, my soul, her heart would break.
She wrung her hands all in her hair,
Just like some lady in despair.

7 "Go dig my grave both wide and deep,
A marble stone at my head and feet,
And on my breast a turtle dove
To show the world that I died for love."

"The Flying Cloud," K-28, never has been traced
satisfactorily to specific historical events. Some believe it is an amalgamation of two distinct ballads--
one dealing with piracy and the other with slavery. In
any event, it is one of those rare songs describing conditions on board a "slaver." Lou Killen sings an a
cappella version on his Topic recording Ballads and
Broadsides, 12T126. The text is from Captain Archie S.
Spurling of Maine, who learned it from a Nova Scotian
acquaintance. It is printed in Fannie Hardy Eckstorm
and Mary Winslow Smyth, Minstrelsy of Maine (Boston:
Houghton Mifflin Co., 1927), pp. 214-216.

THE FLYING CLOUD

1 My name is Edward Holleran, as you may understand,
I was born in County Waterford, in Erin's lovely
    land;
I being young and in my prime, my age scarce
    twenty-one,
My parents doted on me, I being their only son.

2 My father bound me to a trade in Waterford gay
    town,
He bound me to a cooper there, by the name of
    William Brown.

I served my master faithfully for eighteen months
    or more,
When I shipped on board the <u>Ocean Queen</u>, bound down
    to Valparaiso shore.

3 When we reached Valparaiso shore I fell in with
    Captain Moore,
  Commander of the <u>Flying Cloud</u>, belonging to
    Trimore.
  He kindly asked me if I would consent on a slaving
    voyage to go,
  To the burning plains of Africa, where the sugar
    cane do grow.

4 The <u>Flying Cloud</u> was as fine a ship as ever sailed
    the seas,
  Or ever spread a white topsail before the gentle
    breeze;
  Her sails all white as the driven snow, on them
    she bears no stain,
  With twenty-nine brass mounted guns, she carries
    beaft her main.

5 The <u>Flying Cloud</u> was a Spanish ship, five hundred
    ton or more,
  She was built to outsail any ship leaving Columbian
    shore.
  I've often watched this gallant ship, when the wind
    blew abaft her main,
  With royals and skysails set aloft, run sixteen
    off the reel.

6 It's when we reached the African shore for a load
    of slaves,
  It would have been better for those poor souls if
    they were in their graves.
  We run their bodies up on deck and stowed them
    down below,
  Eighteen inches to a man was all that they could
    go.

7 Three days after we set sail from the African shore,
  With eighteen hundred of those poor souls from
    their native place,
  When a plague and fever came on board that swept
    them half away;
  We run their bodies up on deck and throwed them
    in the sea.

8 "Square the yards, run before the wind, till we
      reach the Cubean shore,"
   And we sold them to the planters there to be slaves
      forevermore,
   The rice and cotton fields to sow, beneath the
      burning sun,
   To lead a long and dreary life till their course
      was run.

9 It's now our money it is all gone, we put to sea
      again,
   When Captain Moore came up on deck and says this
      to his men;
   "There is gold and silver to be had, if you'll come
      along with me,
   We'll hoist aloft the pirate flag and scour the
      raging sea."

10 We all agreed but five young men, these we had to
      land,
   Two of them were Boston men, two more from New-
      foundland,
   The other was an Irish boy belonging to Trimore,
   I wish to God I'd joined those men and gone with
      them to shore.

11 Many's the ship we robbed and plundered down along
      the Spanish Main,
   Caused many a widow and orphan child in sorrow to
      remain;
   We made the crews all walk the plank, gave them a
      watery grave,
   For the saying of our Captain was, "Dead men tell
      no tales."

12 Chased we were by many's the ship, by liners and
      frigates too,
   But all in vain astern of us their burning shot
      they flew;
   All in vain a-leeward of us their cannon roared
      so loud,
   All in vain it was for them to catch the Flying
      Cloud.

13 Until an English man-of-war from Donglon hove in
      view,
   She fired a shot across our bows, a signal to heave
      to.
   We gave to her no answer, boys, but ran before the
      wind,

When a chase-ball struck our mainmast, and then we
soon fell behind.

14 "Clear the decks," the order was, as she ran up
alongside,
And soon acrost our quarter-deck there flowed a
crimson tide.
We fought till Captain Moore was slain and eighty
of our men,
When a bombshell set our ship on fire, we was
forced to surrender then.

15 So here's a health to yonder shady grove and the
girl that I adore,
Her voice, like music in my ear, will never cheer
me more;
I ne'er will kiss her ruby lips, nor press her
lily-white hand,
For I must die a scornful death all in some foreign
land.

16 So next to Newgate I was taken, bound down in irons
strong,
For the robbing and plundering of ships at sea down
in the Spanish Main.
'Twas drinking and bad company that made a wretch
of me,
So young men all a warning take and shun bad
company.

"High Barbary," K-33, is an analogue to Child 285,
"The George Aloe and the Sweepstake." It is attributed
to Charles Didbin (1745-1814) who wrote songs for the
British navy. Not surprisingly, the ballad has been
found in oral tradition along the coast of North America
from Maine to Florida. One of the most lyrical recordings of the song was by Burl Ives, with Tony Mottola on
guitar, in 1950. Joe Hickerson records a contrasting
version on <u>Drive Dull Care Away</u>, <u>Volume II</u>, Folk-Legacy
Records FSI-59. The text, from the <u>Forget-me-not</u>
<u>Songster</u>, Turner and Fisher publishers, circa 1840-50,
p. 215, is the probable source of most versions.

HIGH BARBARY

1 Two lofty ships from Old England came,
Blow high, and blow low, and so sailed we;
One was the <u>Prince of Luther</u>, and the other <u>Prince</u>
<u>of Wales</u>,
Crusing down on the coast of Barbary.

2 Up aloft, up aloft, the jolly boatswain cries,
    Blow high, blow low, and so sailed we;
Look ahead, look astern, look the weather and the
    lee,
    Look along down on the coast of Barbary.

[repeat lines 2 and 4 as in stanza one for the
following stanzas]

3 There's none upon the stern, there's none upon the
    lee,
    But there is a ship at windward, a lofty ship at
    sea,

4 Oh, hail, oh, hail, that lofty tall ship,
    Are you a man of war, or a privateer, said she,

5 Oh, I am no man of war or privateer, said she,
    But I'm a jolly pirate, a-looking for my fee,

6 Broadside and broadside a long time they lay,
    Till the Prince of Luther shot all the pirate's
    mast away,

7 Oh, quarter! oh, quarters! these pirates did cry,
    But the quarters that we gave them, we sank them
    in the sea.

    "Jack the Jolly Tar," K-40, I, is an analogue of
the Child 67 ballad "Glasgerion." The original tale
featured a lord, lady and harper. The broadside transformed the characters into a squire, a farmer's (or
lawyer's) daughter and a tarry sailor--more pedestrian
perhaps, but more survivable as a song. The following
is a collated variant from several sources including
the late A. L. (Bert) Lloyd's on Haul On the Bowlin',
an out-of-print Stinson ten inch LP, SLP #80. Most
American versions lack the completeness of the British
texts.

JACK THE JOLLY TAR

1 As a sailor was walkin' one fine summer day,
    A squire and a lady were making their way;
    And the sailor he heard the squire say:
    "Tonight with you I plan to stay."
        With me do me Ama, ding me Ama, do me Ama, day.

[repeat last line after each stanza]

2 "You must tie a string all around your finger,
   With the other end of the string hanging out the
        window;
   I'll just slip by and pull that string,
   And you must come down and let me in."

3 Says Jack to himself, "I've a mind to try
   To see if a poor sailor he can win the prize."
   So he showed up and he yanked that string
   And the lady came down and let old Jack in.

4 Well the squire came by, he was humming a song,
   Thinking to himself how it wouldn't be long;
   But when he got there, no string he found,
   Behold his hopes were all dashed to the ground.

5 Well early next morning, it was just getting light,
   The lady jumped up in the bed in a terrible fright,
   For there lay Jack in his tarry old shirt,
   Behold his face was all covered in dirt.

6 "What do you want you tarry sailor
   Breaking in a lady's bedroom to steal her
        treasure?"
   "Well no," says old Jack, "I just pulled that
        string
   And you came down, mam, and let me in."

7 The sailor he said, "Oh, forgive me I pray,
   I'll steal away very quiet at the dawn of the day."
   "Oh, no," says the lady, "don't go too far,
   For I never will part from my jolly Jack tar."

CRIME

     Crime is a major theme in the classic ballads, so
also in the broadsides. "Sam Hall," L-5, features an
unrepentant murderer, who, on the gallows, curses everyone present. It is based on the early eighteenth century British song, "Jack Hall," about a chimney sweep
who was hanged for burglary in 1701. Collector Frank
Kidson concluded that a British comic singer in the
1840's revised the story along present day lines.
Version A is based on the original tale and is sung by
Colyn Davies on Cockney Music Hall Songs and Reci-
tations, Tradition TLP1017. The opening stanza is
printed for contrast with the coarser American text, B,
similar to Bill Bender's rendition on an early Stinson
LP, Frontier Ballads and Cowboy Songs, SLP18.

A - JACK HALL

My name it is Jack Hall, a chimney sweep,
Oh, my name it is Jack Hall, a chimney sweep;
And I rob both great and small
And my life must pay for all, when I die.

B - SAM HALL

1 Now, my name is Samuel Hall, Sam Hall,
Oh, my name is Samuel Ha-a-all;
Oh, my name is Samuel Hall, and I hate you one and
all,
You're a bunch of muckers all, blast your eyes!

2 Now, I killed a man they said, so they said,
Oh, I killed a man they said, yes they said;
I killed a man they said, and I left him layin'
dead,
'Cause I bashed his bloody head, blast his eyes!

3 Now, they put me in the quad, in the quad,
Oh, they put me in the qua-a-ad;
Oh, they put me in the quad, and they left me there,
by God,
Fastened to a chain and rod, blast their eyes!

4 Now, the preacher he did come, he did come,
Oh, the preacher he did come, he did come;
Oh, the preacher he did come, and he looked so
doggone glum
As he talked of kingdom come, blast his eyes!

5 And the sheriff he come too, he come too,
Oh, the sheriff he come too, he come too;
Oh, the sheriff he come too, with his yellow boys
and blue,
Sayin', "Sam, I'll see you through," blast your
eyes!

6 Oh, it's up the rope I go, I go,
It's up the rope I go, up I go;
Oh, it's up the rope I go, while you critters
down below
Are sayin', "Sam, I told you so," blast your eyes!

7 Oh, it's a swingin' I must go, I must go,
It's a swingin' I must go-o-o;
It's a swingin' I must go, just because she loved
him so,
Just because she loved him so, blast her eyes!

8 I must hang until I'm dead, dead, dead,
  I must hang until I'm de-e-ad;
  I must hang until I'm dead, 'cause I killed a man,
      they said,
  And left him layin' dead, blast his eyes!

"Brennan On the Moor," L-7, is based on the exploits of an eighteenth century Irish highwayman. Its
popularity in North America extended to Missouri, the
origin of the text. Reprinted from Ballads and Songs,
Collected by the Missouri Folk-Lore Society, edited by
H. M. Belden, by permission of the University of Missouri Press, University of Missouri Studies, Volume IX,
No. 1, p. 284.

BRENNAN ON THE MOOR

1 "Tis of a fearless Irishman
  The story I will tell;
  His name was Willie Brennan,
  In Ireland he did dwell.
  'Twas in the Cumberland Mountains
  He commenced his wild career,
  And many a wealthy nobleman
  Before him shook with fear.

2 A brace of loaded pistols
  He carried night and day;
  He never robbed a poor man
  Upon the king's highway,
  But when he'd taken from the rich
  Like Durban and Black Bess,
  He always divided
  With the widow in distress.

3 Now Willie met with a packman
  By the name of Julius Bunn.
  They travelled on together
  Till day began to dawn.
  When Julius found his money gone,
  Likewise his watch and chain,
  He encountered Billy Brennan
  And robbed him back again.

4 Now Willie finding the packman
  As good a man as he,
  He took him on the king's highway
  A companion for to be.
  Then Julius threw his pack away
  Without any more delay

107

And proved a faithful comrade
Unto his dying day.

5 One day upon the king's highway
  As Willie sat him down,
  He met the mayor of Cortial
  One mile outside of town.
  The mayor knew his features,
  And "I think, young man," said he,
  "Your name is Billy Brennan.
  You must come along with me."

6 Now Willie's wife she being in town
  Provisions for to buy,
  When she saw her Willie
  She began to weep and cry.
  You ought to seen the token--
  As soon as Willie spoke
  She handed him a blunderbuss
  From underneath her cloak.

7 Now of this loaded blunderbuss
  The truth I'll unfold;
  He made the mayor to tremble
  And robbed him of his gold.
  A hundred pounds were offered
  For his apprehension there.
  His horse, saddle, and bridle
  To the mountains he did tear.

8 Now Willie being an outlaw
  Upon the mountain high,
  With infantry and cavalry
  To catch him they did try.
  He laughed at them, he scoffed at them
  Till at last he has to say
  "A false-hearted young girl
  Did beastly me betray."

9 "Twas in the town of Tipperary,
  The country of Claymore,
  That Willie and his comrade
  Were made to suffer sore;
  They lay out in the briers
  That grew up in an open field.
  And they received twelve wounds
  Before it's they would yield.

10 Now Willie he was taken,
   With strong irons he was bound,
   They took him to the Commeral jail

Where strong walls did him surround.
The jury found him guilty
And the judge made this reply:
"For robbing on the king's highway
You are condemned to die."

11 "Here's to my wife and children,
Who long may mourn for me;
Here's to my aged father,
Who has shed tears for me;
Here's to my aged mother,
Who tore her locks and cried,
Saying, "'Twere better, Billy Brennan,
In your cradle you had died."

"The Rambling Boy," L-12, has been widely recorded.
In October of 1928, the McMitchen-Layne String Orchestra
cut one of the first versions on shellac for Columbia.
It remained unissued until Rounder Records included it
on Gid Tanner and His Skillet Lickers: "The Kickapoo
Medicine Show," Rounder 1023. The text follows:

THE RAMBLING BOY

1 I was raised a wreck [rake] and a rambling boy,
To many a shore there I've been.
To London City I paid my way,
And I lost my money in a gambling way.

2 Was there that I married me a loving wife,
And I loved her as dear as I loved my life.
I dressed her up in silks so gay,
And she taught me to rob on the road highway.

3 I bought my ticket in Greenville town,
And on that train when I sat down,
The whistle blew, and the train rolled on,
In about five days I landed home.

4 I robbed that train, I do declare,
I robbed it on James Island Square.
I robbed it of ten thousand pounds,
One night while I was rambling round.

5 And now, I am compelled to die,
For me, my true love will weep and cry.
Her tears so sweet and her tears so free,
But they won't save me from the gallows tree.

6 Now, when I'm dead, go bury me deep,
Place a marble stone at my head and feet;

And on my grave place the wings of a dove
To prove to the world that I died for love.

"Whiskey In the Jar," L-13 A, has regained much of
its popularity, thanks to its inclusion in the repertoire of many young urban singers. A fine Irish version
was included on the out-of-print Riverside album, _Irish
Street Songs_ by Patrick Galvin. The text is from the
tradition of Sarah Gunning. She learned "Captain Devin"
from her mother in Kentucky and recorded it on _Girl of
Constant Sorrow: Sarah Ogan Gunning_, FSA-26 (used by
permission of Folk-Legacy Records, Sharon, Conn.).

CAPTAIN DEVIN

1 As I was a-going across King's Mountain
  I met Captain Devin, and his money he was counting.
  First I pulled my pistol, and then I pulled my
       saber,
  Saying, "Stand and deliver, for I am your bold
       deceiver."

  chorus:
       With your musha-ringa-row
       And right to my loddy,
       Right to my loddy,
       Oh, there's whiskey in the jar.

2 I picked up his gold, feeling gay and jolly,
  I picked up his gold, took it home to Loddy.
  Told her all about it, thought she never would
       deceive me,
  But the devil's in the women and they never can
       be easy.

3 I went to Molly['s] chamber for to take a slumber,
  I went to Molly chamber, cold and hungry.
  Laid down to take a nap, not thinking any matter.
  She discharged both of my pistols and filled them
       full of water.

4 Next morning very early, between six and seven,
  There I was surrounded for killing Captain Devin.
  Reached for my pistol but found I was mistaken,
  For my pistols was discharged and a prisoner I
       was taken.

As Laws indicates, there is a close connection between "Botany Bay," L-16 A, and "The Boston Burglar,"
L-16 B. Both ballads are in the North American tradition although, as might be expected, the second is

much more common. Version A represents "Botany Bay" and is from a London broadside of about 1800. B is a Kentucky variant of the "Boston Burglar" retitled the "Louisville Burglar," a common practice to fit the tale to a local community or region. It was recorded by the Hickory Nuts in the late 1920's and was reissued on County Records 522, Old-Time Ballads from the Southern Mountains.

A - BOTANY BAY

1 Come all you men of learning,
  And a warning take by me,
  I would have you quit night walking,
  And shun bad company.
  I would have you quit night walking,
  Or else you'll rue the day,
  You'll rue your transportation, lads,
  When you're bound for Botany Bay.

2 I was brought up in London town
  And a place I know full well,
  Brought up by honest parents
  For the truth to you I'll tell.
  Brought up by honest parents,
  And rear'd most tenderly,
  Till I became a roving blade,
  Which proved my destiny.

3 My character soon taken was,
  And I was sent to jail,
  My friends they tried to clear me,
  But nothing could prevail.
  At the Old Bailey Sessions,
  The judge to me did say,
  "The jury's found you guilty, lad,
  So you must go to Botany Bay."

4 To see my aged father dear,
  As he stood near the bar,
  Likewise my tender mother,
  Her old grey locks to tear;
  In tearing of her old grey locks,
  These words to me did say,
  "O, Son! O, Son! what have you done,
  That you're going to Botany Bay?"

5 It was on the twenty-eighth of May,
  From England we did steer,
  And, all things being safe on board,
  We sail'd down the river, clear.

111

And every ship that we pass'd by,
We heard the sailors say,
"There goes a ship of clever hands,
And they're bound for Botany Bay."

6 There is a girl in Manchester,
A girl I know full well,
And if ever I get my liberty,
Along with her I'll dwell.
O, then I mean to marry her,
And no more to go astray;
I'll shun all evil company,
Bid adieu to Botany Bay.

B - LOUISVILLE BURGLAR

1 Raised up in Louisville,
A city you all know well.
Raised up by honest parents,
The truth to you I'll tell.
Raised up by honest parents,
Raised most tenderly,
Til I became a burglar
At the age of twenty-three.

2 My character was taken
And I was sent to jail.
The people found all in vain,
To get me out on bail.
The jury found me guilty;
The clerk he wrote it down.
The judge passed the sentence
And sent me to Frankfort town.

3 They put me on an east bound train
One cold December day.
And as I passed the station
I could hear those people say:
"Yonder goes a burglar,
For some big crime I know,
For some big crime or other
To Frankfort town must go."

4 And saw my aged father
A-pleading at the bar.
I saw my dear old mother
A-dragging at her hair;
Dragging at those old grey locks,
The tears were streaming down;
She says, "My son, what have you done
To [be] sent to Frankfort town?"

5 I have a girl in Louisville,
  A girl that I love well.
  If ever I get my liberty,
  Long life with her I'll dwell;
  If ever I get my liberty,
  Bad company I will shun,
  With playing cards and gambling,
  And also drinking rum.

6 To you who have your liberty,
  Pray keep it while you can.
  Don't walk about the streets at night,
  Or break the laws of man.
  For if you do you'll truly will,
  You'll find yourself like me,
  Serving out your twenty-one years
  In the state penitentiary.

"The Wild Colonial Boy," L-20, recounts the adventures of an Irish immigrant to Australia. Although the ballad is best known in northeastern United States and Nova Scotia, Rosalie Sorrels obtained the following variant from Mrs. Dora Lawrence of Nampa, Idaho. Sorrels sings it on Folk Songs of Idaho and Utah, Folkways FH 5343 (used by permission of Folkways Records).

THE WILD COLONIAL BOY

1 'Twas of a wild colonian boy, Jack Dolan was his
    name;
  He was born in Ireland's sunny clime in a place
    called Castlemain.
  He was his father's only son, his mother's only
    joy,
  So dearly did his parents love that wild colonian
    boy.

2 'Twas at the age of sixteen years he left his
    native home,
  And to Australia's sunny clime, a bushranger to
    roam.
  And at the age of eighteen years he began his wild
    career;
  He robbed the rich, he helped the poor, he stopped
    Judge Black with joy,
  And he trembling gave his gold up to the wild
    colonian boy.

3 'Twas on a bright May morning, young Jackie rode
    along,
  A-listening to the mocking birds a-singing their

noted song.
Up rode three bold policemen: Kelly, Davis, and
  Fitzroy,
The three rode out to capture that wild colonian
  boy.

4 "Surrender, Jack Dolan, you see there's three to
    one!
  Surrender in the Queen's name, you are her plunder-
    ing son."
  He drew a pistol from his side and he waved that
    little toy;
  "I'll fight, but I'll not surrender," said the
    wild colonian boy.

5 He fired a shot at Kelly, and it brought him to the
    ground,
  But in return from Kelly's gun he received a fatal
    wound.
  A bullet sharp, it pierced his heart, from the
    pistol of Fitzroy,
  And that's the way they captured this wild colonian
    boy.

"Jack Donahue,"(Donahoe) L-22, apparently reached
the United States from Australia, at least that is what
John Lomax surmised about the variant he collected from
a black undertaker in Austin, Texas. John Greenway recorded an Australian version of this song (and the preceeding one) on Australian Folksongs and Ballads, Folkways FW 8718. The text is from John A. and Alan Lomax
(eds.), Cowboy Songs and Other Frontier Ballads (New
York: The MacMillan Co., 1938), pp. 209-212 (used by
permission of Alan Lomax).

JACK DONAHOE

1 Come, all you bold undaunted men,
  You outlaws of the day,
  It's time to beware of the ball and chain,
  And also slavery.
  Attention pay to what I say,
  And verily if you do,
  I will relate you the actual fate
  of bold Jack Donahoe.

  refrain:
    Then come, my hearties, we'll roam the
      mountains high!
    Together we will plunder, together we will die!

114

We'll wander over mountains, we'll wander over
    plains,
For we scorn to live in slavery, bound down
    with iron chains.

2 He took to rob on the King's highway;
  We heard the people say
  They were afraid to go that road
  By either night or day!
  And every day the newspapers
  Were filled with something new
  Concerning this bold highwayman
  Whom they called Jack Donahoe.

3 He scarcely had landed, as I tell you,
  Upon Australia's shore,
  Than he became a real highwayman,
  As he had been before.
  There was Underwood and Mackerman,
  And Wade and Westley too,
  These were four associates
  Of bold Jack Donahoe.

4 But Donahoe was taken
  In the middle of his prime,
  And he was sentenced to be shot
  For an outrageous crime;
  He left the police behind him
  And several soldiers too;
  Until the fatal day came round
  They lost bold Donahoe.

5 Jack Donahoe who was so brave
  Rode out one afternoon,
  Knowing not that the pain of death
  Would overtake him soon.
  So quickly then the horse police
  From Sydney came to view;
  "Begone from here, you cowardly dogs,"
  Says bold Jack Donahoe.

6 Says Donahoe to his comrade,
  "If you'll prove true to me
  We'll either fight until we die
  Or gain the victory!
  Be of good corage, stout and bold;
  Be loyal, firm, and true,
  For today we'll fight for victory!"
  Said bold Jack Donahoe.

7 "Oh, no!" said cowardly Westley,
  "To that I can't agree.
  Cannot you see there's nine of them
  Against just you and me?
  But if we wait we'll be too late,
  The battle we'll surely rue."
  "Begone from me, you cowardly whelp,"
  Said bold Jack Donahoe.

8 The captain and the sergeant
  Stopped then to decide.
  "Do you intend to fight us,
  Or unto us resign?"
  "To surrender to such cowardly dogs
  Is more than I will do;
  This day I'll fight if I lose my life,"
  Said bold Jack Donahoe.

9 The captain and the sergeant
  The men they did divide.
  They fired from behind him
  And also from each side;
  It's six police he did shoot down
  Before the fatal ball
  Did pierce the heart of Donahoe
  And cause bold Jack to fall.

10 "I'd rather roam these hills and dales
   Like a wolf or kangaroo,
   Than one hour for government!"
   Cries bold Jack Donahoe.
   And when he fell, he closed his eyes,
   He bid the world adieu.
   Come all you boys, and sing the song
   Of bold Jack Donahoe.

LOVERS: OPPOSITION AND DECEPTION

This category includes ballads that record familial opposition to lovers as well as those that describe the numerous deceptions and disguises used by the participants in the game of love.

"The Drowsy Sleeper," M-4, has been widely collected in North America and with many variations. It is related to the native American ballad "The Silver Dagger," G-21, while the song "Katie Dear" or "Who's That Knocking?" seems to be an amalgamation of the two.

116

"The Drowsy Sleeper" has been traced to an ancient pagan ritual in Britain which required the prospective husband to visit his bride-to-be secretly and spend the night with her. The bride's parents offered only ritualistic opposition to this "Night Visit." Once the custom died out, it is thought that the ballad was re-interpreted by stressing parental opposition to the lovers.[1] There are numerous endings to the variants--some tragic, some happy.

Version A is of the latter type, sung by Monroe Presnell on The Traditional Music of Beech Mountain, North Carolina, Vol. I, FSA-22 (used by permission of Folk-Legacy Records, Sharon, Conn.). B was recorded by Kentuckian B. F. Shelton in 1927 and combines the "Katie Dear" amalgamation with the lyrical song "I Was Born In East Virginia." C is similar to The Carter Family's "Who's That Knocking?" from their 1938-1942 transcription series on the Mexican radio station XERA. Recorded on The Carter Family On Border Radio, JEMF101 (the John Edwards Memorial Foundation). See Chapter Four for a version of "Silver Dagger."

A - AWAKE, AWAKE, MY OLD TRUE LOVER

1 Awake, awake, my old true lover;
   Awake, arise, it's almost day.
   How can you bear those soft, soft sleeping,
   And your true love going away?

2 Oh, who is that a-knocking at my window?
   I pray you, tell to me.
   It's me, it's me, your old true lover;
   Awake, arise, come pity me.

3 Go love, go and ask your father
   If this night you could be my bride.
   If he says no, so return and tell me;
   [It will] be my last time ever bother thee.

4 I can't go and ask my father,
   For he's on his bed of rest,
   And by his side there lies a weapon
   To kill the one that I love best.

---

[1]For a more complete account see: The Carter Family On Border Radio, JEMF101, and the enclosed booklet, pp. 12-13.

5 Go love, go and ask your mama
  If this night you could be my bride.
  If she says no, so return and tell me;
  Be my last time ever bother thee.

6 I can't go and ask my mama
  And tell her of your love so dear.
  You may go and court some other
  And whisper softly in her ear.

7 I will go to some wide river,
  Spend my days, my months and years;
  Eat anything but the green growing willow,
  Also drink from my flowing tears.

8 Come back, come back, my old true lover
  And stay a little while with me.
  I will forsake my dear old mother
  And go along by the side of thee.

B - OH, MOLLY DEAR

1 Oh, once I lived in old Virginny
  To North Carolina I did go.
  There I saw a nice young lady,
  Oh, her name I did not know.

2 Her hair was black and eyes were sparkling,
  On her cheek her diamond rare,[?]
  And on her breast she wore a lily
  To mourn of tears that I have shed.

3 Oh, when I'm sleep I dream about her,
  When I wake I see no rest.
  Every moment seems like an hour,
  Oh, the pains that cross my breast.

4 Oh, Molly dear, go ask your mother,
  'Tis my bride can ever be.
  And if she says no, come back and tell me
  And never more will I trouble thee.

5 Last night as I laid on my pillow,
  Last night as I laid on my bed,
  Last night as I laid on my pillow,
  I dreamed that fair young maid was dead.

6 No, I won't go ask my mother,
  She's lying on her bed of rest.
  And in one hand she holds a dagger
  To kill the man that I love best.

7 Now go and leave me if you want to,
  And from me you will be free.
  For in your heart you love another,
  And in my grave I'd rather be.

C - WHO'S THAT KNOCKING?

1 Who's that knocking at my window?
  Knocks so loud and won't come in?
  It is your own true hearted lover,
  Rise you up and let him in.

2 Go 'way, go 'way, don't wake my mother,
  For love's a thing she can't endure.
  She's been the ruin of many a lover.
  She'll be the ruin of many more.

3 Go way, go way, don't wake my father.
  For he is on his bed of rest,
  And on his breast he carries a weapon
  To kill the one that I love best.

4 I wish I was a little sparrow.
  I'd circle like a turtle dove.
  I'd fly away to a lonely valley,
  And settle down in the land of love.

"The Bold Soldier," M-27, is thought to be connected to Child 7, "Earl Brand," and may be a broadsider's parody of the older ballad. An Arkansas variant, "The Valiant Soldier," is sung by Sam Hinton on The Songs of Men, Folkways FA 2400 (used by permission of Folkways Records).

THE VALIANT SOLDIER

1 Oh, I'll tell you of the soldier, that lately came
     from war,
  He courted a lady so rare and so fair;
  Her riches was so great, they scarcely could be
     told
  But still she loved her soldier because he was so
     bold.

2 As they went to the church and returned home again,
  There they saw her father and seven armed men.
  "Oh," cried the lady, "I fear we'll both be slain!"
  "Fear nothing at all," said the soldier again.

3 Up rode her old father and says, "Is this the way
  You bring a scandal to my family?

119

You might have been some young gentlemen's wife,
But now in yonders valley I aim to end your life!"

4 The soldier drew his pistol, he hung it by his
     side,
  And swore that "we'd get married no matter what
     betide."
  He drew out his sword, he cause it for to rattle,
  And the lady held the horses while the soldier
     fought the battle.

5 The first one he come to, he run it through his
     brain,
  The next one he come to, he served him the same.
  "Let's run," cried the others, "for I fear we'll
     all be slain!
  To fight a valiant soldier I see it's all in vain."

6 "Hold on," says the old man, "now don't you be so
     bold,
  And you shall have my daughter and five thousand
     pounds of gold."
  "Fight on," cried the lady, "the sum it is too
     small."
  "Hold your hand," says the old man, "and you can
     have it all."

7 He took the soldier with him, he called him his
     heir.
  T'wasn't from a willing mind, but only out of fear.
  "Here's my land and money and here's my house and
     home,
  It shall all be at your command when I am dead and
     gone."

8 Come all the young ladies that has gold laid up in
     store,
  And never slight a soldier because he is so poor;
  For a soldier he's a gentleman both handsome,
     strong and free,
  And he'll fight for his true love as well as
     liberty.

"William and Dinah," M-31 A, and its comic variant
"Vilikins and His Dinah," M-31 B, have entered the North
American tradition, although the music hall parody is
the most popular. The tune was stolen to fit the well-
known gold rush ballad "Sweet Betsy from Pike." Logan
English learned a humorous version from singers on his
father's Kentucky farm. He sings it on Kentucky Folk
Songs and Ballads, Folkways FA 2136 (used by permission

120

of Folkways Records).

WILLIAM AND DINAH

1 There was a silk merchant in London did dwell,
  He had one lone daughter, a pretty fair gal;
  Her name it was Dinah, past sixteen years old,
  And a very large fortune of silver and gold.

    refrain:
        Sing too ree lie early, lie early lie oh,
        Sing too ree lie early, lie early lie oh,
        Sing too ree lie early, lie early lie oh.

2 Well, Dinah were a-sittin' in the garden one day,
  Her papa came to her, these words he did say:
  "Go dress yourself, Dinah, in silk corgilee,
  I'll bring you a husband both gallant and gay."

3 "Oh, papa, oh, papa, I hain't made up my mind,
  For to get married I don't feel inclined.
  All my riches I'll freely give o'er
  If I can stay single a year or two more."

4 "Oh, daughter, oh, daughter," this old man replied,
  "If you don't consent to be this young man's bride,
  All your riches to the nearest of kin,
  And it shan't be to the benefit of one single
      thing."

5 Well, William were a-walkin' in the garden one day,
  He spied his dear Dinah a-layin' on clay,
  With a cup of cold poison down by her side,
  He could swear his dear Dinah were poisoned and
      died.

6 Well, he called his dear Dinah ten thousand times
      o'er,
  And he kissed her cold corpus ten thousand times
      more.
  Then he drunk up the poison like a lover so brave,
  Now William and Dinah both lie in one grave.

There is an amusing "Dutch" variant in which
Katrina chokes on a sausage. The last two stanzas are
from Earl J. Stout, Folklore from Iowa (Memoirs of the
American Folklore Society, Vol. XXIX), p. 54 (used by
permission).

Now as Hans Dunder chanced to pass by the door,
He saw his Katrina lying dead on the floor;

The big bologna sausage lay there by her side
And he said, "I'll be damned 'twas by this thing
    she died."

Now all you young fellers take a warning from me,
Be careful whose girl you go for to see;
And all you young ladies what court in the passage,
Think of Hans and Katrina and the big bologna
    sausage.

Some ballad buffs have criticized Child unjustly
for not including "The Bramble Briar," M-32, in his collection. It certainly meets his critical tests as well
as "Lord Lovel" or dozens more admitted to his canon.
The explanation is simple--no broadsides were known.
Apparently then, oral tradition brought the ballad to
North America where it has received remarkable currency
under various titles: "In Bruton Town," "In Seaport
Town," and the following, "In Zepo Town." Traditionalist Liza Shelton from North Carolina recorded the ballad
on Folkways FA 2309, Old Love Songs and Ballads (used by
permission of Folkways Records).

                    IN ZEPO TOWN

1 In Zepo Town there lived a merchant.
  He had three sons and a daughter dear,
  And among them all was the prettiest boy.
  It was the daughter's dearest dear.

2 One evening they were in a room courting,
  Their oldest brother chanced to hear.
  He goes and tells his other brother:
  "Let's deprive her of her dearest dear."

3 So they rose up so early next morning,
  A game of hunting was agreed to go.
  But little did he think of a bloody murder,
  A game of hunting he agreed to go.

4 They wandered over hills and valleys,
  And through a many of a place unknown,
  Till at last they became to a ditch of briars,
  And there they killed him dead alone.

5 So they returned home late in the evening,
  Their sister inquiring for the service boy:
  "Oh, we got him lost in the wildwoods hunting,
  No more of him could we ever find."

6 While she lie upon her pillow,
   The service boy appeared in a dream.
   Says: "Your brothers killed me rough and cruel,
   All wallowed in a gore of blood.

7 "But since your brothers has been so cruel,
   To rob and steal your own sweet love,
   One grave deserves both of our bodies;
   I'll stay with you as long as life."

8 So she returned home late in the evening,
   Her brothers asked her where she'd been:
   "Just hold your peace you deceitful villains,
   For one alone you both shall hang."

9 Her brothers being deep convicted
   To jump in a ship and find relief.
   The winds did blow and the waves overcome them,
   Their graves was both in the deep blue sea.

"Edwin In the Lowlands Low," M-34, once again
demonstrates how the folk process can keep a ballad
alive by a few skillful adjustments. In early English
versions the young lady lives in a castle; in the following text from North Carolina she resides in a boarding house; similarly, the English sailor becomes a
Southern Appalachian driver boy. "Young Emily" is from
the recording by Doug Wallin on Folkways FA 2418,
Dillard Chandler: The End of an Old Song (used by permission of Folkways Records).

                    YOUNG EMILY

1 Young Emily was a pretty fair miss,
   She loved a driver boy
   Who drove the stage some gold to get,
   Down in the low lands low.
   [repeat lines 3 and 4]

2 My father owns a boarding house,
   All on yon river side.
   Go there, go there,
   And enter in this night with me abide.

3 Be sure you tell them nothing,
   Nor let my parents know
   That your name is young Edmond,
   Who drove in the low lands low,
   [repeat lines 3 and 4, similarly in stanzas 4-10]

                        123

4 Young Edmond fell to drinking
  Until he went to bed.
  He did not know they swore that night
  That they would cut off his head.

5 Young Emily in her chamber,
  She had an awful dream.
  She dreamed she saw young Edmond's blood
  Go flowing like a stream.

6 Young Emily rose in the morning
  A-puttin' on her clothes.
  She's goin' to find her driver boy,
  Who drove in the low lands low.

7 Oh father, oh dear father,
  You'll die a public show
  For the murdering of that driver boy,
  Who drove in the low lands low.

8 Away then to some coun-se-lor
  To let the deed be known,
  Of the murder of her driver boy,
  Who drove in the low lands low.

9 Them coats that hang on the mountain,
  They look so blue and true.
  They remind me of my driver boy,
  Who drove in the low lands low.

10 Them fish that swim in the ocean,
   Swim o'er my true love's breast.
   His body's in the gentle motion,
   And I hope his soul's at rest.

"Jack Monroe," N-7, is the first ballad in this
section featuring the disguises and deceptions of
lovers. Its strong appeal among the folk is demon-
strated by its widespread currency from New York to
Texas. Popularized previously by Joan Baez as
"Jackaroe," Grateful Dead featured it on their 1981
album Reckoning, Arista A2L8604. The text is from
George Davis' eloquent Folkways album, When Kentucky Had
No Union Men, FA 2343 (used by permission of Folkways
Records).

JACK MONROE

1 Oh, come all you good people,
  Here's a story you should know,
  Of a girl named Polly,

And a boy named Jack Monroe.
    Oh, and a boy named Jack Monroe.

2 They fell in love so madly,
And had named their wedding day,
And swore that nothing, darling,
Could tear our love away.
    Oh, could tear our love away

3 Her parents they got angry,
And said she must obey.
They spent ten thousand dollars,
To carry Jack away.
    Oh, to carry Jack away.

4 Polly she went down in town,
All dressed in crimson and gray,
Bargained with a captain,
To carry her away.
    Oh, for to carry her away.

5 She stepped up to the captain,
Her money all in her hand,
Saying: "Please kind captain,
Send me to the far off land.
    Oh, send me to the far off land."

6 "Your body is too slender
Your fingers are too small,
Your cheeks too red and rosy,
To face a cannonball.
    Oh, to face a cannonball.

7 "Since this is your intention,
Your name I'd like to know."
She answered very politely:
"My name is Jack Monroe.
    Yes, my name is Jack Monroe."

8 "I know my body's slender,
My fingers they are small,
But it wouldn't change my countenance,
To see ten thousand fall.
    Oh, for to see ten thousand fall."

9 Then Polly she set sailin',
And soon did come to land.
Among the dead and dying,
She found her darling man.
    Oh, she found her darling man.

125

10 She picked him up all in her arms,
   And carried him to a town,
   And hired a wealthy surgeon,
   To heal his deathly wound.
        Oh, to heal his deathly wound.

11 This couple they got married,
   In the land of Germany.
   This couple they got married.
   And why not you and me?

"The Handsome Cabin Boy," N-13, is rare in the
North American tradition. Some singers were apparently
embarrassed to sing it for collectors. They should not
have been; it is a clever story. The following is an
example of the new way traditional material is assimi-
lated. Gordon Bok obtained it from Bete Franklin while
on the schooner Owl; Franklin picked it up from a recording. Bok sings it on A Tune For November, FSI-40
(used by permission of Folk-Legacy Records, Sharon,
Conn.).

THE HANDSOME CABIN BOY

1 It's just a pretty female
  As you may understand,
  Her mind being bent on rambling
  Unto a foreign land;
  She dressed herself in sailor's clothes,
  Or so it does appear,
  And she signed with a captain
  To serve him for a year.

2 The captain's wife she being on board,
  She seemed in great joy
  To think the captain had engaged
  Such a handsome cabin boy,
  That now and then she'd slip him a kiss
  And she'd have liked to toy,
  But 'twas the captain found out the secret
  Of the handsome cabin boy.

3 Whose cheeks they were like roses
  And her hair all in a curl.
  The sailors often smiled and said
  He looked just like a girl.
  But eating of the captain's biscuits
  Her color did destroy,
  And the waist did swell of pretty Nell,
  The handsome cabin boy.

4 "Twas down the Bay of Biscay
   Our gallant ship did plow.
   One night amongst the sailors
   A hell of a flurry and row;
   It tumbled the men from out their hammocks,
   Their sleep it did destroy,
   Terrible cursing and the moaning of
   The handsome cabin boy.

5 "Oh, doctor, dear, oh, doctor,"
   The cabin boy did cry,
   "My time has come, I am undone,
   And I must surely die."
   The doctor came a-running
   And smiling at the fun,
   For to think a sailor lad should have
   A daughter or a son.

6 The sailors, when they heard the news,
   They all did stand and stare.
   The child belonged to none of them,
   They solemnly do swear.
   The captain's wife, she says to him,
   "My dear, I wish you joy,
   For 'tis either you or I have betrayed
   The handsome cabin boy."

7 Now, sailors, take your tot of rum
   And drink success to trade,
   And likewise to the cabin boy
   That was neither man nor maid.
   Here's hoping the wars don't rise again
   Our sailors to destroy,
   And here's hoping for a jolly lot more
   Like the handsome cabin boy.

   "The Dark-Eyed Sailor," N-35, is an example of a
lover's trick. In "The Bailiff's Daughter of Islington"
the young woman disguised herself to test her true-love.
In this ballad it is the young man's turn to test the
fidelity of his love. While touring England in 1947,
Paul Clayton learned it from a singer known only as
Jack. Clayton performs it on British Broadside Ballads
In Popular Tradition, Folkways FW 8708 (used by permission of Folkways Records).

                THE DARK EYED SAILOR

1 It's of a comely young lady fair,
   Who was walking out for to take the air,
   She met a sailor whilst on her way,

                        127

So I paid attention, so I paid attention
To hear what they did say.

2 He said, "Pray lady, why roam alone,
The day's far spent and the night's coming on."
She said, whilst tears from her eyes did fall,
"Twas the dark-eyed sailor, twas the dark-eyed
   sailor
That proved my downfall.

3 "Tis two long years since he left the land,
A golden ring he took off my hand,
We broke the token, here's half with me,
Whilst the other lay rolling, whilst the other
   lay rolling
At the bottom of the sea."

4 Said William, "Lady, drive him from your mind,
There's other sailors as good you'll find,
Love turns aside and soon cold doth grow,
Like a winter's morning, like a winter's morning,
With the ground all covered with snow."

5 These words did Phoebe's young heart inflame,
She said, "Upon me you shall play no game;"
She drew a dagger and loud did cry:
"For my dark-eyed sailor, for my dark-eyed sailor
A maid I live and die.

6 "But still," said Phoebe, "I ne'er disdain
A tarry sailor, but treat the same;
Come drink his health, here's a piece of coin
For this dark-eyed sailor, for the dark-eyed sailor
Still claims this heart of mine.

7 "His coal-black eye and his curly hair,
His pleasing tongue did my heart ensnare;
Genteel he was, not a rake like you,
To advise a maiden, to advise a maiden,
To slight the jacket blue."

8 Half the ring did bold William show,
She seemed distracted midst joy and woe,
"Oh, welcome, William, I've land and gold
For my dark-eyed sailor, for my dark-eyed sailor,
So manly, true and bold."

9 Now in a cottage down by the sea
They joined in wedlock and well agree,
All maids be true whilst your love's away;

For a cloudy morning, for a cloudy morning,
Brings forth a sunshine day.

TRUE-LOVERS AND FALSE TRUE-LOVERS

Themes of universal interest headline this section
which selects a handful of ballads from the eighty-one
catalogued by Laws.

One of the best known in North America is "The
Foggy Dew," 0-3. Burl Ives popularized the ballad on
radio programs and recordings in the 1940's and 1950's.
It is a favorite of Sandy Paton who writes: "While it
is realistically frank, it is certainly not a bawdy
song. Indeed, it manages to be both tender and lusty
at the same time, combining a sympathetic understanding
of human fraility with a not unsympathetic touch of
humor." The quotation is from the accompanying booklet
to Sandy and Caroline Paton, Folk-Legacy EGO-30, from
which the text is taken (used by permission of Folk-
Legacy Records, Sharon, Conn.).

THE FOGGY DEW

1 When I was an old bachelor,
   I followed a roving trade.
   All the harm that ever I done,
   I courted a serving maid.
   I courted her one summer season,
   And part of the winter, too.
   And many's the time I rolled my love
   All over the foggy dew.

2 One night, as I lay in my bed
   A-taking my barm of sleep,
   This pretty fair maid she came to me,
   And bitterly she did weep.
   She wept, she cried, she tore her hair,
   Saying, "Alas, what shall I do?
   For this night I'm resolved to sleep with you,
   For fear of the foggy dew."

3 So, all the first part of the night
   How we did sport and play.
   And all the latter part of the night
   Close in my arms she lay.
   And when it came to broad daylight,
   She cried, "I am undone."
   I said, "Hold your tongue, you foolish young thing,
   For the foggy dew is gone.

129

4 "Supposing you should have a child,
   'Twould make you laugh and smile.
   Supposing you should have another,
   'Twould make you think awhile.
   Supposing you should have another,
   Another, another one, too.
   It would make you leave off your foolish young
       tricks
   And think of the foggy dew."

5 I loved that girl with all of my heart,
   Loved her as I loved my life.
   And in the latter part of the year
   I made her my lawful wife.
   I never told her of her faults,
   And never intend to,
   For many's the time, as she winks and smiles,
   I think of the foggy dew.

"Seventeen Come Sunday," 0-17, is a merry courtship
ballad popular on both sides of the Atlantic. The original broadside ended on an almost too happy note, so
apparently traditional singers decided "to fix it up"
by fashioning a more realistic and evasive ending.
This change is shown in the two texts printed: A is the
last two stanzas from the H. P. Such broadside; and B
is the full text from traditionalist Seamus Ennis as
learned by Paul Clayton. Clayton sings it on British
Broadside Ballads in Popular Tradition, FW 8708 (used
by permission of Folkways Records).

A - SEVENTEEN COME SUNDAY

Soldier, will you marry me?
   Now is your time or never,
For if you do not marry me
   I am undone for ever,
       With my ru rum ra.

Now I'm with my husband dear,
   Where the wars are alarming,
Drum and fife is my delight,
   And a merry man in the morning,
       With my ru rum ra.

B - WHEN COCKLE SHELLS MAKE SILVER BELLS

1 As I roved out one bright May morning,
   One May morning merrily;
   As I roved out one bright May morning,
   One May morning merrily;

I met a maid upon the way,
She was her mamma's darling.

refrain:
    With my rurum rah, fol the diddle-la
    Starry diddle-all lee di-dee-do.

2 Her shoes were black and her stockings white,
And her hair shines like the silver;
[repeat lines 1 and 2]
She has two nice bright sparkling eyes
And her hair hangs o'er her shoulder.

3 "What age are you my pretty fair maid,
What age are you my darling?"
[repeat lines 1 and 2]
She answered me quite modestly,
"I'm sixteen years next Monday morning.

4 "And will you come to my momma's house,
The moon shines bright and clearly?
[repeat lines 1 and 2]
Open the door and let me in
And dada will not hear me."

5 She took me by the lily-white hand
And led me to the table.
[repeat lines 1 and 2]
There's plenty wine for the soldiers here
As far as they can take it.

6 And she took my horse by the bridle right
And brought him to the stable.
She took my horse by the bridle right
And brought him to the stable.
There's plenty hay for soldier's horses
As far as they are able.

7 And she went up and dressed in bed
And dressed soft and hazy.
She went up and dressed in bed
And dressed soft and hazy.
And I went up to tuck her in,
Cryin', "Lassie, are you comfortable?"

8 And I slept in the house till the break of day
And in the morning early--
I slept in the house till the break of day
And in the morning early--
I got up and put on my shoes
Crying, "Lassie, I must leave you."

9 "And when will you return again
    Or when will we get married?
    When will you return again
    Or when will we get married?"
    "When cockle shells make silver bells
    That's the day we'll marry."

"The Lady of Carlisle," 0-25, has a novel twist to
it. Our heroine chooses between two lovers by tossing
a fan into a lions' den. The one who retrieves the fan
gains the lady! Surely you can think up another ending
for this potboiler. A variant, "Carolina Lady," is sung
by Dillard Chandler on Folkways FA 2418, Dillard
Chandler: The End of an Old Song (used by permission of
Folkways Records).

CAROLINA LADY

1 It's in Carolina there lived a lady,
    She was most handsome and gay.
    And she determined to be a lady
    And no man could her betray.

2 At length there was two loving brothers
    And on them she placed her heart's delight.
    One of them was a brave lieutenant,
    A brave lieutenant, a man of war.

3 The other was a bold sea captain,
    He belonged on a ship called Colonel Kar.
    It's up spoke this handsome lady,
    Saying, "I can not be but one man's bride,
    But if you'll meet me tomorrow morning,
    On this question we'll decide."

4 She called for her horse and coaches,
    And they were ready at her command.
    Off together these three did ramble
    Until they came to the lions' den.

5 Well, there they stopped and they halted,
    These two brothers musing round.
    It was for the space of half an hour
    She lie senseless on the ground.

6 When at last she did recover,
    She threw her fan in the lions' den.
    Saying, "Which of you to gain a lady
    Would return to me my fan?"

132

7 It's up spoke this bold sea captain,
   Raised his voice high above.
   Saying, "Madam, I'm a man of honor,
   And I will not lose my life for love."

8 It's up spoke this brave lieutenant,
   Raised his voice high above.
   Says, "Madam, I'm a man of honor,
   I will return your fan or die."

9 Down in the lions' den he ventured.
   Them lions they looked so over him.
   He hooped, he reached around among them,
   Till at last he did return.

10 When she saw her love a-coming,
   And no harm to him was done.
   She threw herself all on his bosom,
   Saying, "Here young man's the prize you've won."

"The Girl Volunteer," O-33, is another variation
of the female warrior theme. Sarah Ogun Gunning learned
"May I Go With You, Johnny?" from her mother who took it
for a Civil War song. Gunning sings it on Girl of
Constant Sorrow, Folk-Legacy FSA-26 (used by permission
of Folk-Legacy Records, Sharon, Conn.).

MAY I GO WITH YOU, JOHNNY?

1 The war it is started and Johnny must go.
   "May I go with you, Johnny?" "Oh, no, my love, no."
   "Oh, no, my love, no, that's what grieves my heart
       so.
   May I go with you Johnny?" "Oh, no, my love, no.

2 "Your waist is too slender, your fingers too small,
   Your cheeks too red and rosy to face the cannon-
       ball."
   "To face the cannonball, that's what grieves my
       heart so.
   May I go with you Johnny?" "Oh, no, my love no."

3 "I know my waist is slender, I know my fingers
       small,
   But I don't believe I'd tremble to see ten thousand
       fall.
   To see ten thousand fall, that's what grieves my
       heart so.
   May I go with you, Johnny?" "Oh, no, my love, no."

133

4 "I'll pull off my dresses, men clothing I'll put on
  And go to the army to stay with my John.
  To stay with my John, that would give my heart
    rest.
  May I go with you, Johnny?" "Oh, yes, my love,
    yes."

5 "Yes, my love, yes, that's what gives my heart
    rest.
  May I go with you, Johnny?" "Oh, yes, my love,
    yes."

"A-Growing," O-35, or "Daily Growing" or "The
Trees They Do Grow High" is not as common in North
America as it is in Great Britain. That is unfortunate,
for it is one of the most beautiful of all the broadsides and equals the Child ballads in intensity and
poetic quality. It is much older than most broadsides,
dating back to at least the 1630's. The text is a composite based mainly on the singing of Harry Richards of
Somerset and Mrs. Joiner of Chiswell Green in the early
twentieth century. It is printed in R. Vaughan Williams
and A. L. Lloyd (eds.), The Penguin Book of English Folk
Songs (Harmondsworth: Penguin Books, 1959), p. 99 (used
by permission).

THE TREES THEY GROW SO HIGH

1 The trees they grow so high and the leaves they
    grow so green.
  The day is past and gone, my love, that you and I
    have seen.
  It's a cold winter's night, my love, when I must
    bide alone,
  For my bonny lad is young but a-growing.

2 As I was a-walking by yonder church wall,
  I saw four and twenty young men a-playing at the
    ball.
  I asked for my own true love but they would not
    let him come,
  For they said the boy was young, but a-growing.

3 "O father, dearest father, you've done to me much
    wrong.
  You've tied me to a boy when you know he is too
    young."
  "O daughter, dearest daughter, if you'll wait a
    little while,
  A lady you shall be, while he's growing.

134

4 "We'll send your love to college, all for a year
      or two,
    And then perhaps in time the boy will do for you.
    I'll buy you white ribbons to tie about his waist,
    To let the ladies know that he's married."

5 And so early in the morning at the dawning of the
      day,
    They went out into the hayfield to have some sport
      and play,
    And what they did there, she never would declare,
    But she never more complained of his growing.

6 And at the age of sixteen he was a married man,
    And at the age of seventeen she brought to him a
      son,
    And at the age of eighteen the grass grew over him,
    And that soon put an end to his growing.

Another example of the broadside ballad at its
finest is "Molly Bawn," O-36. The plot parallels the
ancient tale of Cephalus and Procris in which Cephalus
mistakes Procris for an animal and kills her with his
spear. Phillips Barry concludes that the ballad is
based on Gaelic lore. Immigrants carried it to colonial
North America where it was printed in Jamieson's cir-
cular letter of 1799. A more recent popularization
occurred in 1963 with the release of the Peter, Paul and
Mary recording.

The two versions printed are from oral tradition.
"Molly Bawn" is by Sarah Cleveland, learned from her
mother and uncle, and recorded on Folk-Legacy FSA-33,
Ballads and Songs of the Upper Hudson Valley (used by
permission of Folk-Legacy Records, Sharon, Conn.).
"Molly Bonder" was collected by Bruce Buckley from a
"singing Irish family" in Adams County, Ohio. Buckley
sings it on Ohio Valley Ballads, Folkways FA 2025 (used
by permission of Folkways Records).

A - MOLLY BAWN

1 Come all you young hunters who follow the gun,
    Beware of late shooting by the setting of the sun.
    Jimmy Randall, the squire, was a-fowling in the
      dark;
    He aimed at his true love and ne'er missed his
      mark.

2 Being late in the evening when the shower came on,
    She ran under a green bush the shower to shun.

135

With her apron around her, he took her for a swan,
But, oh, and alas, wasn't she Molly Bawn?

3 He went to his home and he threw down his gun,
Crying, "Uncle, dear uncle, I have shot Molly Bawn.
I've shot that fair maiden, the pride of my life.
It was my intention to make her my wife."

4 The night before the trial her ghost did appear,
Saying, "Father, dear father, Jimmy Randall shall
go clear.
With my apron around me, he took me for a swan,
But, oh, and alas, wasn't I Molly Bawn?"

5 The girls of old England were all very glad
That the flower of Killarney was shot and killed
dead.
If we gather them together and stand them in a row,
Molly Bawn will shine among them like a mountain of
snow.

B - MOLLY BONDER

1 Come all you young huntsmen that handles a gun
And ever go a-hunting at the down setting sun,
I will tell to you a story that happened of late
Concerning pretty Molly whose beauty was great.

2 Molly Bonder was a-walking when a shower came on,
She went under a beech tree the shower to shun.
Jimmy Ramsel was a-hunting all fowling in the dark,
When he shot his own true love and he missed not
the mark.

3 He ran along to her and threw his gun down,
Saying, "Molly, truest Molly, I shot Molly Bond.
She was the fairest jewel, the joy of my life,
I always intended to make her my wife."

4 He ran home to his uncle and threw his gun down,
Cryin', "Uncle, dearest uncle, I've shot Molly Bond
Come and go along with me and for yourself see.
Yonder lies her body under a green growing tree."

5 Out spoke his old uncle with locks all so gray,
Saying, "Stay at home Jimmy and don't run away."
Saying, "Stay at home Jimmy your trial to stand,
Perhaps you'll come clear by the laws of this
land."

6 The day of Jimmy's trial Molly's ghost did appear,
  Saying, "Squire, dearest squire, Jimmy Ramsel come
      clear.
  He shot me and he killed me, the fault was my own,
  With my apron tucked around me he took me for a
      swan."

7 All the girls in this country they made themselves
      glad,
  When they heard of Molly Bonder her beauty being
      dead.
  He said, "Take all from around me and place them
      in a row,
  Molly shone through them like a mountain of snow."

   The first of the false true-love ballads, "The
Green Bushes," P-2, is best known in the Maritime Pro-
vinces of Canada and in New England. The text is from
Richard Hartlan of Nova Scotia as collected by Helen
Creighton. Margaret Christl and Ian Robb interpret it
on The Barley Grain for Me, FSC-62 (used by permission
of Folk-Legacy Records, Sharon, Conn.).

                THE GREEN BUSHES

1 All early, all early, all into the Spring,
  You hear the birds whistle and nightingales sing.
  I spied a fair damsel and sweetly sang she,
  Down by some green bushes, or chance to meet me.

2 "Oh, it's where are you going, my pretty fair
      maid?"
  "I'm in search of my true love, kind sir," and she
      said:
  "But if you will go with me, and we can agree,
  I'll leave my own Jimmy and follow with thee."

3 "I will buy you rich dresses, fine silks and fine
      gowns;
  I will buy you rich dresses, all flounced to the
      ground.
  I will buy you rich dresses, all flounced to the
      knee,
  If you'll leave your own Jimmy and follow with me."

4 "I don't want your fine jewels, fine silks or fine
      house.
  Do you think I'm so foolish as to marry for
      clothes?
  But if you will go with me, and we can agree,
  I will leave my own Jimmy and follow with thee.
                    137

5 "It is time to be leaving, young man if you please,
It is time to be leaving from under these trees.
But my true love is coming in yonder, I see,
A-whispering and singing, all joys to meet me."

6 And when he got there and he found she was gone,
He looked like a lamb and he cried out forlorn,
"She is gone and she's left me, forsaken I'll be.
Here's adieu to green bushes where'er you be."

"A Rich Irish Lady" or "The Sailor From Dover,"
P-9, is related to Child 295, "The Brown Girl," but
separate in that the plot situation is reversed. It is
widespread in North America. Hedy West's version was
handed down in her family from her great-grandmother,
Talitha Prudence Sparks Mulkey, and recorded on Old
Times and Hard Times, Folk-Legacy FSA-32 (used by permission of Hedy West).

A RICH IRISH LADY

1 A rich Irish lady, from London she came,
A beautiful damsel called Saro by name.
There was a young merchant worth thousands a year
Come courting this beautiful damsel so fair.

2 But her beauty being lofty and her portion so high
That on this young merchant she scarce cast her
    eye.
"Oh Saro, oh Saro, oh Saro," said he,
"I'm sorry that my love and yours can't agree.

3 "And now, if your hatred don't turn into love,
I know that your beauty my ruin shall prove."
"Oh, no, I don't hate you nor no other man,
But to say that I love you is more than I can.

4 "So you can retire and quit this discourse,
For I never will have you unless I am forced."
Oh, scarcely six weeks had rolled over and passed
When this beautiful damsel fell sick at the last.

5 She was tangled in love and she knew not for why,
She sent for this young man she once did deny.
"Oh, am I the doctor, you've sent for me here,
Or am I the young man that you now love so dear?"

6 "Oh, yes, you're the doctor can kill and can cure,
And without your assistance, I'm ruined for sure."
"Oh Saro, oh Saro, oh Saro," said he
"Now don't you remember when I courted thee?

7 "You slighted, denied me, through scorn and
      disdain,
   And now I'll reward you for what's past and gone."
   "For what's past and gone, love, forget and
      forgive,
   And let me have longer on this earth to live."

8 "Oh, no, I won't Saro, and during your life,
   But I'll dance on your grave when yo're laid in
      the earth."
   Oh, off of her finger pulled diamond rings three,
   Saying, "Take these and wear them while dancing
      on me."

9 Pretty Saro is dead, as we all might suppose,
   Some other rich woman willed all her fine clothes.
   She's at last made a bed in the wet and cold clay,
   Her red rosy cheeks are now mouldering away.

   "The Rejected Lover," P-10, learned by Howie
Mitchell from Lynn Flickinger while attending Cornell
University, is a collation of several versions in
Sharp. Hear it on Howie Mitchell, Folk-Legacy FSI-15
(used by permission of Folk-Legacy Records, Sharon,
Conn.).

                 THE REJECTED LOVER

1 I once knew a pretty girl
   And I loved her as my life,
   And I'd freely give my heart and hand
   To make her my wife,
   Oh, to make her my wife.

2 Well, she took me by the hand
   And she led me to the door,
   And she throwed her arms around me,
   Saying, "You can't come any more,
   Oh, you can't come any more."

3 Well, I'd not been gone for six months
   Before she did complain,
   And she wrote me a letter,
   Saying, "Do come again,
   Oh, do come again."

4 Well, I wrote her an answer,
   Just for to let her know
   That no young man could venture
   Where he once could not go,
   Oh, he once could not go.

                    139

5 So, come all you true lovers,
  Take a warning by me,
  And never place your affection
  On a green growing tree,
  Oh, a green growing tree.

6 For the leaves they will wither
  And the roots they will decay,
  And the beauty of a fair maid
  Will soon fade away,
  Oh, will soon fade away.

"The Nightingale" or "One Morning In May," P-14,
may be connected to a story in Boccaccio's Decameron
(1348-53). North American traditionalists have been
reluctant to admit to the song's double-entendre meaning. Joan Sprung, formerly a member of Roger Sprung's
"Progressive Bluegrassers," sings what she calls a
"folk-processed" version as set to a Jim Rooney tune on
Ballads and Butterflies, Folk-Legacy FSI-60 (used by
permission of Folk-Legacy Records, Sharon, Conn.).
Compare it to the more complete, but florid, variant by
Almeda Riddle on Ballads and Hymns from the Ozarks,
Rounder 0012.

ONE MORNING IN MAY

1 One morning, one morning, one morning in May,
  I spied a young couple a-making their way.
  One was a maiden, a maiden so fair,
  The other a soldier, a brave volunteer.

2 "Good morning, good morning, good morning to thee,
  And where be you going, my pretty lady?"
  "Oh, I'm going walking because it is spring,
  To see waters glide, hear the nightingale sing."

3 They hadn't been standing a moment or two
  When out of his pack-sack a fiddle he drew,
  And the tune that he played made the valleys all
      ring,
  And it sounded more sweet than the nightingales
      sing.

4 "Now," said the soldier, "it is time to leave
      o'er."
  "Oh, no," said the fair maid, "play a tune or two
      more!"
  So he keyed up his fiddle all on the high string
  And he played her the same tune right over again.

5 "Now, handsome soldier, you must marry me."
  "Oh, no pretty fair maid, that never can be,
  For I have a wife and children twice three.
  Two wives in the army are too much for me.

6 "I'll go back to London and stay there a year,
  And often I'll think of you, my little dear.
  And if I return, it will be in the spring
  To see waters glide, hear the nightingales sing."

7 Come all you fair maidens, take a warning from me.
  Never place your affection in a soldier so free,
  For he'll love you and leave you without any ring
  To rock your little baby, hear the nightingales
      sing.

From Nova Scotia to Florida and as far west as
Wyoming, variants of "The Butcher Boy," P-24, have been
uncovered. Its absorption into the folk mainstream was
aided by numerous broadside and songster printings.
Version A is the more or less standard treatment as sung
by Sam Hinton on The Wandering Folk Song, Folkways FA
2401. It contains the well-worn "go dig my grave"
stanza. "The Tavern In the Town," B, is based on a
Cornish version and is from the same source as A (both
used by permission of Folkways Records). "Morning
Fair," C, is an unusual variant by Frank Proffitt, learned from his aunt, Nancy Prather, and sung on Frank
Proffitt of Reese, North Carolina, Folk-Legacy FSA-1
(used by permission of Folk-Legacy Records, Sharon,
Conn.).

                A - THE BUTCHER BOY

1 In Jersey City where I did dwell,
  A butcher's boy I loved so well.
  He courted me both night and day,
  But now with me he will not stay.

2 There is an inn in this same town,
  There my love he sits him down,
  Takes some strange girl upon his knee
  And tells her what he won't tell me.

3 Oh, is that not grief to me,
  That she has silver more than me?
  But her gold will fade and her silver fly,
  And someday she'll be poor as I.

4 She went upstairs and to her bed,
  Nothing to her mother said.

And when her father he came home,
He said, "Where has my daughter gone?"

5 He went upstairs, the door he broke,
Found her hanging by a rope.
He took his knife and he cut her down
And in her bosom these words he found.

6 "Go dig my grave both wide and deep,
With a marble slab at head and feet.
On my breast a turtle dove,
To show the world that I died for love."

B - THE TAVERN IN THE TOWN

1 There is a tavern in the town,
And there my true love sits him down,
And he drinks his wine as merry as can be,
And never, never thinks of me.

[refrain, repeat after each verse]
Fare thee well, for I must leave you.
Do not let the parting grieve thee,
For the time has come for you and I to say
goodbye.
Adieu, adieu, kind friends, adieu.
I can no longer stay with you.
I'll hang my harp on the weeping willow tree,
And may the world go well with thee.

2 He left me for a damsel dark,
Each Friday night they used to spark.
And now he takes that damsel on his knee,
And tells her things that he won't tell me.

3 Go dig my grave both wide and deep,
With marble slab at head and feet.
And on my breast a turtle dove,
To signify that I died for love.

C - MORNING FAIR

1 As I woke up one morning fair
To take a walk all in the air,
I thought I heard my true love say,
"Oh, turn and come my way.

2 "You told me tales, you told me lies,
You courted a girl worth more than I
But gold will fade and silver will fly,
My love for you will never die.

3 "Oh, tell me, Willie, oh, tell me please,
   Do you take her upon your knees
   And hug and kiss her all so free,
   And tell her things you won't tell me?

4 "Is it because that I am poor
   That you turn me far from your door
   To wander out in a cruel dark world
   Because you love a rich man's girl?"

5 She gave me cake, she gave me wine,
   I rode out in her carriage fine.
   She set herself upon my knee
   And begged and kissed me all so free.

6 Her father gives to me his land
   And also of his daughter's hand.
   To give it up a fool I'd be,
   To trade it all for love of thee.

7 She went upstairs, up to her bed,
   A aching was all in her head.
   A rope she tied around the sill,
   They found her hanging, cold and still.

8 There in her bosom was this note,
   All with her pen these words she wrote:
   "Heap up my grave so very high
   So Willie can see as he rides by."

"The Nobleman's Wedding," P-31, strikes a slightly
different note than others in this section in that the
woman dies of remorse after being reminded of her un-
faithfulness by her lover during her wedding reception!
Sara Cleveland learned the following version from her
mother and recorded it on Ballads and Songs of the Upper
Hudson Valley, Folk-Legacy FSA-33 (used by permission
of Folk-Legacy Records, Sharon, Conn.).

TO WEAR A GREEN WILLOW

1 Once I was invited to a nobleman's wedding
   By a false lover that proved so unkind.
   It causes me now to wear a green willow,
   It causes me now to bear a troubled mind.

2 Supper was over and everyone seated,
   Every young man sang his true love a song,
   Until it came to the bride's own fond lover,
   The song that he sang to the bride it belonged.

143

3 Saying, "How can you lie on another man's pillow
As long as you have been a sweetheart of mine?
It causes me now to wear a green willow,
It causes me now to bear a troubled mind."

4 The bride she sat at the head of the table,
Every word she remembered right well,
Until at last she could bear it no longer
And down on the floor at the groom's feet she fell.

5 Saying, "There's one request that I ask as a favor.
As it is the first one, won't you grant it to me?
That this first night I may spend with my mother,
The rest of my life I will spend it with thee."

6 As it was the first one it was truly granted.
Sighing and sobbing she went to her bed.
Early next morning the groom he arose
And went there to find that his Mary was dead.

7 "Oh, Mary, dear Mary, you never have loved me
With a fond heart as I have loved you.
May this be a warning to all men and maidens
To never come between a bride and a groom."

"The Cruel Ship's Carpenter," P-36 A and B, is
better known in North America as "Pretty Polly." Most
versions have drastically reduced the original story.
"Pretty Polly" has been recorded by an assortment of
both traditional and contemporary singers. The text is
from the recording by B. F. Shelton in the late 1920's,
reissued on County Records 522, Old-Time Ballads From
the Southern Mountains.

PRETTY POLLY

1 "Pretty Polly, pretty Polly, would you think it
        unkind,
Pretty Polly, pretty Polly, would you think it
        unkind,
To sit down beside you and tell you my mind."

[repeat line 1 in remaining stanzas]

2 I courted pretty Polly the live long night,
And left the next morning before it was light.

3 I led her over hills to the valley so deep,
At last pretty Polly beginning to weep.

4 "Come on pretty Polly and go along with me,
   Before we get married some pleasures to see."

5 "Oh, Willie, sweet Willie, I fear from your ways,
   The way you around me, you leave me afraid."

6 She went up a-farther to see what she could find,
   A new dug grave and a spade lyin' by.

7 Had no time to study, no time left to stand,
   He stood with a knife though all in his right hand.

8 "Pretty Polly, pretty Polly, you guessing just
       right,
   I dug on your grave six long hours of last night."

9 She threw her arms around him and suffered no
       tears:
   "How can you kill a girl that loves you so dear?"

10 He stabbed her to the heart, her heart blood it
       did flow,
   And into the grave pretty Polly did go.

11 "Oh, Willie, sweet Willie, turn loose of my hand,
   You see my heart blood puddling around where you
       stand."

12 He threw some dirt over her and turned to go home,
   Leavin' nothin' behind him but the birdy to mourn.

13 "Gentlemen and ladies, I bid you farewell,
   For killing pretty Polly it'll send my soul to
       hell."

HUMOROUS AND MISCELLANEOUS

    Many broadsides in this category deal with married
life, others are comic Irish pieces. There is one about
a dying, but still larcenous, miller, and still another
has a race horse discussing strategy with his jockey.

    "The Old Woman of Slapsdam," Q-2, or "There Was An
Old Lady," has a moral for married couples. Horton
Barker learned the ballad from collector John Powell in
the 1930's. Hear it on Horton Barker: Traditional
Singer Folkways FA 2362 (used by permission of Folkways
Records).

THERE WAS AN OLD LADY

1 There was an old lady in our town,
In our town did dwell,
She loved her husband dearly
But another man twice as well.

refrain:
Sing too-de-um, sing too-de-um,
Whack, fol-lolly day.

3 She went down to the butcher shop
To see if she could find,
To see if she could find something
To make her old man blind.

3 She got twelve dozen marrow bones,
She made him suck them all.
Says he, "Old woman, I'm so blind
I cannot see at all."

4 Says he, "I'd go and drown myself,
If only I could see."
Says she, "My dearest husband,
I'll go and show you the way."

5 She bundled him up in his old grey coat,
She took him to the brim.
Says he, "I cannot drown myself
Unless you push me in."

6 The old woman took a step or two back
To give a rolling spring.
The old man stepped a little to the side
And she went tumbling in.

7 She bubbled and gurgled and squawled out
As loud as she could bawl.
Says he, "Old woman I'm so blind
I can't see you at all."

8 The old man being kind-hearted,
For fear that she could swim,
He went and got a very long pole
And pushed her further in.

"Devilish Mary," Q-4, details the war between the
sexes. The zany performance of the ballad at the
Eighth National Fiddle Contest in 1932 won first prize
for Gid Tanner and His Skillet Lickers. The text is
from their 1929 recording, reissued on County Records

146

506, The Skillet Lickers.

DEVILISH MARY

1 When I was young and foolish
  I thought I never would marry,
  Fell in love with a pretty little gal
  And shore'nuff we married.

  refrain:
      Love come-a-dink-come-derry,
      Prettiest gal I'd ever saw,
      Her name was devilish Mary.

2 We both were young and foolish,
  She was just a girlie.
  We both agreed upon the word
  Our wedding day was Thursday.

3 We hadn't been married for about six weeks
  She got mean as the devil.
  Every time I look cross-eyed
  She knocked me in the head with a shovel.

4 We hadn't been married for about six months,
  We both agreed to be parted.
  So she up with a little dust
  And down the road she started.

5 Fill my back with old soap suds,
  Fill my back with stiches,
  She let me know right at the start
  She's gonna wear my britches.

6 If I marry another time
  It's gonna be for love not riches.
  Marry a little gal about two feet high,
  She can't wear my britches.

"Will the Weaver," Q-9, first appeared in a
Scottish broadside in 1793. It has been recorded by Doc
Watson, Paul Clayton, and Mike Seeger among others.
Loman Cansler sings the following variant on Folksongs
of the Midwest, Folkways FH 5330 (used by permission
of Folkways Records).

WILL THE WEAVER

1 "Mother, mother, now I've married,
  How I wish I'd longer tarried,

For my wife she does declare
That the britches she will wear."

2 "Son, oh, son, go home and love her
And to me no more discover.
Give that daughter what's 'er due
And let me hear no more from you."

3 "I'll give her gold, I'll give her silver,
I'll give her all things if she's clever.
'Pon my word, she does rebel,
Take a stick and thrash her well."

4 So, this poor man went home in a blunder.
At the door he wrapped like thunder.
"Who is there?" the weaver cried!
"'Tis my husband, you must hide."

5 So up the chimney he did venture,
Then she let her husband enter.
Soon as the clat began to glow--oh,
Thinking husband would not know.

6 "Oh, wife, oh, wife, give me no reflections,
You've got to go by my directions.
Draw me some beer for I am dry,"
Thus her husband did reply.

7 He searched the house all around and around
And not a soul could there be found.
'Til up the chimney he did gaze
And there he saw the soul amaze.

8 'N there he saw the ragged soul
Stickin' a straddle of the chimney pole.
"Oh, Will, oh, Will, I'm glad I found you
For I'll neither hang nor drown'd you."

9 But thus was thought but nothing spoke,
"I will trifle you with smoke."
So he kicked up a roaring fire
Just to please his own desire.

10 His wife cried out with a free good will,
"Husband! husband! the man you'll kill!
Take him down, spare his life,
For I become your lawful wife."

11 So off the chimney pole he took him,
'Round the room like fun he shook him.

Cryin' out at every stroke,
"Come back no more to stop my smoke."

12 I never saw a chimney sweeper
Half as black as Will the weaver.
His hands, his face, his clothes likewise;
Sent him home with two black eyes.

"The Irish Wake," Q-18, outlines a scheme by Pat
to collect on a life insurance policy, but the consequences of his action soon sink in. Lawrence Older
learned a variant, "Pat Malone," from his father, and
sings it on Adirondack Songs, Ballads and Fiddle Tunes
(used by permission of Folk-Legacy Records,Sharon, Cn.).

PAT MALONE

1 Time was hard in Irish town,
Everything was goin' down,
When Pat Malone was pressed for ready cash.
He, for life insurance, spent
Every dollar to a cent,
Until all of his affairs had gone to smash.
"Now, dear Pat, if you were dead,
That twenty thousand dollars we might take."
So Pat laid down and tried
To make out that he had died
Until he smelled the whiskey at the wake.

Pat Malone forgot that he was dead.
He raised up in his coffin and he said,
"If the wake goes on a minute,
Sure, the corpse he must be in it!
Oh, you gotta get me drunk to keep me dead."

2 They gave to him a sup,
Afterwards they filled him up
And they gently laid him back upon the bed
Till the break of day; everybody felt so gay
They forgot Pat was only playing dead.
Snatched him off the bunk,
Wasn't dead, but awful drunk,
And they threw him in his coffin with a prayer,
Till the driver of the cart says, "Bedad, before
I start,
I'd like to know who'll pay the fare."

Pat Malone forgot that he was dead.
He raised up in his coffin and he said
"If you dare to doubt me credit,

149

You'll be sorry that you said it!
Drive on, or else the corpse'll break your
    head!"

3 So, then they started out
On the cemetery route,
All trying the widow to console,
Until they reached the base
Of Malone's resting place,
And they gently lowered Patrick in the hole.
Pat began to see,
Just as plain as one, two, three,
He'd forgot to reckon on the end.
When the sod begun to drop,
He broke off the coffin top
And quickly to the earth he did ascend.

    Pat Malone forgot that he was dead,
    From the cemetery quickly fled.
    It's a lucky thing, by thunder,
    Pat come nearly going under.
    It's lucky Pat forgot that he was dead.

"The Miller's Will," Q-21, a classic satire on entrepreneurship, is widespread in England and Scotland as well as North America. A Miss Stone of Wise County, Virginia, provided Horton Barker with the version he sings on Horton Barker: Traditional Singer, Folkways FA 2362 (used by permission of Folkways Records).

THE MILLER'S WILL

1 There was an old miller who lived all alone,
He had three sons who were almost grown.
He was about to make his will
And all that he had was a little old mill.
    Hi-lo-diddle-lol-day.

2 The miller called to his oldest son,
"Son, oh, son, I'm almost gone,
And if to you this will I make,
Pray tell me the toll that you aim to take."

3 "Father, you know my name is Heck,
Out of a bushel I'll take a peck.
If my fortune I would make,
Now this is the toll that I mean to take."

4 "Son, oh, son, I'm afraid you're a fool,
You have not learned to follow my rule.

This mill to you I will not give
For by such a toll no man can live."

5 The miller then called to his second son,
"Son, oh, son, I'm almost gone,
And if to you this will I make,
Pray tell me the toll that you aim to take."

6 "Father, you know my name is Ralph,
Out of a bushel I'll take half.
If my fortune I would make,
Now this is the toll that I mean to take."

[stanzas 7 and 8 repeat stanzas 4 and 5, except
8 begins: "The miller then called to his
youngest son."]

9 "Father, you know my name is Paul,
Out of a bushel I'll take it all.
Take all the grain and swear to the sack
And kick the old farmer if he ever comes back."

10 "Glory to God," the old man says,
"I've got one son who's learned my ways!"
"Hallelujah!" the old woman cried,
And the old man straightened out his legs and
        he died.

"Skewball," Q-22, is a tale about an Irish race
horse with a skewbald coloration (blotches of bay on a
white coat), who may well have raced on the plains of
Kildare before the ballad was printed in 1822.   In
North America it is called "Stewball" and even has
entered the black tradition.   In 1976 Joan Baez updated
the story by adding references to the tragedy of the
filly Ruffian who was ahead in her race when she
stumbled and had to be destroyed.   The text is by Cisco
Houston, Cowboy Ballads, Folkways FA 2022 (used by permission of Folkways Records).   Horse and rider do not
converse in the more mundane North American texts.

STEWBALL

1 Stewball was a good horse
And he held a high head,
And the mane on his foretop
Was fine as silk thread.

2 I rode him in England,
I rode him in Spain,

151

And I never did lose boys,
I always did gain.

3 So come all of you gamblers
From near and from far,
Don't bet your gold dollar
On that little grey mare.

4 Most likely she'll stumble,
Most likely she'll fall,
But you never will lose
On my noble Stewball.

5 Sit tight in your saddle,
Let slack on your rein,
And you never will lose boys,
You always will gain.

6 As they were riding
'Bout half way 'round,
The gray mare she stumbled
And fell to the ground.

7 And away out yonder,
Ahead of them all,
Came dancing and prancing
My noble Stewball.

8 Stewball was a good horse,
And he held a high head,
And the mane on his foretop
Was fine as silk thread.

9 I rode him in England,
And I rode him in Spain,
And I never did lose boys,
I always did gain.

"Erin's Green Shores," Q-27, is a political message ballad in which the narrator dreams of a "Goddess of Freedom" who appeals to the Irish people to redress the wrongs of British rule. In Joe Hickerson's version, from Hedy West's north Georgian-Irish heritage, the goddess is the daughter of a freedom fighter from the revolution of 1848. Text: Joe Hickerson: Drive Dull Care Away, Volume II, Folk-Legacy FSI-49 (used by permission of Hedy West and Folk-Legacy Records).

ERIN'S GREEN SHORES

1 One evening for pleasure I rambled
  On the banks of a clear purling stream.
  I sat down in a bed of primroses
  And I quickly fell into a dream.

2 I dreamed I beheld a fair maiden
  Her equal I'd ne'er seen before.
  And she said for the sake of her country
  She had strayed along Erin's green shore.

3 I stepped up and I boldly addressed her,
  "Fair maid won't you tell me your name
  And why in this wild wooded country
  From England through London you came?"

4 "I'm the daughter of Daniel O'Connell
  And from England I lately come o'er.
  And it's for to awaken my brothers
  Who slumbers on Erin's green shore."

5 Her cheeks were like two blooming roses,
  Her teeth like the ivory so white,
  Her eyes were like two sparkling diamonds,
  Or the stars of a clear frosty night.

6 She resembled the riches of Eden
  And green was the mantle she wore.
  And she said for the sake of her country
  She had strayed along Erin's green shore.

MAX HUNTER
Photo by Sandy Paton   Courtesy Folk-Legacy Records

SARAH OGUN GUNNING
Photo by Ellen Stekert   Courtesy Folk-Legacy Records

CHAPTER FOUR

NATIVE AMERICAN BALLADS

North Americans have been singing secular music since the time of the early settlements, notwithstanding religious strictures. Cotton Mather, a Puritan leader in seventeenth century Massachusetts, warned of the growing popularity of "sinful" songs: "I'm informed that the minds and manners of many people about the country are much corrupted by foolish songs and ballads which the hawkers and pedlars carry to all parts of the country."[1] Yet Mather's protests went unheeded; Americans enjoyed music too much. Classic ballads and British broadsides were popular from the beginning. As time passed, Americans constructed new ballads--native American ballads--hardly literary or musical masterpieces, but, nevertheless, indigenous to the continent. These newer ballads suffer from direct comparisons with the older British forms. They are more subjective and sensational; they lack suspense; they are deficient in style--prosaic and concerned with minutia. Time, the necessary element for the folk process to polish the original music, was limited.

On the other hand, native balladry reflects the character of its people. First, they are more democratic and accessible than songs composed in older and more class-oriented societies. Second, the black tradition of Africa and North America has added its unique ingredients to the Anglo-Scots-Irish mix. Finally, American balladry expresses concern for those faced with tragedy. As Laws explains: "Native balladry may be rugged and colorful or commonplace and sentimental; much of it may be inept, some even illiterate, but above all it shows compassion, neighborliness, and concern for other men's misfortunes."[2]

If these newer ballads fail to measure up to Child's standards, there are some musical gems among the rough stones which more than compensate for their de-

---

[1] Quoted in MacEdward Leach, The Ballad Book (New York: A. S. Barnes and Company, Inc., 1955), p. 36.

[2] G. Malcolm Laws, Native American Balladry (Philadelphia: The American Folklore Society, 1964), p. 111.

ficiencies. Two such jewels are "The Buffalo Skinners," a realistic look at the Old West, and "John Henry," a tragic confrontation between man and machine which still has a bearing on our modern technologically-oriented society.

This chapter is organized along the guide lines established by G. Malcolm Laws in <u>Native American Balladry</u> (revised edition) where he listed over 250 ballads. He excluded all ballads composed within thirty years of 1964, the date of the revised edition, on the grounds that it was premature to call them traditional. Only ballads collected from singers since 1920 were included, thus eliminating many examples that were traditional earlier (and still may be!). Despite such limitations, and with modifications and additions, this chapter utilizes the classification system of Laws including his letter-number identification scheme.

WAR

"Brave Wolfe," the first of the war ballads in Laws, A-1, may be the oldest native ballad found in twentieth century oral tradition. An account of the battle on the Plains of Abraham near Quebec in 1759, the ballad commemorates Montcalm's defeat by British General Wolfe thereby sealing the fate of the French in North America. The ballad was the work of an obscure broadside poet; but the folk were so struck with the content that it soon entered the oral tradition. The text, based on a Newfoundland variant collected by Elizabeth Bristol Greenleaf in 1929, was recorded by Alan Mills on <u>O' Canada: A History in Song</u>, Folkways FP 3001 (used by permission of Folkways Records).

BRAVE WOLFE

1 Come now, you young men all, and hear my story
Of how bold Wolfe did fall, in all his glory.
On the Plains of Abraham fell this brave hero,
We'll long lament his loss in deepest sorrow.

2 That brave and gallant youth did cross the ocean,
To free America of her division.
He landed at Quebec with all his party,
The city to attack, being brave and hearty.

3 Bold Wolfe drew up his men in a line so pretty
On the Plains of Abraham before the city.

On the plains before the town, where the French
    did meet him,
In double numbers round, all for to beat him.

4 When, drawn up in a line, for death preparing,
And in each other's face, those two armies staring,
Where the cannons on both sides did roar like
    thunder,
And youth, in all its pride, was torn asunder.

5 Where the drums did loudly beat, 'mid colors a-
    flying,
Bold Wolfe did bravely ride, all dangers defying,
When shot from off his horse fell that brave hero,
May we lament his loss that day in sorrow.

6 The guns the ground did shake, where he was lying,
Bold Wolfe he seemed to wake as he was dying.
He lifted up his head as the guns did rattle,
And to his men he said: "How goes the battle?"

7 His aide-de-camp replied: "'Tis in our favor!
Quebec in all her pride, there is none can save
    her,
For 'tis falling in our hands with all her
    treasure!"
"Oh," then replied bold Wolfe: "I died in
    pleasure!"

"Paul Jones, the Privateer," A-3, describes a
battle between the USS Ranger, commanded by John Paul
Jones, and a superior British warship off the Irish
coast in 1778. The title of one variant, "The Stately
Southerner," apparently refers to Jones who, although
born in Scotland, settled in Virginia. Sandy Ives sings
it on Folksongs of Maine, Folkways FH 5323 (used by permission of Folkways Records).

THE STATELY SOUTHERNER

1 'Tis of a stately southerner that carried the
    stripes and stars,
A whistling wind from west-nor'west blew through
    her pitch-pine spars.
Her starboard tack we had on board were heavy on
    the gale,
One autumn night we raised the light on the Old
    Head of Kinsale.

2 What rises on our weather bow? What hangs upon the
      breeze?
   'Tis time our good ship hauled her wind abreast of
      the Saltees.
   And by her wondrous spread of sail, her sharp and
      tapering spars,
   We knew our morning visitor was a British man-of-
      war.

3 Out booms upon the southerner, out booms and give
      her sheet!
   The fastest keel that cuts the deep and the pride
      of the British fleet
   Come bearing down upon us with a high foam at her
      prow.
   Out booms upon the southerner, spread out your
      canvas now!

4 Away! Away! A shower of shot came through our
      rigging and mast,
   The fastest keel that cuts the deep was heading
      our frigate fast.
   Those British tars they gave three cheers from
      the deck of their corvette,
   We answered back with a scornful laugh from the
      deck of our patriot bark.

5 Up spoke our noble captain, a cloud was on his
      brow,
   He said: "My gallant heroes, our great distress
      is now.
   We carry aloft the stars and stripes against that
      British host.
   Paul Jones, the terror of the seas, shall flog
      them on their coast."

6 The morning mist had just arisen that scarce
      obscured the shore,
   A heavy fog hung o'er the land from Erin to
      Kingshore.
   Paul Jones down in North Channel did steer, his
      sharp prow cut the spray.
   We left that British ship astern soon after the
      break of day.

    "James Bird," A-5, was written in 1814 by Charles
Miner, the editor of the Wilkes-Barre newspaper The
Gleaner. It is an accurate account of a marine hero-
turned-deserter during the War of 1812. Following the
battle of Lake Erie, in which Bird had served honorably,
he went AWOL from his unit apparently hoping to join

Commodore Perry, who had been transferred elsewhere. Americans were shocked by the heavy-handed nature of the court martial with its death sentence verdict. The text is from <u>Vivian Richman Sings</u>, Folkways FG 3568 (used by permission of Folkways Records).

JAMES BIRD

1 Sons of freedom, listen to me,
  And your daughters, too, give ear.
  You a sad and mournful story
  As was ever told shall hear.

2 Hull, you know, his troops surrendered
  And defenseless left the west.
  Then our forces quickly assembled,
  The invaders to resist.

3 Among the troops that marched to Erie
  Was the Kingston volunteers,
  Captain Thomas then commanded
  To protect our west frontiers.

4 Soon they came where noble Perry
  Had assembled all his fleet.
  Then the gallant Bird enlisted,
  Hoping soon the foe to meet.

5 But, behold, a ball has struck him,
  See the crimson current flow.
  "Leave the deck!" exclaimed brave Perry.
  "No," cried Bird, "I will not go!"

6 But there came most dismal tidings
  From Lake Erie's distant shore,
  Better far if Bird had perished
  Midst the battle's awful roar.

7 "Dearest parents," read the letter,
  "This will bring sad news to you;
  Do not mourn your first beloved,
  Though this brings his last adieu.

8 "I must suffer for deserting
  From the brig <u>Niagara</u>;
  Read this letter, brothers, sisters,
  'Tis the last you'll hear from me."

9 Lo! he fought so brave at Erie,
  Freely bled and nobly dared;

Let his courage plead his mercy,
Let his precious life be spared.

10 Farewell, Bird, farewell forever,
   Friends and home he'll see no more.
   But his mortal frame lies buried
   On Lake Erie's distant shore.

"The Constitution and the Guerriere," A-6, cele-
brates Captain Hull's victory over Captain Dacres in the
famous naval engagement during the War of 1812. The
bragging, nationalistic lyrics are set to a jaunty tune.
Wallace House sings it on War of 1812, Folkways FP 5002
(used by permission of Folkways Records).

THE CONSTITUTION AND THE GUERRIERE

1 It oftimes has been told
  That the British seamen bold
  Could flog the tars of France so neat and handy,
     oh!
  But they never found their match
  Till the Yankees did them catch,
  Oh, the Yankee boys for fighting are the dandy,
     oh!

2 The Guerriere, a frigate bold,
  On the foaming ocean rolled,
  Commanded by proud Dacres the grandee, oh!
  With as choice an English crew
  As a rammer ever drew,
  Could flog the Frenchmen two to one so handy, oh!

3 When this frigate hove in view,
  Said proud Dacres to his crew,
  "Come, clear the ship for action and be handy, oh!
  To the weather gage, boys, get her."
  And to make his boys fight better,
  Gave them to drink, gunpowder mixed with brandy,
     oh!

4 Then Dacres loudly cries,
  "Make this Yankee ship your prize,
  You can in thirty minutes, neat and handy, oh!
  Twenty-five's enough I'm sure, and
  If you'll do it in a score,
  I'll treat you to a double share of brandy, oh!"

5 The British shot flew hot
  Which the Yankee answered not,

Till they got within the distance they called
   handy, oh!
"Now," says Hull unto his crew,
"Boys, let's see what we can do,
If we take this boasting Briton we're the dandy,
   oh!"

6 The first broadside we poured
Carried her mainmast by the board,
Which made this lofty frigate look abandoned, oh!
Then Dacres shook his head, and
To his officers said,
"Lord! I did't think those Yankees were so handy,
   oh!"

7 Our second told so well
That their fore and mizzen fell,
Which dous'd the royal ensign neat and handy, oh!
"By George," says he, "we're done."
And they fired a lee gun
While the Yankees struck up Yankee Doodle Dandy,
   oh!

8 Then Dacres came on board
To deliver up his sword,
Tho' loath he was to part with it, 'twas handy,
   oh!
"Oh, keep your sword," says Hull,
"For it only makes you dull,
Cheer up and let us have a little brandy, oh!"

9 Now fill your glasses full
And we'll drink to Captain Hull,
And so merrily we'll push about the brandy, oh!
John Bull may toast his fill, but
Let the world say what they will,
The Yankee boys for fighting are the dandy, oh!

"The Texas Rangers," A-8, describes a battle between rangers and Indians, although some versions pit
rangers against Mexicans. Civil War variants name the
enemy either as Yanks or Rebels depending upon the
loyalty of the singer. Finlay Adams of Big Laurel,
Virginia, was the source for Paul Clayton's version on
Cumberland Mountain Folksongs, Folkways FP 2007 (used
by permission of Folkways Records).

                THE TEXAS RANGERS

1 Oh, come all you Texas Rangers
Wherever you may be,

And I'll tell you a story
That happened unto me.

2 At about the age of sixteen
I joined this jolly band.
We marched from western Texas
Down to the Rio Grande.

3 Our captain, he informed us
To what he thought was right.
Before we reached the station
Says, "Boys, you'll have to fight."

4 Oh, I saw the Indians coming,
I heard them give a yell,
My feelings at that moment,
My courage almost fell.

5 We fought them nine long hours
Before the fray was o'er.
The like of dead and wounded
I never saw before.

6 There lay six as noble a rangers
As ever sought the west,
Besides all their comrades
With bullets in their breasts.

7 I then thought of my dear mother,
In tears to me did say,
"To you they are all strangers,
With me you'd better stay."

8 Oh, I then thought that she was childish
And the best she did not know.
My mind was bent on rambling
And I was forced to go.

9 Perhaps you all have mothers,
Likewise a sister, too,
Perhaps you all have sweethearts
To weep and mourn for you.

10 If this be your condition
And you are forced to roam,
I'll tell you from experience
You had better stay at home.

"The Battle of Elkhorn Tavern," A-12, is one of the
few surviving actual battlefield ballads from the Civil
War. To historians,Gettysburg, Antietam or Vicksburg

may be significant campaigns, but the folk usually honor minor skirmishes in obscure locations. Max Hunter sings a related story, "The Battle of Pea Ridge," on Ozark Folksongs and Ballads, Folk-Legacy FSA-11, from which the text is taken (used by permission of Folk-Legacy Records, Sharon, Conn.).

THE BATTLE OF PEA RIDGE

1 It was on March the seventh
In the year of sixty-two,
We had a sore engagement
With Abe Lincoln's crew.
Van Dorn was our commander,
As you remember be.
We lost ten thousand of our men
Near the Indian Territory.

2 Cap' Price come a-riding up the line,
His horse was in a pace.
And as he gave the word "retreat"
The tears rolled down his face.
Ten thousand deaths I'd rather die
As they should gain the field.
From that he got a fatal shot
Which caused him to yield.

3 At Springfield and Carthrage
Many a hero fell.
At Lexington and Drywood,
As near the truth can tell.
But such an utter carnage
As did I ever see
Happened at old Pea Ridge
Near the Indian Territory.

4 I know you brave Missouri boys
Were never yet afraid.
Let's try and form in order,
Retreat the best we can.
The word "retreat" was passed around.
It caused the heathen cry.
Helter-skelter through the woods
Like lost sheep they did fly.

"The Hunters of Kentucky," A-25, was written by Samuel Woodworth in 1822 to honor Andrew Jackson, the hero of the Battle of New Orleans. Jackson partisans used it as a campaign song in the presidential election of 1828. The text is from Election Songs of the United States, sung by Oscar Brand, Folkways FH 5280 (used by

163

permission of Folkways Records). See also Vera Brodsky Lawrence, <u>Music</u> <u>for</u> <u>Patriots</u>, <u>Politicians</u>, <u>and</u> <u>Presidents</u>, p. 212.

THE HUNTERS OF KENTUCKY

1 Ye gentlemen and ladies fair
   That grace this famous city,
   Come listen if you've time to spare
   While I rehearse this ditty.
   And for the opportunity consider yourself lucky
   It is not often that you see a hunter from
      Kentucky.
   Oh, Kentucky, the hunters of Kentucky.

2 Now you all did read in public prints how
      Packenham attempted
   To make our Hickory Jackson wince,
   But soon his scheme repented.
   For Jackson he was wide awake
   And wasn't scared at trifles,
   And well he knew what aim we take
   With our Kentucky rifles.
   Oh, Kentucky, the hunters of Kentucky.

3 Well, bank was raised to hide our breasts,
   Not that we thought of dying,
   But that we always like to rest
   Unless our game is flying.
   Behind it stood our little band,
   None wished it to be greater,
   Every man was half a horse and half an alligator.
   Oh, Kentucky, the hunters of Kentucky.

4 Well, the British found 'twas vain to fight
   Where lead was all their booty
   And so, they wisely took to flight
   And left us all this beauty.
   And so, if danger e'er annoys,
   Remember what our trade is.
   Send for us Kentucky boys
   And we'll protect you, ladies.
   Oh, Kentucky, the hunters of Kentucky.

COWBOYS AND PIONEERS

Some of the finest native ballads describe the trials and tribulations of a genuine breed of rugged individualists--cowboys. "The Cowboy's Lament," B-1, has been discussed previously in Chapter One as part of

164

"The Unfortunate Rake" cycle.

"The Dying Cowboy" or "Bury Me Not On the Lone Prairie," B-2, is a variation of "The Ocean Burial" which was written by the Reverend Edwin H. Chapin and published in 1839. The text is from Joe Hickerson, Drive Dull Care Away, Volume II, Folk-Legacy FSI-59 (used by permission of Folk-Legacy Records, Sharon, Conn.). Compare it to Fields Ward's recording, Bury Me Not On the Prairie, Rounder Records 0036, and to Sandy and Jeanie Darlington, Folk-Legacy FSI-28.

BURY ME NOT ON THE LONE PRAIRIE

1 "O bury me not on the lone prairie,"
These words came low and mournfully
From the pallid lips of a youth who lay
On his dying bed at the close of day.

2 "O bury me not on the lone prairie,
Where the wild coyote will howl o'er me,
Where the buffalo roams on the prairie sea,
O bury me not on the lone prairie.

3 "It makes no difference so I've been told
Where the body lies when life grows cold,
But grant, I pray, one wish to me,
O bury me not on the lone prairie.

4 "I've often wished to be laid when I die
By the little church on the green hillside
By my father's grave, there let me be,
O bury me not on the lone prairie."

5 The cowboys gathered all around the bed
To hear the last word that their comrade said:
"O partners all, take a warning from me,
Never leave your homes for the lone prairie.

6 "Don't listen to the enticing words
Of the men who own large droves and herds,
For if you do, you'll rue the day
That you left your homes for the lone prairie.

7 "O bury me not," but his voice failed there,
But we paid no heed to his dying prayer.
In a narrow grave just six by three
We buried him there on the lone prairie.

8 We buried him there on the lone prairie
Where buzzards fly and the wind blows free,

Where the rattlesnakes rattle, and the tumbleweeds
Blow across his grave on the lone prairie.

9 And the cowboys now as they cross the plains
Have marked the spot where his bones are lain.
Fling a handful of roses o'er his grave
And pray to the Lord that his soul be saved.
    In a narrow grave just six by three
    We buried him there on the lone prairie.

"Little Joe, the Wrangler," B-5, was a favorite of
the editor years before he discovered its folk roots.
N. Howard Thorp claimed to have written it while on a
cattle drive in 1898. Versions by Cisco Houston (Cowboy
Ballads, Folkways FA 2022) and Harry Jackson (The Cowboy, Folkways FH 5723) have been recorded. The text is
from Thorp's 1908 book Songs of the Cowboys.

LITTLE JOE, THE WRANGLER

1 Little Joe, the wrangler, will never wrangle more;
    His days with the "Remuda"--they are done.
'Twas a year ago last April he joined the outfit
    here,
    A little "Texas Stray" and all alone.

2 'Twas long late in the evening he rode up to the
    herd
    On a little brown pony he called Chaw;
With his brogan shoes and overalls a harder look-
    ing kid
    You never in your life had seen before.

3 His saddle 'twas a southern kack built many years
    ago,
    An O. K. spur on one foot idly hung,
While his "hot roll" in a cotton sack was loosely
    tied behind
    And a canteen from the saddle horn he'd slung.

4 He said he'd had to leave his home, his daddy'd
    married twice
    And his new ma beat him every day or two;
So he saddled up old Chaw one night and "Lit a
    shuck" this way
    Thought he'd try and paddle now his own canoe.

5 Said he'd try and do the best he could if we'd
    only give him work
    Though he didn't know "straight" up about a
      cow,

166

So the boss he cut him out a mount and kinder put
    him on
        For he sorter liked the little stray somehow.

6 Taught him how to herd the horses and to learn to
    know them all
        To round 'em up by daylight; if he could
    To follow the chuck-wagon and to always hitch the
    team
        And help the "cosinero" rustle wood.

7 We'd driven to red river and the weather had been
    fine;
        We were camped down on the south side in a bend
    When a norther commenced blowing and we doubled up
    our guards
        For it took all hands to hold the cattle then.

8 Little Joe, the wrangler was called out with the
    rest
        And scarcely had the kid got to the herd
    When the cattle they stampeded; like a hail storm,
    long they flew
        And all of us were riding for the lead.

9 'Tween the streaks of lightning we could see a
    horse far out ahead
        'Twas little Joe, the wrangler in the lead;
    He was riding "old Blue Rocket" with his slicker
    'bove his head
        Trying to check the leaders in their speed.

10 At last we got them milling and kinder quieted down
        And the extra guard back to the camp did go
    But one of them was missin' and we knew at a glance
        'Twas our Little Texas stray poor wrangler Joe.

11 Next morning just a sunup we found where Rocket
    fell
        Down in a washout twenty feet below
    Beneath his horse mashed to a pulp his horse had
    rung the knell
        For our little Texas stray--poor wrangler Joe.

    The best known of the forty-niner gold rush ballads
is "Sweet Betsy From Pike," B-9. Sung to the tune of
"Vilikins and His Dinah," M-31B, it recounts both hardships and amusing diversions on the westward journey to
the California gold fields. The text first appeared in
Put's Golden Songster, San Francisco, 1858. Logan
English sings it on The Days of '49, Folkways FH 5255

(used by permission of Folkways Records).

SWEET BETSY FROM PIKE

1 Oh, don't you remember sweet Betsy from Pike
  Who crossed the wide mountains with her lover Ike,
  With one yoke of oxen and a big yellow dog
  A tall Shanghai rooster and a one-spotted hog.

  refrain:
      Singing too-ral-i-early, li-early, li-ay,
      [repeat 3 times]

2 Out on the prairie one bright starry night
  They broke out the whiskey and Betsy got tight.
  She sang and she shouted, she danced o'er the
      plain,
  And made a great show for the whole wagon train.

3 The Injuns come down in a wild yelling horde,
  And Betsy got scared they would scalp her adored.
  Behind the front wagon wheel Betsy did crawl,
  And fought off the Injuns with musket and ball.

4 They soon reached the desert, where Betsy give out,
  And down in the sand she lay rolling about.
  While Ike in great terror looked on in surprise,
  Saying, "Get up now Betsy, you'll get sand in your
      eyes."

5 The wagon tipped over with a terrible crash,
  And out on the prairie rolled all sorts of trash.
  A few little baby clothes done up with care
  Looked rather suspicious, though 'twas all on the
      square.

6 The Shanghai run off and the cattle all died,
  The last piece of bacon that morning was fried.
  Poor Ike got discouraged, and Betsy got mad,
  The dog wagged his tail and looked wonderfully sad.

7 One morning they climbed up a very high hill
  And with great wonder looked down into old Placer-
      ville.
  Ike shouted and said, as he cast his eyes down,
  "Sweet Betsy, my darling, we've come to Hangtown."

8 Long Ike and sweet Betsy attended a dance
  Where Ike wore a pair of his Pike County pants.

Sweet Betsy was covered with ribbons and rings,
Said Ike, "You're an angel, but where are your
    wings?"

9 A miner said, "Betsy, will you dance with me?"
"I will that, old hoss, if you don't make too free.
But don't dance me hard, don't you want to know
    why?
Doggone you, I'm chock-full of strong alkali."

10 Long Ike and sweet Betsy got married of course,
But Ike, getting jealous, obtained a divorce.
And Betsy, well satisfied, said with a shout,
"Goodbye you big lummox, I'm glad you backed out."

Generations of Americans were raised on the myths
of the Cattle Frontier, first in dime novels, then in
motion pictures, and more recently on television. Cowboys were portrayed as violent men--dead shots with
rifles and revolvers--but generous, brave and honest.
They were young and handsome, white and sleek, romantic
lovers, agile horsemen, impeccable dressers, and even
well-educated. "The Buffalo Skinners," B-10, exposes
many of these myths with its realistic account of a
buffalo hunt. Echoing the sentiments of pioneer song
collector John Lomax, Carl Sandburg described the
ballad's lyrics as "blunt, direct, odorous, plain and
made-to-hand, having the sound to some American ears
that the Greek language of Homer had for the Greeks of
that time."[1]

"The Buffalo Skinners" is a reworking of "Canaday
I-0," C-17, a lumberjack ballad based on an English sea
song, "Canada I. 0." Woody and Arlo Guthrie recorded
variants of "The Buffalo Skinners," while Ed McCurdy
sang a dramatic version on Songs of the Old West,
Elektra EKL-112. The text is by Harry Tuft from The
Continuing Tradition, Volume 1: Ballads, Folk-Legacy
FSI-75 (used by permission of Folk-Legacy Records,
Sharon, Conn.). See the annotated edition by the Fifes
of Thorp, Songs of the Cowboys for a complete analysis.

THE BUFFALO SKINNERS

1 Come all you good-time cowboys,
And listen to my song,
I pray you not grow weary,

---

[1]Carl Sandburg, The American Songbag, p. 270.

I'll not detain you long.
Concerning some young cowboys
Who did agree to go
And spend the summer pleasantly
On the range of the buffalo.

2 'Twas in the town of Jacksboro,
In the year of '73,
A man by the name of Crego
Came stepping up to me.
Says, "How d'you do, young feller,
And how'd you like to go.
And spend the summer pleasantly
On the range of the buffalo?"

3 Well, it's me being out of employment
To old Crego I did say,
"This going out on the buffalo range
Depends upon the pay.
But, if you will pay good wages
And transportation, too,
Then maybe I will go with you
To the range of the buffalo."

4 "Oh, yes, I pay good wages
And transportation, too,
If you will come along with me
And work the season through.
But if you do grow homesick
And try to run away,
Well, you'll starve to death out on the range,
And you'll also lose your pay."

[next stanza from other sources]

5 It's now our outfit was complete,
Seven able-bodied men,
With navy six and needle-gun,
Our troubles did begin.
Our way it was a pleasant one,
The route we had to go,
Until we crossed Pease River
On the range of the buffalo.

6 Well, it's now we crossed Pease River, boys,
Our trouble's just begun.
First old buffalo that I skinned,
Christ, how I cut my thumb!
While skinning the damned old stinkers
Our lives they were no go,

For the outlaws waited to pick us off
From the hills of Mexico.

7 Well, he fed us on such sorry chuck,
I wished myself was dead,
Old beans and hardtack
And rotten sour bread.
The mosquitos and the chinches,
I tell you boys, no show,
For God's forsaken the buffalo range
And the damned old buffalo.

8 Well, the season was near over, boys,
And old Crego, he did say
The crowd had been extravagant,
We were in debt to him that day.
Well, we coaxed him and we argued,
But still it was no go,
And we left his damned old bones to bleach
On the range of the buffalo.

9 And it's now we've crossed Pease River, boys,
And homeward we are bound.
No more in that hell-fired country
Will ever we be found.
Go home to our wives and sweethearts,
Tell others not to go.
God's forsaken the buffalo range
And the damned old buffalo.

"Joe Bowers," B-14, is another gold rush ballad in
the style of "Sweet Betsy From Pike." Lumberjacks and
cowboys have reworked the story to fit their circumstances. The text is from The Days of '49, sung by
Logan English, Folkways FH 5255 (used by permission of
Folkways Records).

JOE BOWERS

1 My name it is Joe Bowers, I've got a brother Ike,
I come from old Missouri, yes all the way from
    Pike.
I'll tell you why I left there, and how I came to
    roam,
And leave my poor old mammy, so far away from home.

2 I used to love a gal there, they called her Sally
    Black,
I axed her for to marry, she said it was a whack.

171

Says she to me, "Joe Bowers, before we hitch for life,
You oughter have a little home to keep your little wife."

3 Says I, "My dearest Sally, oh Sally, for your sake,
I'll go to Californy and try to raise a stake."
Says she to me, "Joe Bowers, oh you're the chap to win,
Give me a kiss to seal the bargain," and she threw a dozen in.

4 I shall ne'er forget my feelin's when I bid adieu to all,
Sally cotched me round the neck, and I began to bawl.
When I got in, they all commenced--you ne'er did hear the like,
How they all took on and cried, the day I left old Pike.

5 When I got to this country, I hadn't nary red,
I had such wolfish feelings, I wished myself most dead.
But the thoughts of my dear Sally soon made them feelings git,
And whispered hopes to Bowers--Lord, I wish I had 'em yet!

6 At length I went to minin', put in my biggest licks,
Come down upon the boulders just like a thousand bricks.
I worked both late and early, in rain, and sun and snow,
But I was working for my Sally, so 'twas all the same to Joe.

7 I made a very lucky strike, as the gold itself did tell,
And saved it for my Sally the gal I loved so well.
I saved it for my Sally that I might pour it at her feet,
That she might kiss and hug me, honey, and call me something sweet.

8 But one day I got a letter from my dear, kind brother, Ike.
It came from old Missouri, sent all the way from Pike.

It brought me the darndest news as ever you did
    hear,
My heart is almost bustin', so, pray, excuse this
    tear.

9 It said my Sal was fickle, that her love for me had
    fled.
That she had married a butcher, whose hair was
    awful red!
It told me more than that--oh, it's enough to make
    one swear--
It said Sally had a baby and that baby had red
    hair!

10 Now I've told you all that I could tell, about
    this sad affair,
'Bout Sally marryin' the butcher, and the butcher
    had red hair.
Now whether 'twas a boy or girl, the letter never
    said,
It only said its cussed hair was inclined to be
    red!

Although not included in Laws, "The Days of '49"
is a gold rush ballad of high quality and has entered
the oral tradition from the Ozarks to the Adirondacks.[1]
If "The Buffalo Skinners" cuts through the romanticism
of life on the range, then "The Days of '49" similarly
depicts the cruel conditions facing the gold seekers.
Again, the text is from the memorable Folkways album
by Logan English, The Days of '49, FH 5255 (used by
permission of Folkways Records).

THE DAYS OF '49

1 I'm old Tom Moore from the bummer's shore
In the good old golden days.
They call me a bummer and a ginsot, too,
But what care I for praise?
I wander around from town to town
Just like a roving sign,
And the people all say, "There goes Tom Moore
Of the days of '49."

_____

[1]It is listed in Laws, Native American Balladry,
under "ballad-like pieces" in Appendix III, 277. It was
rejected because it was "weak or disunified in narrative
action."

chorus:
> In the days of old, in the days of gold,
> How oftimes I repine--
> For the days of old when we dug up the gold
> In the days of '49.

2 My comrades, they all loved me well,
A jolly saucy crew.
A few hard cases I will admit,
Though they were brave and true.
Whatever the pitch they would never flinch,
They would never fret nor whine.
Like good old bricks, they stood the kicks
In the days of '49.

3 There was old Lame Jess, a hard old cuss,
Who never did repent.
He never was known to miss a drink
Nor to ever spend a cent.
But old Lame Jess, like all the rest,
To death he did resign
And in his bloom went up the flume
In the days of '49.

4 There was Poker Bill, one of the boys,
Who was always in for a game,
Whether he lost or whether he won,
To him it was all the same.
He would ante up and draw his cards,
He would go you a hatful blind.
In the game with death Bill lost his breath,
In the days of '49.

5 There was New York Jake, the butcher's boy,
He was always getting tight.
And every time that he'd get full
He was spoiling for a fight.
But Jake rampaged against a knife
In the hands of old Bob Stein,
And over Jake they held a wake,
In the days of '49.

6 There was Ragshag Bill from Buffalo,
I never will forget,
He would roar all day and he'd roar all night
And I guess he's roaring yet.
One night he fell in a prospect hole
In a roaring bad design.
And in that hole he roared out his soul
In the days of '49.

7 Of all the comrades that I've had
There's none that's left to boast.
And I'm left alone in my misery
Like some poor wandering ghost.
And as I pass from town to town
They call me the rambling sign:
"There goes Tom Moore, a bummer shore,
Of the days of '49."

Rarely are supernatural ballads native to North
America, but "Tying a Knot In the Devil's Tail," B-17,
is a humorous description of an encounter between two
whiskey-soaked cowboys and the devil. Satan is out to
capture souls, but he fails to reckon with lassos.
Source: Cisco Houston, Cowboy Ballads, Folkways FA 2022
(used by permission of Folkways Records).

TYING A KNOT IN THE DEVIL'S TAIL

1 Way high up in the Sierra peaks
Where the yellow pines grow tall,
Sandy Bob and Buster Jiggs
Had a round-up camp last fall.

2 They took their horses and their runnin' irons
And maybe a dog or two,
And they 'lowed they'd brand all the long-eared
calves
That came within their view.

3 Well, many a long-eared dogie
That didn't hush up by day,
Had his long ears whittled and his old hide
scorched
In a most artistic way.

4 Then one fine day said Buster Jiggs
As he throw'd his cigo down:
"I'm tired of cow biography
And I 'lows I'm goin' to town."

5 They saddles up and they hits them a lope
Fer it wa'nt no sight of a ride,
An' them was the days when an old cow hand
Could oil up his old insides.

6 They starts her out at the Kentucky bar
At the head of the whiskey row.
And they winds her up at the depot house
Some forty drinks below.

7 They sets her up and turns her around
   And goes her the other way,
   And to tell you the Lord foresaken truth
   Them boys got drunk that day.

8 Well, as they was a-headin' back to camp
   And packin' a pretty good load,
   Who should they meet but the devil himself
   Come prancin' down the road.

9 Now the devil he said: "You cowboy skunks
   You better go hunt your hole,
   'Cause I come up from the hell's rim-rock
   To gather in your souls."

10 Said Buster Jiggs: "Now we're just from town
   An' feelin' kind of tight,
   And you ain't gonna get no cowboy souls
   Without some kind of a fight."

11 So he punched a hole in his old throw-rope
   And he slings her straight and true,
   And he roped the devil right around the horns,
   He takes his dallies true.

12 Old Sandy Bob was a reata-man
   With his rope all coiled up neat,
   But he shakes her around and he builds him a loop
   And he ropes the devil's hind feet.

13 They threw him down on the desert ground
   While the irons was a-gettin' hot.
   They cropped and swallow-forked his ears
   And branded him up a lot.

14 They pruned him up with a dehorning saw
   And knotted his tail for a joke.
   Rode off and left him bellowing there,
   Knecked up to a lilac-jack oak.

15 Well, if you ever travel in the Sierra peaks
   And you hear one awful wail,
   You'll know it's nothin' but the devil himself
   Raisin' hell about the knots in his tail.

LUMBERJACKS AND SAILORS

   Some of the most lyrical and emotional of the
native ballads were written by lumberjacks, mainly of
Irish extraction, living in the relative isolation of

lumber camps dotting the northern woods. While the ballads of sailors are as vigorous and spirited as those of the lumberjacks, they lack the substance and drama of them.

"The Jam On Gerry's Rocks," C-1, recounts a familiar theme among lumberjack ballads--the drowning of the hero. It probably dates from the Civil War period when Canadians were employed as rivermen along the Penobscot River in Maine, the apparent birthplace of the ballad. The text is a Minnesota variant from Franz Rickaby, Ballads and Songs of the Shanty-Boy, (Cambridge, Mass.: Harvard University Press, 1926), p. 11.

THE JAM ON GERRY'S ROCK

1 Come all ye true born shanty-boys, whoever that ye
      be,
  I would have you pay attention and listen unto me,
  Concerning a young shanty-boy so tall, genteel and
      brave.
  'Twas on a jam on Gerry's Rocks he met a wat'ry
      grave.

2 It happened on a Sunday morn as you shall quickly
      hear.
  Our logs were piled up mountain high, there being
      no one to keep them clear.
  Our boss he cried, "Turn out, brave boys. Your
      hearts are void of fear.
  We'll break that jam on Gerry's Rocks, and for
      Agonstown we'll steer."

3 Some of them were willing enough, but others they
      hung back.
  'Twas for to work on Sabbath they did not think
      'twas right.
  But six of our brave Canadian boys did volunteer
      to go
  And break the jam on Gerry's Rocks with their
      foreman, young Monroe.

4 They had not rolled off many logs when the boss
      to them did say,
  "I'd have you be on your guard, brave boys. That
      jam will soon give way."
  But scarce the warning had he spoke when the jam
      did break and go,
  And it carried away these six brave youths and
      their foreman, young Monroe.

177

5 When the rest of the shanty-boys these sad tidings
       came to hear,
   To search for their dead comrades to the river they
       did steer.
   One of these a headless body found, to their sad
       grief and woe,
   Lay cut and mangled on the beach the head of young
       Monroe.

6 They took him from the water and smoothed down his
       raven hair.
   There was one fair form amongst them, her cries
       would rend the air.
   There was one fair form amongst them, a maid from
       Saginaw town.
   Her sighs and cries would rend the skies for her
       lover that was drowned.

7 They buried him quite decently, being on the
       seventh of May.
   Come all the rest of you shanty-boys, for your
       dead comrade pray.
   'Tis engraved on a little hemlock tree that at his
       head doth grow,
   The name, the date, and the drowning of this hero,
       young Monroe.

8 Miss Clara was a noble girl, likewise the rafts-
       man's friend.
   Her mother was a widow woman lived at the river's
       bend.
   The wages of her own true love the boss to her did
       pay,
   And a liberal subscription she received from the
       shanty-boys next day.

9 Miss Clara did not long survive her great misery
       and grief.
   In less than three months afterwards death came to
       her relief.
   In less than three months afterwards she was called
       to go,
   And her last request was granted--to be laid by
       young Monroe.

10 Come all the rest of ye shanty-men who would like
       to go and see,
   On a little mound by the river's bank there stands
       a hemlock tree.

The shanty-boys cut the woods all around. These
    lovers they lie low.
Here lies Miss Clara Dennison and her shanty-boy,
    Monroe.

"The Little Brown Bulls," C-16, supposedly was composed in the early 1870's in a northwestern Wisconsin
logging camp. The text is from the singing of Sam
Eskin. He was a pioneer folk singing roamer and rambler
who, in the 1930's, lugged a cumbersome disc recorder
with him on his collecting hunts. From Loggers' Songs
and Sea Shanties, Folkways FA 2019 (used by permission
of Folkways Records).

THE LITTLE BROWN BULLS

1 Not a thing in the woods had McClusky to fear
  As he swung his gored stick o'er the big spotted
      steers.
  They were young, sound and quick, girding eight
      foot and three.
  Said McClusky the Scotsman, "They're the laddies
      for me!"

2 Oh, it's next came Bull Gordon, the skidding was
      full
  When he hollered, "Wah-hush!" to his little brown
      bulls.
  They were short-legged and shaggy, girding six
      foot and nine.
  "Too light," said McClusky, "to handle our pine.

3 "For it's three to the thousand our contract does
      call.
  Our skidding 'tis good and our timber 'tis tall."
  Said McClusky to Gordon, "To make the day full
  I will skid two to one of your little brown bulls."

4 "Oh no," said Bull Gordon, "that you never can do,
  But mind you, my laddie, you'll have your hands
      full,
  Though your big spotted steers are the pets of the
      crew,
  When you skid one more log than my little brown
      bulls."

5 O the day was appointed, and soon did draw nigh,
  For twenty-five dollars their fortunes to try.
  Both eager and anxious that morning, 'twas found,
  The boss and the scaler appeared on the ground.

179

6 With a whoop and a holler came McClusky in view
  With the big spotted steers, the pets of the crew,
  Saying, "Chew your cuds well, boys, and keep your
    mouths full,
  For today we will conquer the little brown bulls."

7 Then up came Bull Gordon with a pipe in his jaw,
  And the little brown bulls with a cud in their
    jaws.
  Said Gordon to Sandy, "We've nothing to fear,
  For we'll never be beat by the big spotted steers."

8 Well at sundown that evening the foreman did say,
  "Turn in, boys, turn in, you've enough for today--
  All numbered and scaled, each man and his team."
  And we thought that we knew which had knocked down
    the beam.

9 When supper was over, McClusky appeared
  With a belt ready made for big spotted steers.
  To make it he'd tore up his best mackinaw,
  He was bound to conduct it according to law.

10 Then up jumped the scaler: "Hold on, boys, you're
    wild!
  The big spotted steers are behind just a mile.
  You've skidded one hundred and ten and no more,
  While Gordon has beat you by ten and a score."

11 How the boys they all hollered and McClusky did
    swear!
  As he pulled out in handfuls his long yellow hair.
  Said: "I'll just kill them and take off their
    skins,
  And I'll dig them a grave and I'll tumble them in!"

12 So here's to Bull Gordon and Big Sandy John
  For the biggest days' work on the Wolf River was
    done.
  So fill up your glasses and fill them plumb full,
  And we'll drink to the health of the little brown
    bulls.

"Canaday I-O," C-17, is the progenitor of the
classic cowboy ballad "The Buffalo Skinners," B-10. It
is an 1854 reworking of a tasteless British song,
"Canada I. O.," by Ephriam Braley of Hudson, Maine. The
text is from another "down Easterner," Mrs. Annie V.
Marston, as printed in Fannie Hardy Eckstorm and Mary
Winslow Smyth, Minstrelsy of Maine (Boston: Houghton
Mifflin Co., 1927) pp. 22-23.

1 Come all ye jolly lumbermen, and listen to my song,
But do not get discouraged, the length it is not
    long,
Concerning of some lumbermen, who did agree to go
To spend one pleasant winter up in Canada I O.

2 It happened late one season in the fall of fifty-
    three,
A preacher of the gospel one morning came to me;
Said he, "My jolly fellow, how would you like to go
To spend one pleasant winter up in Canada I O?"

3 To him I quickly made reply, and unto him did say:
"In going out to Canada depends upon the pay.
If you will pay good wages, my passage to and fro,
I think I'll go along with you to Canada I O."

4 "Yes, we will pay good wages, and will pay your
    passage out,
Provided you sign papers that you will stay the
    route;
But if you do get homesick and swear that home
    you'll go,
We never can your passage pay from Canada I O.

5 "And if you get dissatisfied and do not wish to
    stay,
We do not wish to bind you, no, not one single day.
You just refund the money we had to pay, you know,
Then you can leave that bonny place called Canada
    I O."

6 It was by his gift of flattery he enlisted quite a
    train,
Some twenty-five or thirty, both well and able men;
We had a pleasant journey o'er the road we had to
    go,
Til we landed at Three Rivers, up in Canada I O.

7 But there our joys were ended, and our sorrows did
    begin;
Fields, Phillips and Norcross they then came
    marching in;
They sent us all directions, some where I do not
    know,
Among those jabbering Frenchmen up in Canada I O.

8 After we had suffered there some eight or ten long
    weeks

We arrived at headquarters, up among the lakes;
We thought we'd find a paradise, at least they told
   us so,
God grant there may be no worse hell than Canada
   I O!

9 To describe what we have suffered is past the art
   of man,
   But to give a fair description I will do the best
   I can;
   Our food the dogs would snarl at, our beds were on
   the snow,
   We suffered worse than murderers up in Canada I O.

10 Our hearts were made of iron and our souls were
   cased with steel,
   The hardships of that winter could never make us
   yield;
   Fields, Phillips and Norcross they found their
   match, I know,
   Among the boys that went from Maine to Canada I O.

11 But now our lumbering is over and we are returning
   home,
   To greet our wives and sweethearts and never more
   to roam,
   To greet our friends and neighbors; we'll tell
   them not to go
   To that forsaken G__ D__ place called Canada I O.

"Peter Amberley," C-27, is a true story of a run-
away who left his home on Prince Edward Island to work
in the woods near Boiestown, New Brunswick. A local
poet, John C. Calhoun, recorded Amberley's tragic ending
in 1881. According to Sandy Ives, the ballad rivals
"The Jam On Gerry's Rock" for top popularity among lumberjack songs in the Northeast. "Peter Emberly" is from
Sandy Ives, Folksongs of Maine, Folkways FH 5323 (used
by permission of Folkways Records).

PETER EMBERLY

1 My name is Peter Emberly as you may understand,
   I was born on Prince Edward's Island down by the
   ocean strand.
   In eighteen hundred and eighty when the leaves
   wore a brilliant hue
   I left my native island, my fortune to pursue.

2 I landed in New Brunswick in the lumbering
   counteree,

182

I hired to work in the lumbering woods on the
Sou'west Miramichi;
I hired to work in the lumbering woods and bring
the tall spruce down,
And while loading two-sleds in a yard I got my
fatal wound.

3 Adieu unto my father, 'twas he that drove me here;
He used to treat me very mean, his punishment was
severe.
Don't ever press a boy too hard to try to keep him
down;
'Twill only cause him to leave home when he is far
too young.

4 Adieu unto my best friend, I mean my mother dear;
Adieu to Prince Edward's Island and the Island
girls so dear.
Oh little did my mother think as she sang lullaby,
What countries I might travel to or what death I
might die.

5 Now there is just one more thing that in this world
I crave;
It's that some holy father will come and bless my
grave.
Nearby the city of Boiestown my mouldering bones do
lay,
A-waiting for the saviour's call on that great
judgement day.

Shifting to sea balladry, "Fifteen Ships on
Georges' Banks," D-3, memorializes the tragic events of
February 24, 1862, when fifteen ships foundered in high
winds off the coast of Newfoundland. Crews from
thirteen of the ships perished. The text is from Gordon
Bok's Folk-Legacy album Bay of Fundy, FSI-54 (used by
permission of Folk-Legacy Records, Sharon, Conn.).

FIFTEEN SHIPS ON GEORGES' BANKS

1 I pray you pay attention and listen to me
Concerning all those noble men who drownded in the
sea.
'Twas in the month of February, in 1862,
Those vessels sailed from Gloucester, with each a
hardy crew.

2 The course was East-South-East they steered, Cape
Ann being out of sight;

183

They anchored on the Banks that night with everything all right.
But on the 24th at night, the wind come on to blow,
The seas rose up like mountain-tops, which proved
their overthrow.

3 The thoughts of home and loving ones did grieve
their hearts full sore,
For well convinced were all these men they'd see
their homes no more.
No tongue can ever describe the scene, the sky was
full of snow,
And fifteen ships did founder there, and down to
bottom go.

4 A hundred forty-nine brave friends, who lately left
the land,
Now they sleep on Georges' Bank, in the rough and
shifting sand.
One hundred and seventy children these men have
left on shore,
And seventy mournful widows their sorrows to
endure.

5 So, now you'd think with gloomy thoughts, as on
life's path you roam,
Of many's the happy hours and days you've spent
with them at home.
For you they left their native shore, for you the
seas did roam,
For love and duty called them forth to leave their
happy home.

6 So, now adieu to Georges' Bank, my heart it doth
despise,
For many's the gale I've seen out there, and heard
those widows cry.
And now I bid you all adieu, dry up your tearful
eye,
Prepare to meet your God above, and dwell beyond
the skies.

"The Red Iron Ore," D-9, recalls the victory of the
schooner E. C. Roberts in a race with the Exile and
other vessels during the last days of the combination
sail-and-steam iron ore carriers on the Great Lakes in
the late 1860's and early 1870's. The text is from
Vivien Richman Sings, Folkways FG 3568 (used by permission of Folkways Records). For a graphic description
of a more turbulent time on the Great Lakes in 1975,
listen to Gordon Lightfoot's "The Wreck of the Edmund

184

Fitzgerald" on <u>Summertime Dream</u>, Reprise MS2246.

THE RED IRON ORE

1 Come all you bold sailors that follow the Lakes,
On an iron ore vessel your living to make.
I shipped in Chicago, bid adieu to the shore,
Bound away to Escanaba for red iron ore.
    Derry down, down, down, derry down.

2 In the month of September, the seventeenth day,
Two dollars and a quarter is all they would pay.
And on Monday morning the <u>Bridgeport</u> did take
The <u>E. C. Roberts</u> away out in the lake.

3 Next morning we hove alongside the <u>Exile</u>,
And soon was made fast to an iron ore pile,
They lowered their chutes and like thunder did
    roar,
They spouted into us that red iron ore.

4 Some sailors took shovels while others got spades,
And some took wheelbarrows, each man to his trade,
We looked like red devils, our fingers got sore,
We hated Escanaba and that blamed iron ore.

5 The tug <u>Escanaba</u> she towed out the <u>Minch</u>,
The <u>Roberts</u> she thought she had left in a pinch,
And as she passed us, she bid us goodbye,
Saying, "We'll meet you in Cleveland next Fourth
    of July!"

6 Across Saginaw Bay the <u>Roberts</u> did ride,
With the dark and deep water rolling over her side.
Now for Port Huron the <u>Roberts</u> must go,
Where the tug <u>Katie Williams</u> she took us in tow.

7 Now the <u>Roberts</u> is in Cleveland, made fast stem
    and stern,
And over the bottle we'll spin a big yarn.
But Captain Harvey Shannon had ought to stand treat
For getting into Cleveland ahead of the fleet.

8 Now my song is ended, I hope you won't laugh,
Our dunnage is packed and all hands are paid off.
Here's a health to the <u>Roberts</u>, she's staunch,
    strong and true,
Not forgotten the bold boys that comprise her crew.

    "The Titanic," D-24, probably should be assigned
to the ballad category of "Tragedy," for it concerns

the calamitous maiden voyage, in 1912, of the White Star
liner described as "unsinkable." The numerous recorded
versions of the ballad attest to its widespread popu-
larity--from shellac discs of the 1920's and 1930's by
Ernest V. Stoneman, Vernon Dalhart, Ma Rainey, and
William and Versey Smith, to more recent LP's by Hobart
Smith, Pete Seeger, and Happy and Artie Traum.

In addition to the lines of class protest found in
most variants, there are black versions in which Jack
Johnson, black heavyweight boxing champion, is refused
a first class berth ("I ain't haulin' no coal"). He rejects lesser accommodations and remains in England--one
of the few times segregation benefits minorities! The
text is by Hobart Smith, a Southern Appalachian traditionalist, from his Folk-Legacy recording FSA-17 (used
by permission of Folk-Legacy Records, Sharon, Conn.).

THE TITANIC

1 On one Sunday morning, just about one o'clock,
  This great Titanic boat begin to reel and rock.
  People on board begin to cry,
  Saying, "My Lord, I'm bound to die!"
  Wasn't it sad when that great ship went down?

    chorus:
        Awful sad when that great boat went down.
        Husbands and wives, little children lost their
            lives.
        Wasn't it sad when that great ship went down?

2 Ship was leaving England, pulling for the shore;
  Rich they declared they would not ride with the
      poor.
  Put the poor below;
  They's the first ones had to go.
  Wasn't that sad when that great ship went down?

3 Builders kept building, declared what they would
      do:
  Gonna build a boat the waters couldn't break
      through.
  God had the power at his hand,
  Showed to the world it would not stand.
  Wasn't it sad when the great ship went down?

"The Coast of Peru," D-26, is one of several
whaling ballads sung by New Bedford, Massachusetts,
whalers in the mid-nineteenth century. Bernie Klay
sings this explicit version on the Folkways album The X

Seamens Institute Sings at the South Street Seaport,
FTS 32418 (used by permission of Folkways Records).

THE COAST OF PERU

1 Come all ye young fellows that bound after sperm,
Come all ye bold seamen that's rounded the horn.
Our captain has told us, and we hope says true,
That there's plenty of sperm whale on the coast of
    Peru.

2 We've weathered the horn and we're now off Peru,
We're all of one mind to endeavor to do,
Our boats they're all ready, our masthead's all
    manned,
Our rigging rove light me boys and our signals all
    planned.

3 It was early one morning we heard the brave shout,
As the man on the lookout cried out,
"There she spout!" "Where away," says our captain,
    "and where do she lay?"
"Two points to our lee bow not a mile away."

4 And it's call up hands me lads and be of good
    cheer,
Put your tubs in your boats boys, have your
    bowlines all clear,
Sway up on them boats now, jump in me brave crew,
Lower away now and after her try the best you can
    do.

5 Well, the waist boat got down and she made a good
    start,
"Lay on," says the harpooner, "for I'm hell for
    long darts,
Now bend on them oars boys, and make your boat fly,
But one thing be dread of, keep clear of his eye."

6 Oh, we give him one iron and the whale he went
    down,
But as he come up boys, our captain bent on,
And the next harpoon struck and the line sped away,
But whatever the whale done he give us fair play.

7 Oh, he raced and he sounded, he twist and he spin,
But we fought him alongside and we got our lance
    in,
Which caused him to vomit and the blood for to
    spout,

187

And in ten minutes time me boys he rolled both
    fins out.

8 We towed him alongside and with many a shout,
  We soon cut him in and begun to try out,
  Now the blubber is rendered and likewise stowed
      down,
  And it's better to us me boys than five hundred
      pounds.

9 Now we're bound into Tumbez in our manly power,
  Where a man buys a whorehouse for a barrel of
      flour,
  We'll spend all our money on those pretty girls
      ashore,
  And when it's all gone me boys, we'll go whaling
      for more.

"The Ship That Never Returned," D-27, was written
by the prolific composer Henry Clay Work in 1865. It
quickly entered the folk tradition spawning numerous
variants and parodies including "M. T. A.," popularized
by The Kingston Trio during the folk revival craze of
the 1950-1960's. The original song was the musical
ancestor of "The Wreck of the Old 97," G-2 (see later).
The text, from Kentucky, was published in Carl Sandburg,
The American Songbag (New York: Harcourt Brace
Jovanovich, Inc., 1955), pp. 146-147.

THE SHIP THAT NEVER RETURNED

1 On a summer's day while the waves were rippling,
    with a quiet and a gentle breeze;
  A ship set sail with a cargo laden for a port
      beyond the sea.

  chorus:
      Did she ever return? No, she never returned,
          and her fate is still unlearned,
      But a last poor man set sail commander, on a
          ship that never returned.

2 There were sad farewells, there were friends for-
    saken, and her fate is still unlearned,
  But a last poor man set sail commander on a ship
      that never returned.

3 Said a feeble lad to his aged mother, "I must
    cross that deep blue sea,
  For I hear of a land in the far off country where
      there's health and strength for me."

188

4 'Tis a gleam of hope and a maze of danger, and our
      fate is still to learn,
   And a last poor man set sail commander, on a ship
      that never returned.

5 Said this feeble lad to his aged mother, as he
      kissed his weeping wife,
   "Just one more purse of that golden treasure, it
      will last us all through life.

6 "Then we'll live in peace and joy together and
      enjoy all I have earned."
   So they sent him forth with a smile and blessing
      on a ship that never returned.

CRIME

     The next three categories of native ballads, crime,
murder and tragedy, have fascinated audiences for generations revealing the human passion for sensationalism
and the macabre. The favorite criminal ballad in North
America must be "Jesse James," E-1-2. The folk have
transformed the real-life desperado into a courageous
and generous ballad hero in the tradition of the legendary Robin Hood. First, the ballad recalls selected exploits of the James brothers and their criminal band,
and then it concentrates on Jesse's murder by the "dirty
little coward" Robert Ford. Again, as with the green-
clothed hero of Sherwood Forest, the folk identify with
the anti-establishment nature of James.

     The text is a collation of several sources as sung
by George and Gerry Armstrong and others on Golden Ring,
Folk-Legacy FSI-16 (used by permission of Folk-Legacy
Records, Sharon, Conn.).

                    JESSE JAMES

1 Jesse James was a man that was knowed through all
      the land,
   For Jesse he was bold and bad and brave;
   But that dirty little coward that shot down Mister
      Howard
   Has went and laid poor Jesse in his grave.

   chorus:
      Oh, I wonder where my poor old Jesse's gone;
      Oh, I wonder where my poor old Jesse's gone.

                        189

> I will meet him in that land where I've never
>   been before,
> And I wonder where my poor old Jesse's gone.

2 Jesse and his brother Frank, they robbed the
     Gallatin bank
  And carried the money from the town;
  It was in that very place that they had a little
     race
  And they shot Captain Sheets to the ground.

3 It was on a Wednesday night and the moon was
     shining bright,
  They robbed the Glendale train;
  And the agent, on his knees, delivered up the keys
  To the outlaws, Frank and Jesse James.

4 It was on a Friday night and the moon was shining
     bright;
  Bob Ford had been hiding in a cave.
  He had ate of Jesse's bread; he had slept in
     Jesse's bed,
  But he went and laid poor Jesse in his grave.

5 Jesse James was alone a-straightening up his home;
  Stood on a chair to dust a picture frame.
  When Bob Ford fired the ball that pulled Jesse
     from the wall
  And he went and laid poor Jesse in his grave.

6 Jesse James has gone to rest with his hands upon
     his breast;
  There's many a man that never knowed his face.
  He was born one day in the county of Clay
  And he come from a solitary race.

Like Jesse James, Cole Younger began his infamous
career with Quantrell's Missouri guerrilla forces during
the Civil War. The ballad "Cole Younger," E-3, is less
sympathetic and more straightforward than the legends
surrounding Jesse James. Dock Boggs recorded the
following version for Mike Seeger in 1964. It was released on Dock Boggs, Volume Two, Folkways FA 2392 (used
by permission of Folkways Records).

COLE YOUNGER

1 I am a noted bandit,
  Cole Younger is my name,
  To many a death procession
  My friends I brought to shame.

190

2 Of robbing of a Northfield bank's
   A thing I can't deny.
   Now I'm a poor prisoner,
   In the Stillwater jail I lie.

3 The first of my many robberies
   I will relate to you,
   Was a poor Californian miner,
   And the same will surely rue.

4 I taken from him his money
   And I told him to go his way,
   The same will check my conscience
   Until my dying day.

5 I went home
   And brother Bob did say,
   "We'll buy fine horses
   And together ride away."

6 We started out for Texas
   That good old Lone Star State,
   All on the new prairie
   The James boys we did meet.

7 With knives and revolvers
   We all set out to play,
   A-drinking good corn whisky, boys,
   To pass the time away.

8 The Union Pacific
   We first did surprise,
   A-murdering of your own heart's blood
   Would bring tears to your eyes.

9 Brother Bob was shot and wounded,
   All in Northfield he did die.
   All on the new prairie
   There the bullion lie.

One of the most realistic of all the criminal
ballads is "Sam Bass," E-4. It traces the adventures
of Bass from his birth in Indiana, to his move to
Denton, Texas, to the formation of his gang of train
robbers, and finally to his betrayal and death in Round
Rock, Texas. N. Howard Thorp credited authorship to a
John Denton of Gainsville, Texas, in 1879. Alan Lomax
sang a splendid version on Tradition TLP 1029, Texas
Folksongs, from John A. and Alan Lomax, Cowboy Songs
and Other Frontier Ballads. Alan acclaimed it "the

191

finest ballad Texas ever produced." The text is from Thorp's 1908 collection <u>Songs</u> <u>of</u> <u>the</u> <u>Cowboys</u>.[1]

SAM BASS

1 Sam Bass was born in Indiana, it was his native
   home
  And at the age of seventeen, young Sam began to
   roam
  He first went down to Texas, a cow-boy bold to be
  A kinder hearted fellow, you'd scarcely ever see.

2 Sam used to deal in race stock, had one called the
   Denton mare
  He watched her in scrub races, took her to the
   County Fair.
  She always won the money, wherever she might be
  He always drank good liquor, and spent his money
   free.

3 Sam left the Collins ranch in the merry month of
   May
  With a herd of Texas cattle the Black Hills to see.
  Sold out in Custer City and all got on a spree
  A harder lot of cow-boys you'd scarcely ever see.

4 On the way back to Texas, they robbed the U. P.
   train
  All split up in couples and started out again.
  Joe Collins and his partner were overtaken soon
  With all their hard earned money they had to meet
   their doom.

5 Sam made it back to Texas all right side up with
   care
  Rode into the town of Denton his gold with friends
   to share.
  Sam's life was short in Texas 'count of robberies
   he'd do
  He'd rob the passengers coaches the mail and express too.

---

[1] For more information see: Austin E. and Alta S. Fife (eds.), <u>Songs</u> <u>of</u> <u>the</u> <u>Cowboys</u> <u>by</u> N. Howard ("Jack") <u>Thorp</u> (Clarkson N. Potter, Inc., New York, 1966), 112-120. Also check the authoritative notes by Charles Edward Smith in <u>Ohio</u> <u>Valley</u> <u>Ballads</u>, Folkways Records FA 2025.

6 Sam had four bold companions, four bold and daring
    lads
  Underwood and Joe Jackson, Bill Collins and Old
    Dad.
  They were four of the hardest cow-boys that Texas
    ever knew
  They whipped the Texas Rangers and ran the boys in
    blue.

7 Jonis borrowed of Sam's money and didn't want to
    pay
  The only way he saw to win was to give poor Sam
    away
  He turned traitor to his comrades they were caught
    one early morn
  Oh what a scorching Jonis will get when Gabriel
    blows his horn.

8 Sam met his fate in Round Rock July the twenty-
    first
  They pierced poor Sam with rifle balls and emptied
    out his purse
  So Sam is a corpse in Round Rock, Jonis is under
    the clay
  And Joe Jackson in the bushes trying to get away.

The initial stanzas of "Sidney Allen," E-5, describe a court room shoot-out in Hillsville, Virginia,
in 1912. As Judge Massie was sentencing Floyd Allen to
one year in prison for interference in an arrest case,
twenty relatives and friends of Floyd, including Sidney
and Claude Allen, opened fire. When the smoke from the
two hundred or so shots cleared, the judge, the sheriff
and the prosecuting attorney lay dead. The Richmond
(Virginia) Times-Dispatch offered a revealing explanation:

> The psychology of the Allens is simply that
> of unbridled individualism, setting itself above
> all social control. This was partly due to the
> frontier and mountain environment, wherein each
> man makes his own laws and executes them by brute
> force. And partly it is attributed to the iso-
> lation and interdependence of a clan. The
> border raids and reprisals of Scotland's history
> show to what ferocious lengths this anarchy of
> individual liberty can go. It is a survival
> of clan feeling.[1]

---

[1] Quoted by Charles Edward Smith in Ohio Valley
Ballads, Folkways Records FA 2025.

The Allens escaped from the courtroom, but were later recaptured. Floyd and Claude were sentenced to death and Sidney received a life sentence.

According to Charles Edward Smith, the ballad is related to "Casey Jones" which, in turn, is connected to an earlier black blues number, "Been On the Cholly So Long." Source: Bruce Buckley, Ohio Valley Ballads, Folkways FA 2025 (used by permission of Folkways Records).

SIDNEY ALLEN

1 Come all you good people if you want to hear
The story of a famous mountaineer.
Sidney Allen was the fellow's name,
In a courthouse he won his fame.

2 The caller called the jury right at half past nine,
Sidney Allen was a prisoner and he was on time.
He mounted to the bar with a pistol in his hand,
Sent Judge Massie to the promised land.

3 Now, just a moment later and the place was in a
   roar,
The dead and dying they were lying on the floor.
With a thirty-eight special, a thirty-eight Colt,
Sidney backed that sheriff up agin the wall.

4 The sheriff saw he was in a mighty bad place,
A mountain man was starin' him right in the face.
He turned to the window and then he said:
"In a moment, Lord, and we'll all be dead."

5 Sidney saddled up his pony and away he did ride,
His friends and his relatives were ridin' by his
   side.
They all shook hands and swore they would hang
Before they'd give up to that Coulton gang.

6 Sidney Allen wandered and he travelled all around
Till he was captured in a western town.
Taken to the station with a ball and chain,
They put poor Sidney on an eastbound train.

7 They arrived at Sidney's home about eleven forty-
   one;
He met his wife and daughter and two little sons.
They all shook hands and knelt down to pray,
Saying, "Lord, don't take our daddy away."

8 The people were all gathered from far and near
  To see poor Sidney sentenced to the electric chair;
  But to their great surprise the judge he said:
  "He's a-goin' to the penitentiary instead."

In 1881 President James A. Garfield was murdered
by a disappointed office seeker. "Charles Guiteau,"
E-11, immortalized the assassin when the song entered
the folk tradition from Pennsylvania to Florida and
westward to Utah. The ballad was based on "John T.
Williams," a broadside from the 1870's, which, in turn,
borrowed from an 1858 murder ballad "The Lamentation of
James Rodgers," the chorus of which follows:

My name is James Rodgers--the same I ne'er deny,
  Which leaves my aged parents in sorrow for to cry,
  It's little ever they thought, all in my youth and
      bloom,
  I came into New York for to meet my fatal doom.

Compare the preceding to the chorus in E-11, keeping in mind what Arlo Guthrie once said about the folk
process: "To me the term 'folk process' is a good word
for plagiarism or something like it, people stealing
tunes and ideas from each other." The abridged text of
"Charles Guiteau" was recorded in the late 1920's by
Kelly Harrell and the Virginia String Band (reissued on
Old-Time Ballads from the Southern Mountains, County
Records 522).

                    CHARLES GUITEAU

1 Come all you tender Christians, wherever you may
      be,
  And likewise pay attention from these few lines
      from me.
  I was down at the depot to make my getaway,
  And Providence being against me, it proved to be
      too late.

2 I tried to play off insane but found it would not
      do,
  The people all against me it proved to make no
      show.
  Judge Cox he passed the sentence, the clerk he
      wrote it down,
  On the thirtieth day of June to die I was condemn-
      ed.

chorus: [also repeat after stanzas 3 and 4]
     My name is Charles Guiteau
     My name I'll never deny.
     To leave my aged parents
     To sorrow and to die.
     But little did I think
     While in my youthful bloom,
     I'd be carried to the scaffold
     To meet my fateful doom.

3 My sister came in prison to bid her last farewell,
  She threw her arms around me, she wept most bitter-
     ly.
  She said, "My loving brother today you must die
  For the murder of James A. Garfield upon the
     scaffold high."

4 And now I mount the scaffold to bid you all adieu,
  The hangman now is waiting, it's a quarter after
     two.
  The black cap is o'er my face, no longer can I see,
  But when I'm dead and buried dear Lord remember me.

"The Rowan County Crew," E-20, details the origins
of a bitter political feud between the Tolliver and
Martin forces in Rowan County, Kentucky, in the 1880's.
Following the murder of Martin (the concluding episode
in the ballad), the lootings and killings increased,
culminating in a gun battle on Railroad Street in the
town of Morehead in which the Martin partisans defeated
the Tolliver faction. The text is from Bruce Buckley,
Ohio Valley Ballads, Folkways FA 2025 (used by permission of Folkways Records). Note the corruption in
the third line, first stanza. The original read: "and
her many heinous deeds."

THE ROWAN COUNTY CREW

1 Come all young men and maidens, dear mothers,
     fathers too,
  I'll relate to you the history of the Rowan County
     Crew,
  Concerning bloody Rowan and many a heathen be,
  Oh, friends, please pay attention, remember how it
     read.

2 'Twas in the month of August all on election day,
  John Martin he was wounded they say by Johnny Day.
  But Martin couldn't believe it, he said it was not
     so.

196

He said it was Frank Tolliver that struck the
fatal blow.

3 Martin had recovered, some months had gone and
past,
When in the town of Morehead these two men met at
last.
Tolliver and a friend or two all through the
streets did walk;
They seemed to be in trouble with no one which to
talk.

4 They stepped up to Judge Carter's grog shop, they
stepped up to the bar,
But little did he think my friends he'd met his
fatal hour.
The sting of death was nigh him when Martin came
through the door,
A few words passed between them concerning the
row before.

5 The people got excited, began to leave the room,
When a ball from Martin's pistol laid Tolliver in
the tomb.
His friends soon gathered round him, his wife to
weep and wail,
Soon Martin was arrested and hurried off to jail.

6 They put him in the jail at Rowan there to detain
awhile,
In the hands of law and justice to bravely stand
his trial.
The people talked of lynching him, at present it
did fail,
Soon Martin was removed to the Winchester jail.

7 Someone forged an order, their names I do not know,
A plan was soon agreed upon, for Martin they did
go.
They went and called upon him, he seemed to be in
dread.
"They've set a plan to kill me," to the jailer
Martin said.

8 They shot and killed Sol Bradley a sober, innocent
man,
An' left his wife and children to do the best they
can.
They shot at young Ed Sizemore although his life
was saved,

He seemed to shun the grog shop, he stood so nigh
the grave.

9 They put the handcuffs on him, his heart was in
distress;
They hurried to the station, pulled up the night
express.
All along the line she lumbered just at her usual
speed;
There were only a few in number to do this dreadful deed.

10 Martin was in the smoking car accompanied by his
wife;
They did not want her present when they took her
husband's life.
But when they arrived at Farmers they had no time
to lose,
Stepped up to the engineer and begged him not to
move.

11 They stepped up to the prisoner revolvers in their
hand;
In death he soon was sinking, he died in iron
bands.
The death of these two men should never be forgot,
Their bodies all pierced and torn by thirty-two
buckshot.

12 I called this as a warning to all young men beware,
Your pistols cause you trouble on that you may de-
pend.
In the bottom of a whiskey glass a lurking devil
dwells,
Burns the breast of those who drink it and sends
their souls to hell.
In the bottom of a whiskey glass a lurking devil
dwells,
Burns the breast of those who drink it and sends
their souls to hell.

Harvey Logan, alias Kid Curry, was second only to
Butch Cassidy in the ranks of "The Wild Bunch," the cut-
throat band of hoodlums who terrorized towns in the
western states during the late nineteenth century.
Logan personally gunned down nine persons including four
sheriffs. As the "Wanted: Dead or Alive" posters multi-
plied, Logan fled eastward to Knoxville where, in 1902,
he was arrested following a pool room scuffle. The
ballad "Harvey Logan," E-21, continues the saga. The
text is basically the one collected by Paul Clayton in

Wise County, Virginia, and recorded by Clayton on <u>Folk-</u><u>songs</u> <u>and</u> <u>Ballads</u> <u>of</u> <u>Virginia</u>, FA 2110 (used by permission of Folkways Records).

HARVEY LOGAN

1 If you folks don't know, well it's I'll tell you
     so,
  Well, it's down in the barroom where all the
    rounders go.
      It's oh, my Babe, my li'l ole Babe. [repeat
        after each stanza]

2 Just playing for money, money wouldn't go right
  When old Harvey Logan he got into a fight.

3 About that time the cops was coming long,
  Well, they stopped at the gate for they knew that
    something was wrong.

4 They hit him over the head, their billies they did
    break,
  He give them the contents of his smokeless thirty-
    eight.

5 Harvey in the jail and his guard not very far,
  Why he threw a lasso over his head and drawed him
    to the bar.

6 He said, "Now jailer, well I've got you after all,
  If you make an outcry, you'll die right in this
    hall."

7 Got the jailer before him and marched him to the
    stair,
  Said, "All I want is the sheriff's big grey mare."

8 He said, "Now, Harvey, you know you've done me
    wrong."
  "Well, hush up that crying and put that saddle on."

9 He mounted his horse and he looked up at the sky,
  Said, "I've gotta be on my way, for the night is
    drawing nigh."

MURDER

Sensationalism attracts an audience and murder
cases generally draw the largest crowds. Agatha Christie
in literature, Alfred Hitchcock in motion pictures and

the Lindbergh baby kidnapping in journalism, all prove
the point. The 1892 trial of Lizzie Borden for the
murder of her parents produced one of the most popular
jingles of all time:

> Lizzie Borden took an axe
> And gave her mother forty whacks;
> When she saw what she had done
> She gave her father forty-one.

The ballad world attracts its share of such stories;
yet, with few exceptions, the native American ballads
sympathize with the victims of the crime and condemn
the actions of the perpetrators.

"The Jealous Lover," F-1, is a highly popular North
American ballad. Unlike most others, it has not been
linked to a specific murder case, while its transmission
has been exclusively by oral means. Incidentally, Woody
Guthrie borrowed the tune and part of the plot for his
popular hit of the 1940's, "Philadelphia Lawyer." Ellen
Stekert obtained the following "Jealous Lover" variant
from her eighty-one year old informant Fuzzy Barhight.
She sings it on Songs of a New York Lumberjack, Folkways
FA 2354 (used by permission of Folkways Records).

A - THE JEALOUS LOVER

1 Way down in yonders valley
  Where the violets fade and bloom,
  There lies my own fair Ellen,
  So silent in the tomb.

2 She's died, not broken hearted,
  Or by disease she fell,
  But in one moment parted
  From the friends she loved so well.

3 One night when the moon shone brighter
  Than it ever shone before,
  Down to this maiden's cottage
  This jealous lover bore.

4 Saying, "Love, come let us wander
  Down in the woods so gay,
  And while we talk, we'll ponder
  Upon our wedding day."

5 Deep, deep into the forrest
  He led his love so gay;

200

Deep, deep into the forrest
Did the jealous lover stray.

6 "Oh, I care not, love to wander
Down in the woods so gay,
I care not, love, for to ponder
Upon our wedding day."

7 "Retreat your way, no never,
These woods no more you'll roam,
So bid farewell forever
To your parents, friends and home."

8 Then down on her knees before him,
She pleaded for her life;
Deep, deep into her bosom
He plunged the fatal knife.

9 "Oh, Willie, I'll forgive you
With my last parting breath,
Oh, Willie, I'll forgive you."
Then she closed her eyes in death.

10 Though a banner waves high o'er her
Until the bugle sounds,
A stranger came and found her
Cold and lifeless on the ground.

Mrs. Ruth Barron of Youngstown, Ohio, learned a
variant of "The Jealous Lover" from her mother Ella
Young Bailey, born in nearby Hubbard, Ohio, in 1893
(used by permission). It is similar to version F of
"The Murdered Girl" in Mary Eddy, Ballads and Songs
from Ohio. Mrs. Barron remembers the following fragment:

B - THE JEALOUS LOVER

1 Now this man's name was Edward,
His name was Edward Blaine,
And he was hung for the murder,
The murder in Sharon's Lane.

2 "Oh, Alice, oh, sweet Alice,
Come down and take a walk
Under the weeping willows
Where we can sit and talk.

. . . .

3 "Now in this woods I've got you
And here you're going to die."

201

Down on her knees before him
She pleaded for her life.

4 Deep, deep into her bosom
He plunged that fearful (fateful) knife,
Saying, "Edward, may God forgive you
For the wrong you've done tonight!"

"Pearl Bryan," F-2, has been confused with "The
Jealous Lover." In actuality, it was based on a sensational murder and trial in the Cincinnati area in the
late 1890's. Pearl was murdered by two dental students,
Scott Jackson and Alonzo Walling. Apparently they were
hired by a minister's son, William Wood, to perform an
abortion on Pearl with whom he had sexual relations.
The pair botched the job and to prevent identification
they removed her head. Nevertheless, Jackson and
Walling were captured, tried, sentenced and hanged.
Wood escaped prosecution and was not even called as a
witness during the trial. As for Pearl's head, it was
never found. The text is from Bruce Buckley, Ohio
Valley Ballads, Folkways FA 2025 (used by permission of
Folkways Records).

PEARL BRYAN

1 Come all you young ladies, a sad story I'll relate,
It happened in Fort Thomas in the old Kentucky
state;
'Twas January the thirty-first this dreadful deed
was done
By Jackson and Walling, how cold Pearl's blood did
run.

2 Oh, little did Pearl Bryan think when she left her
home that day
The grip she carried in her hand would hide her
head away;
She thought it was her lover's hand she could trust
both night and day,
Although it was her lover's hand that stole her
life away.

3 Little did her parents think when she left her
happy home,
This darling girl just in her youth would never
more return;
How sad it would have been to them to have heard
Pearl's lonely voice
At midnight in that lonely spot where those two
boys rejoiced.

202

4 The driver in the seat is all who knows of Pearl's
       sad fate,
   Of poor Pearl Bryan away from home in the old
       Kentucky state;
   Of her aged parents we all know well what fortune
       they would give
   If Pearl was but to them returned her natural life
       to live.

5 In came Pearl Bryan's sister falling on her knees
   Pleading to Scott Jackson, "Oh, my sister's head,
       oh, please;"
   Scott Jackson set a stubborn jaw, not a word would
       he have said,
   "I'll meet my sister in heaven where we'll find
       her missing head."

6 In came Walling's mother pleading for her son,
   "Don't take my son, my only son, from him I can
       not part;"
   The jury reached a verdict and to their feet they
       sprung,
   "For the crime these boys committed they surely
       must be hung."

7 Young ladies now take warning, men are so unjust,
   It may be your best lover but you know not whom
       to trust;
   Pearl Bryan died away from home upon a lonely spot,
   Take heed, take heed believe me, girls, don't let
       this be your lot.

One bizarre version of "Pearl Bryan" ends with this
warning:

       So you girls who fall in love
       You still may be misled;
       Don't take any hasty actions
       Oh, girls, don't lose your head!

"Poor Omie" or "Little Omie Wise," F-4, details the
death of an orphan girl by her lover, Jonathan Lewis, in
Randolph County, North Carolina. Lewis was arrested,
but escaped and by the time he was recaptured most of
the witnesses had died or had left the county. Lacking
positive evidence, the jury acquitted Lewis. In the
late 1920's the Red Fox Chasers recorded a version
similar to the Vernon Dalhart pop release, a variant of
the related ballad "Naomi Wise," F-31. It was reissued
in 1967 on Red Fox Chasers, County Records 510. The
text is from Betty Smith's collated version on Songs

Traditionally Sung In North Carolina, Folk-Legacy FSA-53 (used by permission of Folk-Legacy Records, Sharon, Conn.).

OMIE WISE

1 I'll tell us all a story about Omie Wise,
How she was deluded by John Lewis' lies.

2 He promised to marry her at Adams' springs;
He'd give her some money and other fine things.

3 He gave her no money, but flattered the case.
Says, "We will get married, there'll be no
disgrace."

4 She got up behind him; away they did go.
They rode 'til they came where the Deep River
flowed.

5 "Now Omie, little Omie, I'll tell you my mind.
My mind is to drown you and leave you behind."

6 "Oh, pity your poor infant and spare me my life.
Let me go rejected and not be your wife."

7 "No pity, no pity," the monster did cry.
"On Deep River's bottom your body will lie."

8 The wretch he did choke her as we understand.
He threw her in the river below the mill dam.

9 Now Omie is missing as well all do know,
And down to the river a-hunting we'll go.

10 Two little boys were fishing just at the break of
dawn.
They spied poor Omie's body come floating along.

11 They arrested John Lewis, they arrested him today.
They buried little Omie down in the cold clay.

12 "Go hang me or kill me, for I am the man
Who murdered poor Naomi below the mill dam."

"On the Banks of the Ohio," F-5, has connections
to British broadsides, but Laws regarded it as a native
ballad. The folk have changed the story's location to
fit local interest, for example: "On the Banks of the
Old Pedee," "The Old Shawnee" and "On the Banks of the
Old Tennessee." The Iron Mountain String Band recorded

a version on <u>Walkin' In the Parlor</u>, Folkways FA 2477, while in 1927 Red Patterson's Piedmont Log Rollers released a disc with lyrics similar to the text.

ON THE BANKS OF THE OHIO

1 I asked my love to take a walk,
  Just a walk a little ways.
  And as we walked along we talked,
  When shall be our wedding day?

2 We walked beneath the whispering pines,
  My heart was filled with love divine.
  And as we neared the river side,
  I asked her when she'd be my bride.

3 "Just only say that you'll be mine
  In a little home we'll build so fine,
  Down beside where the waters flow,
  Down on the banks of the Ohio."

4 "As for your bride I can never be
  For another has prepared for me."
  And as she drew her hands from mine,
  My heart it bled with sad repine.

5 I drew my knife across her breast
  And in my arms she dearly pressed,
  Crying, "Oh, please don't murder me
  For I'm not prepared to die."

6 I took her by her golden curls
  And dragged her down to the river side.
  And as I threw her into drown
  I watched her as she floated down.

7 I got home 'tween twelve and one,
  Thinking, "Oh, what a deed I've done.
  I murdered the girl that I loved so well
  Because she would not be my bride."

"Rose Connoley," F-6, meets a dreadful fate: she is poisoned by wine and then stabbed with a dagger. The famous team of Grayson and Whitter recorded the details in 1927. The Iron Mountain String Band titled the ballad "Willow Garden" on their 1975 album <u>Walkin' In the Parlor</u>, Folkways FA 2477 (used by permission of Folkways Records).

WILLOW GARDEN

1 Down in the willow garden
  Where me and my love did meet,
  There we lay a-courting,
  My true love fell asleep.

2 I had a bottle of the burglar's wine
  And that my love did not know;
  There I murdered that poor little girl
  Down on the banks below.

3 I stabbed her with my dagger
  Which was a bloody knife;
  I throwed her into the river
  Which was a terrible sight.

4 My daddy always told me
  That money would set me free
  If I would murder that poor little girl
  Whose name is Rose Connely.

5 Now he sits by his cabin door
  A-wiping his tear stained eyes,
  A-thinking about his own dear son
  Up on the scaffold high.

6 My race is run beneath the sun
  And hell is waiting for me,
  For I did murder that poor little girl
  Whose name is Rose Connely.

"Lula Viers," F-10, is a remarkably accurate account of a drowning in Kentucky. The ballad had to be written shortly after the arrest of John Coyer, or Colliers, since the murderer was released to join the army (World War I was raging) and never did stand trial. Bruce Buckley sings the following account on Ohio Valley Ballads, Folkways FA 2025 (used by permission of Folkways Records).

LULA VIERS

1 Come all you good people and stand real close
      around,
  I'll tell to you a story about a pretty young girl.
  Her name was Lula Viers in Auxier she did dwell,
  A town in old Kentucky, a place you all know well.

2 Come all you young people and stand real close
      around,

I'll tell to you a story how Lula Viers was
    drowned.
She loved a young John Colliers, engaged to be his
    wife;
He ruined her reputation, and stole away her life.

3 For Lula was persuaded to leave her dear old home,
Bound the morning train with John Colliers for to
    roam.
They went to Elkhorn city just sixteen miles away
And stayed there at a hotel until the break of day.

4 When the night began to fall, they walked out for
    a stroll,
'Twas in the month of December, the winds were
    blowing cold.
They stood down by the river, the waters running
    cold;
Johnny Colliers said to Lula, "In the bottom you
    must go."

5 "Oh, Johnny, you can't mean it, oh, surely it can't
    be;
How can you be the murderer of a helpless girl like
    me?"
She kept humblin' and beggin', before him she did
    kneel,
But around her neck he tied a piece of railroad
    steel.

6 He threw her in the river 'til the bubbles rose
    around;
With the bustle of the sunball and a sad and mourn-
    ful sound,
John Colliers hurried to the depot, he bound the
    train for home;
He thinking that the murder would never, never be
    known.

7 Someone sent out a report, his name was Edwin Din;
They printed it in the papers and around the world
    it went.
They took her out of the river and carried her off
    to town,
With railroad steel around her neck that weighed
    about sixty pounds.

8 Oh, when the mother got the news she was sittin'
    in her home;
She quickly rose from her chair and ran to the
    telephone

207

Saying, "I will call headquarters, and then I'll
     go and see
If that could be my daughter, but surely it can't
     be."

9 When the mother got there, described the clothes
     she wore;
When she saw the body she fainted to the floor.
John Colliers was arrested, condemned without a
     bail,
Probably the electric chair will send him off to
     Hades.

"Poor Ellen Smith," F-11, describes the Forsyth
County, North Carolina, murder of Ellen Smith by her
lover, Peter DeGraff, in 1892. Version A is the well-
known variant as recorded on Glen Neaves and the Virginia Mountain Boys, Folkways FA 3830. B is by traditionalist Pete Steele who learned it from Andy
Whitaker of Shelbyville, Kentucky, and recorded it on
Folkways FS 3828, Banjo Tunes and Songs: Pete Steele
(both texts used by permission of Folkways Records).

A - POOR ELLEN SMITH

1 Poor Ellen Smith
How was she found
Shot through the heart,
Lyin' cold on the ground.

2 Her clothes were ragged,
Her curls on the ground,
Blood marked the spot
Where poor Ellen was found.

3 They picked up her body,
And away they did go
To the lonesome old graveyard,
I'll see her no more.

4 I got a letter yesterday
I read it today.
Said the flowers on her grave
Had all faded away.

5 They took up them rifles,
They hunted me down.
They found me a loafin'
Around in through town.

6 I been in this prison
  For twenty long years.
  Each night I see Ellen
  Through my bitter tears.

7 The warden just told me
  That soon I'll be free
  To go to her grave
  'Neath that old willow tree.

8 I'm goin' back home,
  I'll stay when I go.
  On poor Ellen's grave
  Pretty flowers I'll sow.

9 Poor Ellen Smith,
  How she was found,
  Shot through the heart,
  Lyin' cold on the ground.

B - POOR ELLEN SMITH

1 Oh, it's poor Ellen Smith
  This poor girl she was found
  With a ball through her heart,
  Lying cold upon the ground.

2 I was saw on Friday,
  Before that sad day,
  They picked up her cold body
  And carried hit away.

3 Oh, they gathered their Winchesters,
  They chased me all around,
  They found this poor boy
  In the fur edge of town.

4 Oh, they send me to Frankfurt
  I've been there before,
  I wore the ball and chain
  'Till it made my ankles sore.

5 I courted her through years
  For to make her my wife,
  I loved her too dearly
  To take her precious life.

6 Some day before long
  We'll stand before the bars,
  And when God tries our case,
  We'll shine like a star.

209

"The Lawson Murder," F-35, recollects the mass murder of a mother and her six children by the forty-three year old husband, C. D. Lawson, in Walnut Cove, North Carolina, in 1929. In spite of the copyright granted to Wiley Morris, the ballad entered the folk tradition in North Carolina and Virginia. An incomplete text is sung by Glen Neaves on Ballads and Songs of the Blue Ridge Mountains, Asch AH 3831 (used by permission of Folkways Records). A more intact version exists on The Blue Sky Boys, Rounder Records, 02144.

THE LAWSON MURDER

1 It was on one Christmas evening,
   The snow was on the ground,
   Was a home in North Carolina
   Where this murder' he was found.

2 His name was Charlie Lawson
   And he had a loving wife;
   Well, we'll never know what caused him
   To take his family's life.

3 They say he killed his wife at first
   And the little ones did cry,
   "Please, Papa, won't you spare our lives
   For it is too hard to die?"

4 But the raging man could not be stopped,
   He would not heed their call;
   He kept on firing fatal shots
   Until he killed them all.

5 They were buried in a crowded grave
   While the angels watched up above;
   Come home, come home, you little ones
   To the land of peace and love.

The final murder ballad is undoubtedly the best known of all. "The Murder of Laura Foster," F-36, was the preeminent pop hit of 1958-1959 largely due to The Kingston Trio's version, "Tom Dooley." The ballad dates to 1866 in Wilkes County, North Carolina, where Thomas C. Dula brutally murdered his fiancee. The sordid case involved another woman, possible pregnancy, and a suspected case of venereal disease. In the end Dula was hanged. The text is by Frank Proffitt from his Folk-Legacy album Frank Proffitt, FSA-1 (used by permission of Folk-Legacy Records, Sharon, Conn.). This is not the version Proffitt sang to Frank Warner in 1938 and subsequently printed by John A. and Alan Lomax.

It was the Warner/Lomax variation of the Proffitt ballad which The Kingston Trio recorded with such success.

TOM DOOLEY

1 Hang your head, Tom Dooley,
  Hang your head and cry;
  You killed little Laurie Foster,
  Poor boy, you're bound to die.

2 You met her on the mountain,
  There you took her life;
  You met her on the hillside,
  You stobbed her with a knife.

3 Hang your head, Tom Dooley,
  Oh, hang your head and cry;
  You killed little Laurie Foster,
  Poor boy, you're bound to die.

4 This time tomorrow,
  Reckon where I'll be?
  Down in yonders valley
  A-hanging on a white oak tree.

5 Hang you head, Tom Dooley,
  Oh, hang your head and cry;
  You killed little Laurie Foster,
  Poor boy, you're bound to die.

6 This time tomorrow,
  Reckon where I'll be?
  Hadn't a-been for Grayson
  I'd a-been in Tennessee.

7 Hang your head, Tom Dooley,
  Hang your head and cry;
  You killed little Laurie Foster,
  Poor boy, you're bound to die.

8 You met her on the mountain,
  It was there, I suppose,
  There you went and killed her
  And then you hid her clothes.

9 Hang your head, Tom Dooley,
  Oh, hang your head and cry;
  You killed little Laurie Foster,
  Poor boy, you're bound to die.

10 I'll take down my banjo,
   I'll pick it on my knee,
   For this time tomorrow
   It'll be no use to me.

11 Hang your head, Tom Dooley,
   Hang your head and cry;
   You killed little Laurie Foster,
   Poor boy, you're bound to die.

TRAGEDY

Tragedy obviously is not limited to cases of crime
and murder. Wrecks, mine cave-ins and personal calami-
ties also caught the attention of the ballad makers.
Sometimes they treated these disasters in a carefree and
sprightly manner. This seemed to be all the more reason
for the folk to sympathize with the central character as
certainly was true in our first example. John Luther
"Casey" Jones of Cayce, Kentucky, died April 30, 1900,
when his crack Illinois Central mail train plowed into
a freight which had not quite cleared the main line.
The tragedy gave birth to the perennial favorite ballad
of Americans, "Casey Jones," G-1.

Apparently it was composed by Wallace Saunders, a
black engine worker who serviced Casey's locomotives at
the Canton, Mississippi, roundhouse. The ballad was reworked later into a popular song by two vaudevillians,
Seibert and Newton. Since then, dozens of variations
have been written by both blacks and whites. The rock
group Grateful Dead even concocted a drug-oriented
mutation with references to cocaine and watching "your
speed." Version A is a collation from various sources
by Joe Hickerson on Drive Dull Care Away, I, Folk-Legacy
FSI-58 (used by permission of Folk-Legacy Records,
Sharon, Conn.). B is the sexually-oriented performance
by Fury Lewis using two sides of a 78 disc from 1928,
"Kassie Jones."

A - CASEY JONES

1 Early in the mornin', well it looked like rain,
  Round the bend come a gravel train;
  On the train was a-Casey Jones,
  He's a good old rounder but he's dead and gone.
      Well he's dead and gone
      And he's dead and gone
      He's a good old rounder but he's dead and
          gone.

2 Now Casey Jones was a good engineer,
   Said to his fireman, "Never fear,
   Pour on the water and shovel that coal,
   Stick your head out the window see the drivers
       roll.
       See the drivers roll,
       See the drivers roll,
       Stick your head out the window see the
           drivers roll."

3 Now Casey looked ahead and what did he see?
   Round the bend came the eight-eighteen;
   Casey said, "Fireman you'd better jump,
   These two locomotives they are bound to bump.
       They are bound to bump
       They are bound to bump
       These two locomotives they are bound to bump."

4 Should'a been there for to see the sight,
   Jumpin' and yellin', black and white;
   Some were crippled and some were lame,
   But that six wheel driver had to bear the blame.
       Had to bear the blame
       Had to bear the blame
       That six wheel driver had to bear the blame.

5 Casey Jones said before he died,
   "Just two trains that I never tried;"
   The boys said, "Casey, what can they be?"
   "The Southern Pacific and the Santa Fe.
       And the Santa Fe
       And the Santa Fe
       The Southern Pacific and the Santa Fe."

6 Casey Jones said before he died,
   "Just two drinks that I never tried;"
   The boys said, "Casey, what can they be?"
   "A glass o' water and a cup of tea.
       Well a cup of tea
       And a cup of tea
       Glass of water and a cup of tea."

7 Early in the morning well it looked like rain
   Round the bend come a gravel train;
   On the train was Casey Jones,
   He's a good old rounder but he's dead and gone.
       Well he's dead and gone
       And he's dead and gone
       He's a good old rounder but he's dead and
           gone.

B - KASSIE JONES

1 I woke up this mornin', four o'clock;
  Mr. Kassie tol' the fireman get his boiler hot.
  Put on your water, put on your coal,
  Put your head out the window, see my drivers roll,
    See my drivers roll;
  Put your head out the window, see my drivers roll.

2 Lord, some people said Mr. Kassie couldn't run;
  Let me tell you what Mr. Kassie done.
  He left Memphis was a quarter to nine,
  Got into Newport News it was dinner time,
    Was dinner time;
  Got into Newport News it was dinner time.

3 I sold my gin, I sold it straight,
  Police run to my woman's gate;
  She comes to door, she nod her head,
  She made me welcome to the foldin' bed,
    To the foldin' bed,
  Made me welcome to the foldin' bed.

4 Lord, people said to Kassie, "You runnin' over
    time;
  You got another loser with the one-o-nine."
  Kassie said, "It ain't in mind
  I run any closer 'less I make my time."

5 Said to all the passengers, "Better keep yourself
    hid,
  Natural born shaker like Cheney did,
    Like Cheney did,
  I'm a natural born shaker like Cheney did."

6 Mr. Kassie run his engine into a mile of the place;
  Number four stabbed him in the face;
  The sheriff told Kassie, "Well, you must leave
    town."
  Free to my soul I'm Alabama bound,
    Alabama bound,
  Free to my soul I'm Alabama bound.

7 Mrs. Kassie said she dreamt a dream
  The night she borrowed the sewin' machine;
  The needle got broke, she could not sew;
  She loved Mr. Kassie 'cause told me so,
    Told me so,
  Loved Mr. Kassie 'cause told me so.

8 There was a woman named Miss Alice Fry
   Says, "I'm goin' to ride with Mr. Kassie 'fore I
       die.
   I ain't good lookin', but I takes my time;
   I'm a ramblin' woman with a ramblin' mind,
       Got a ramblin' mind."

9 Kassie looked at his water, water was low,
   Looked at his watch, watch was slow;
       On the road again,
   Natural born eas'man on the road again.

10 Lot of people tell by the sort of moan
   <u>Man</u> at <u>the</u> <u>throttle</u> [?] Mr. Kassie Jones,
       Mr. Kassie Jones.

11 Mr. Kassie said before he died,
   One more road that he wanted to ride;
   People tell Kassie, "Which road?" Said he:
   "The Southern Pacific and the Sankta Fe,
       Sankta Fe."

12 This mornin' I heard someone was dyin'
   Mrs. Kassie's children on the doorstep cryin',
   "Mama, mama, I can't keep from cryin'
   Papa got killed on the Southern Line,
       On the Southern Line;
   Papa got killed on the Southern Line."

13 "Mama, mama, how can it be?
   Killed my father in the first degree."
   "Children, children, won't you hold your breath,
   You'll draw another pension from your father's
       death,
       From your father's death."
       On the road again,
   I'm a natural born eas'man on the road again.

14 Tuesday mornin' it looked like rain;
   Around the curve came a passenger train.
   Under the bar lay Kassie Jones,
   Good ole engineer, but he's dead and gone,
       Dead and gone.
       On the road again,
   I'm a natural born eas'man on the road again.

15 I left Memphis to spread the news,
   Memphis women don't wear no shoes;
   Had it written in the back of my shirt
   Natural born eas'man don't have to work

215

Don't have to work;
I'm a natural born eas'man don't have to work.

Comic versions of "Casey Jones" conclude:

Mrs. Casey set on her bed a-sighin',
Just received a message that Casey was dyin';
Said, "Go to bed, children, and hush your cryin',
'Cause you got another papa on the Salt Lake Line."

Another railroad disaster occurred in 1903 near Danville, Virginia, when the Southern Railway's crack mail train "Old 97" derailed. Vernon Dalhart's 1926 smash pop reworking of the story for Victor became involved in endless court battles over authorship. No clear-cut verdict was ever reached. This was as it should have been, for "The Wreck of the Old 97," G-2, clearly had antecedents. Henry Clay Work's 1865 composition "The Ship That Never Returned" has a similar melody (see D-27, under the "lumberjacks and sailors" section in this chapter). And then in the 1950's, an obscure regional ballad from the Ohio Valley surfaced, "The Rarden Wreck of 1893." Charles Edward Smith suggests that it was the "musical and mood link" between the Work ballad and "Old 97." Listening to all three ballads would convince the most skeptical of critics.

Version A is "The Wreck of the Old 97" as recorded by Cisco Houston on 900 Miles and other R. R. Songs, Folkways FP 13. B is "The Rarden Wreck of 1893" recorded by Bruce Buckley, with notations by Charles Edward Smith, on Ohio Valley Ballads, Folkways FA 2025 (both used by permission of Folkways Records).

A - THE WRECK OF THE OLD 97

1 Well he gave him his orders at Monroe, Virginia,
Sayin', "Steve, you're way behind time,
This is not thirty-eight but its old ninety-seven
You must put her into Danville on time."

2 He turned and said to the black greasy fireman,
"Just shovel on a little more coal,
And when we cross that White Oak Mountain
You can watch old ninety-seven roll."

3 It's a mighty rough road from Lynchburg to
    Danville,
On a line on a three mile grade,
It was on this grade that he lost his average,
You can see what a jump he made.

216

4 He was going down that grade makin' ninety miles
      an hour,
   When his whistle broke into a scream--
   They found him in the wreck
   With his hand on the throttle, he was scalded to
      death by the steam.

5 Now, ladies, you must take warning,
   From this time now on learn,
   Never speak harsh words to your true loving husband
   He may leave you and never return.

B - THE RARDEN WRECK OF 1893

1 It was on a summer's eve when the wind was sighin'
   Through the branches of the trees,
   A train rolled out for Cincinnati
   On the old C. P. and V.

2 They'd been switching cars and sending back signals
   When the engineer took flight;
   For he was killed at Rarden station,
   That's why he never come back.

   chorus:
         Did he ever come back?
         No, he never come back;
         His fate was easy learned,
         For he was killed at Rarden station,
         That's why he never returned.

3 The engineer was poor George Glasgow
   He was runnin' number four;
   And little he thought when he left Portsmouth
   That he'd run that train no more.

4 He was runnin' into Rarden station
   Eleven minutes late;
   And when he saw the switch was opened
   He leaped blindly to his fate.

5 The fireman's name was little Robert Little
   He was kindlin' up a fire;
   And when he started to rush through
   He was crushed between the cars.

6 He'd been shoveling coal in the fiery furnace
   His face it was all black;
   And he was killed at Rarden station
   That's why he never come back.

"The Avondale Mine Disaster," G-6, is a true account of the death of 110 men and boys in the anthracite mines near Wilkes-Barre, Pennsylvania, in 1869. Helen Schneyer, who calls it one of her favorite ballads, sings a version based on a broadside in George Korson, Pennsylvania Songs and Legends. She recorded it on Ballads, Broadsides & Hymns, Folk-Legacy FSI-50 (used by permission of Folk-Legacy Records, Sharon, Conn.).

THE AVONDALE MINE DISASTER

1 Good Christians all, both great and small,
   I pray you lend an ear,
   And listen with attention while
   The truth I will declare.

2 When you hear this lamentation,
   It will cause you to weep and to wail
   About the suffocation
   In the mines of Avondale.

3 On the sixth day of September,
   Eighteen sixty-nine,
   Those miners all then got a call
   To go work in the mine.

4 But little did they think that day
   That death would soon prevail
   Before they would return again
   From the mines of Avondale.

5 The women and the children
   Their hearts were filled with joy
   To see their men go to their work
   And likewise every boy.

6 But a dismal sight in broad daylight
   Soon made them all turn pale,
   When they saw the breaker burning
   O'er the mines in Avondale.

7 From here and there and everywhere
   They gathered in a crowd,
   Some tearing at their clothes and hair
   And shouting right out loud.

8 "Get out our husbands and our sons,
   For death is going to steal
   Their lives away without delay
   In the mines of Avondale."

9 But, oh, alas there was no way
   One single soul to save,
   For there is no second outlet
   In that subterranean cave.

10 No tongue can tell the awful fright
   And horror that prevailed
   Among those dying victims
   In the mines of Avondale.

11 A consultation then was held,
   They called for volunteers
   To go down in that dismal shaft
   And seek their comrades dear.

12 Two Welshmen brave without dismay
   And courage without fail
   Went down that shaft without delay
   To the mines of Avondale.

13 But when the bottom they had reached
   And sought to make their way,
   One of them died from want of air
   And the other without delay.

14 Did give the sign to hoist him up,
   Where he told the dreadful tale
   That all were lost forever
   In the mines of Avondale.

15 Sixty-seven was the number
   That they at first had found;
   It seemed they were bewailing
   Their fate beneath the ground.

16 They found the father with his son
   Wrapped in his arms, so pale;
   It was a heart-rending scene
   In the mines of Avondale.

17 Now to conclude and make an end,
   Their number I'll pen down:
   One hundred and ten of brave strong men
   Were smothered under ground.

18 They are in that grave till their last day
   And their widows may well bewail,
   And the orphans' cries still rend the skies
   All around o'er Avondale.

"Springfield Mountain," G-16, at one time was considered "America's first native ballad." Today we know better and simply designate it as an early North American ballad. It was based on an actual incident near Farmington, Connecticut, in 1761. Twenty-two year old Timothy Myrick died from a rattlesnake bite inflicted while he was mowing a hayfield. He was buried at Springfield Mountain (Wilbraham), Massachusetts. The incident was immortalized in Joseph Fiske's Rhymed Almanac for 1765. By 1832, at the latest, a ballad had been composed and within a few years Joseph Spear created the first of many parodies. Version A is a serious variant from 1849, and B is the Spear parody. Both are from Sam Hinton's Folkways album The Wandering Folk Song, FA 2401 (used by permission of Folkways Records).

A - SPRINGFIELD MOUNTAIN

1 In Springfield Mountain there did dwell
  A likely lad, I knew full well.
  Leftenant Myrick's only son,
  A likely lad of twenty-one.

2 One early morning this lad did go
  Down in the meadow the hay to mow.
  He scarce had mowed twice round the field
  When a pizen sarpint bit his heel.

3 Soon as he felt that deadly wound
  He threw his scythe down on the ground.
  Straightway for home was his intent,
  Crying aloud still as he went.

4 The neighbors round, his voice did hear,
  But none to him did thus appear.
  Thinking for workmen he did call,
  And so alone this lad did fall.

5 His careful father as he went
  Seeking his son was his intent.
  And soon his only son he found,
  Cold as a stone upon the ground.

6 In seventeen hundred and sixty-one
  'Twas this sad accident was done.
  Let it be warning unto all
  To be prepared when God doth call.

B - SPRINGFIELD MOUNTAIN

1 In Springfield Mountain, there did dwell
A likely lad, I knowed him well.
Leftenant Myrick's only son,
A likely lad of twenty-one.

chorus:
Ri too dee noo, ri too dee nay,
Ri too dee noo, ri toodle de day.

2 Now one fine day this lad did go
Down in the meadow, the hay to mow.
He scarce had mowed twice round the field
When a pesky sarpint bit his heel.

3 "Oh, Johnny dear, why did you go
Down in the meadow the hay to mow?"
"Oh, Molly dear, I thought you knowed,
When the hay gets ripe, it must be mowed!"

4 Now Molly had two ruby lips
With which the pizen she did sip.
But Molly had a rotten tooth--
And so the pizen killed them both.

5 And so they died, guv up the ghost,
And off to Heaven they did post
A-crying loud still as they went:
"Oh, cruel, cruel ser-pi-ent!"

6 Now all young men this warning take,
And don't get bit by no rattlesnake.
And mind, when you're in love, don't pass
Too near to patches of tall grass.

"Young Charlotte," G-17, is an unreal tragedy hardly based on an actual incident unless the two lovers were ingesting forbidden substances. Betty Smith learned the ballad from a Library of Congress recording by Dr. I. G. Greer of Thomasville, North Carolina. She sings it on Songs Traditionally Sung in North Carolina, Folk-Legacy FSA-53 (used by permission of Folk-Legacy Records, Sharon, Conn.).

YOUNG CHARLOTTE

1 Young Charlotte lived on a mountain side
In a wild and lonely spot.
Not a dwelling house for five miles 'round,
Except her father's cot.

2 On many a pleasant winter's night
   Young folk would gather there.
   Her father kept a social house,
   And she was young and fair.

3 It was New Year's Eve, the sun was low,
   Joy beamed in her bright blue eyes,
   As to the window she would go
   To watch the sleighs pass by.

4 It was New Year's Eve, the sun was down,
   Joy beamed in her bright blue eyes.
   She watched until young Charlie's sleigh
   Came swiftly dashing by.

5 In a village fifteen miles away
   There's a merry ball tonight.
   The air was dreadful, chilly cold,
   But her heart was warm and bright.

6 "Oh, daughter dear," the mother said,
   "This blanket around you fold.
   'Tis a dreadful night to go abroad;
   You'll catch your deathly cold."

7 "Oh, no, oh, no," the daughter cried,
   And she laughed like a gypsy queen.
   "To ride in a sleigh all muffled up
   I never would be seen."

8 Her cloak and bonnet soon were on;
   They stepped into the sleigh,
   And round the mountain side they went
   For many miles away.

9 "Such a night," said Charles, "I never knew;
   These lines I scarce can hold."
   And Charlotte said, in a very feeble voice,
   "I'm growing very cold."

10 He cracked his whip, he urged his steed
   Much faster than before,
   Saying, "It's five long, dreadful miles to go
   And it's over ice and snow.

11 "How fast," said Charles, "the frosty ice
   Keeps gathering on my brow."
   And Charlotte said, in a very feeble voice,
   "I'm growing warmer now."

12 He drove up to the ballroom door,
Stepped out and reached his hand.
He asked her once, he asked her twice,
He asked her three times o'er.

13 "Why sit you there like a monument
That has no power to move?"
He took her hand in his, oh, God,
And it was deathly cold.

14 Young Charlie knealt down by her side
And the bitter tears did flow.
"My own, my true intended bride
I never more shall know."

15 He twined his arms about her neck
And the bitter tears did flow.
And his thoughts returned to the place where she
said,
"I'm growing warmer now."

"The Silver Dagger," G-21, is related to the British broadside "The Drowsy Sleeper," M-4. (See Chapter Three for a brief discussion and three variants of M-4.) "The Silver Dagger" has been recorded by such diverse singers as The Carter Family, Sarah Ogun Gunning and Paul Joines, on the one hand, and Dave Van Ronk and Joan Baez on the other. Gunning's version is on Rounder Records 0051, The Silver Dagger. The text is by Paul Joines from the excellent anthology by Eric Davidson, Paul Newman and Caleb Finch, Ballads and Songs of the Blue Ridge Mountains: Persistence and Change, Asch Records AH 3831 (used by permission of Folkways Records).

THE SILVER DAGGER

1 Young men and maids, pray lend attention
To these few lines that I shall write,
A comely youth that I shall mention
Who courted a lady fair and bright.

2 As soon as the parents came to know it,
They strove to part them night and day,
To part him from his own dear jewel,
For she was poor they had heard them say.

3 This damsel being both fair and pretty,
She saw the grief that he went through.
She wandered forth and left the city
Some pleasant shady grove to view.

4 Then she pulled out a silver dagger
  And pierced it through her own true heart,
  Saying, "Let this be a faithful warning
  Never to young true-love part."

5 Her true-love lost out in the thicket,
  He thought he heard his true-love's voice.
  He ran to her like one distracted,
  Saying, "Oh, my love, I am quite lost."

6 Her eyes like stars were brightly beaming,
  Said, "Oh, my love, you've come too late.
  Prepare to meet me on Mount Zion
  Where all our love can be more great."

7 Then he picked up the bloodstained weapon
  And pierced it through his own true breast,
  And thus did say as he did stagger,
  "Farewell my love, I'm gone to rest."

The ballad "Floyd Collins," G-22, recalls the 1925 episode of a young man trapped in a cave-in near Mammoth Cave, Kentucky. For over two weeks the folk followed the sensational press coverage of the doomed rescue attempts. The traumatic story produced several popular recordings that eventually entered the folk process. Paul Clayton collected several variants in North Carolina and Virginia and collated them on Cumberland Mountain Folksongs, Folkways FP 2007 (used by permission of Folkways Records).

FLOYD COLLINS

1 Come all you young people and listen to what I
    tell,
  The fate of Floyd Collins, a lad you all knew well.
  His face was fair and handsome, his heart was true
    and brave,
  His body now lies sleeping in a lonely sandstone
    cave.

2 How sad, how sad the story, it fills our eyes with
    tears,
  Its memory, too, will linger for many, many years.
  The broken hearted father who tried his boy to save
  Will now weep tears of sorrow at the door of
    Floyd's cave.

3 Oh, mother, don't you worry, dear father don't be
    sad,

I'll tell you all my troubles in an awful dream
    I've had.
I dreamed I was a prisoner, my life I could not
    save,
I cried, "Oh, must I perish within this silent
    cave."

4 "Oh, Floyd," cried his mother, "don't go, my son,
    don't go,
T'would leave us broken hearted if this should
    happen so."
But Floyd did not listen to advice his mother gave,
So his body now lies sleeping in a lonely sandstone
    cave.

5 His father often warned him from follies to desist,
He told him of the danger and of the awful risk.
But Floyd would not listen to that advice he gave,
So his body now lies sleeping in a lonely sandstone
    cave.

6 Oh, how the news did travel, oh, how the news did
    go,
It travelled through the people and over the radio.
A rescue party gathered, his life they tried to
    save,
But his body now lies sleeping in a lonely sand-
    stone grave.

7 The rescue party labored, they worked both night
    and day
To move the mighty barrier that stood within the
    way.
To rescue Floyd Collins, this was their battle cry,
"We'll never, no we'll never, let Floyd Collins
    die."

8 But on that fatal morning the sun rose in the sky,
The workers still were busy, "We'll save him by and
    by."
But, oh, how sad the ending, his life they could
    not save,
His body there was sleeping in a lonely sandstone
    cave.

9 Young people, oh, take warning, this is for you
    and I,
We may not be like Collins, but you and I must die.
It may not be a sandstone grave in which we find
    our tomb,

But at the mighty judgement we too must meet our doom.

When little Kathy Fiscus fell into a dry pipe-well in 1949, the folk had the first ingredient for another ballad of tragedy. Within a week seven songs memorializing the disaster were submitted to music publishers. One or more were recorded on small hillbilly or regional record labels which apparently were the source for Mrs. Lily Maggard's traditional interpretation. In 1956 Paul Clayton visited Letcher County, Kentucky, where he heard Maggard sing the ballad of "Kathy Fiscus." The text is from Cumberland Mountain Folksongs, Folkways FP 2007 (used by permission of Folkways Records). The folk process lives on!

KATHY FISCUS

1 On April the eighth, the year forty-nine,
Death claimed a little child so pure and so kind.
Kathy, they called her, met death that day,
I know it was God that called her away.

2 Playmates for Kathy were all having fun,
The story was told, they all started to run.
As they looked back, she was not there,
It's so sad to think of this tragic affair.

3 Thousands were there from far and from near,
Workmen they struggled against all their fears,
But after two days they felt so weak,
They called down to Kathy but she never did speak.

4 After working so hard both day and night,
Digging forever she came into sight.
The little darling was dead, her life it was gone,
In San Marino there's a heart-broken home.

5 Just like a beast in a forest that day
The abandoned well took Kathy away.
And as I stand alone so humble I bow,
I know Kathy is happy up there with God now.

MISCELLANEOUS

There are additional native ballads that do not fit easily into the preceeding categories. One is "An Arkansas Traveller" or "The State of Arkansas," H-1, a satiric piece collected throughout the Mid-South and as far west as Utah. Collector H. M. Belden believed it

originated among Irish laborers imported to construct
railroad lines in Arkansas. Joe Hickerson confirms this
interpretation in the accompanying booklet to the album
Drive Dull Care Away, Vol. II, Folk-Legacy FSI-39. The
album's version was originally collected by Sam Henry
from a Northern Irish traditionalist who learned it from
a sailor. The text, "Old Arkansas," is by the Iron
Mountain String Band on Walkin' In the Parlor, Folkways
FA 2477 (used by permission of Folkways Records).

OLD ARKANSAS

1 My name is John Joe Hanner
  I come from Buffalo town,
  For nine long years I've wandered
  This whole wide world around.

2 Through ups and downs and miseries
  And some good days I saw,
  But I never knowed what misery was
  'Till I come to Arkansas.

3 I read the morning paper
  'Til my eyes was getting sore,
  A-looking for a job to work
  I read them over and o'er.

4 Said, "Hand me down five dollars, boy,
  And a ticket you shall draw;
  That'll take you safe by the fastest train
  From hell to Arkansas."

5 I told that old conductor,
  "I drink my whiskey raw,
  I'll drink that whole dang state bone dry,
  The state of Arkansas."

6 Up walked a walking skeleton
  He hand me down his paw,
  Says, "Boy, I got a job for you
  In the state of Arkansas."

7 His hair was long and kinky
  Hung on his latern jaw.
  He was a black-eyed son-of-a-bitch
  Who roamed old Arkansas.

8 They paid me fifty cents a day
  Along with board and room.
  Now, I was glad to get that job
  But sorry pretty soon.

9 They fed me on corned dodger
  As hard as any rock.
  My teeth began to loosen,
  My knees begin to knock.

10 I got so thin on fatback
   I could hide behind a straw.
   You bet I was a different lad
   When I left old Arkansas.

11 If I ever see that state again
   I'll hand you down my paw,
   Be looking through a telescope
   From hell to Arkansas.

"The Roving Gambler," H-4, contains lines and phrases that have moved freely from one folksong to another. The text is from the singing of Hedy West on Old Times and Hard Times, Folk-Legacy FSA-32 (used by permission of Hedy West).

THE ROVING GAMBLER

1 I am a roving gambler,
  I've gambled down in town.
  Whenever I see a deck of cards
  I lay my money down.

2 I gambled out in Mexico
  And I've gambled up in Maine.
  I'm going back to Georgia
  And gamble my last game.
      And gamble my last game,
      And gamble my last game,
      I'm going back to Georgia
      And gamble my last game.

3 I went down in the country,
  I did not go to stay.
  I fell in love with a pretty little girl
  And I could not get away.

4 She took me in her parlor
  And cooled me with her fan.
  Whispered low in her mother's ear,
  "I love that gambling man.
      I love that gambling man,
      I love that gambling man,"
      Whispered low in her mother's ear,
      "I love that gambling man."

228

5 "Oh, daughter, my dear daughter,
   How could you ever stand
   To leave your dear old mother here
   And go with a gambling man?"

6 "Oh, mother, my dear mother,
   You know I love you well,
   But the love I have for the gambling man
   No human tongue can tell.
       No human tongue can tell,
       No human tongue can tell,
       The love I have for the gambling man
       No human tongue can tell."

7 My father was a gambler,
   He taught me how to play.
   He taught me how to stand my hand
   To ace, deuce, jack and trey.

8 I gambled out in Mexico,
   And I've gambled up in Maine.
   I'm going back to Georgia
   And gamble my last game.
       And gamble my last game,
       And gamble my last game,
       I'm going back to Georgia
       And gamble my last game.

"The Little Mohea," H-8, is a highly romantic tale that Burl Ives popularized in the late 1940's. Laws concedes that the ballad may not be a "native product," but perhaps a derivitive of the British broadside "The Indian Lass." The text is similar to the 1937 recording by the Hall Brothers.

THE LITTLE MOHEA

1 As I was out walking
   For pleasure one day,
   For sweet recreation
   To pass time away.

2 As I set a-musing
   Myself on the grass,
   Oh, who should I spy
   But a fair Indian lass.

3 She came sit down beside me
   And taking my hand,
   Saying, "You are a stranger
   And in a strange land.

229

4 "But if you will follow
You're welcome to go
And dwell in the cottage
Which I call it my home."

5 The sun was far sinking
Far over the sea,
As I wandered along
With my pretty Mohea.

6 Together did wander
Together did roam,
'Til we came to the cottage
In a cocoanut grove.

7 Then this kind expression
She made unto me,
"If you will consent, sir,
And stay here with me.

8 "And go no more roving
Abroad a salt sea,
I will teach you the language
Of the little Mohea."

9 "Oh, no, my fair maiden
That never could be,
For I have a true lover
In my own country.

10 "I will never forsake her
For I know she loves me,
Her heart is as true
As the little Mohea."

11 It was early one morning,
A morning in May,
When to this fair maiden
These words I did say.

12 "I'm going to leave you
So farewell my dear,
My ship sails are spreading
And home I must steer."

Undoubtedly "The Young Man Who Wouldn't Hoe Corn,"
H-13, was meant to prod lazy farmers; whether or not it
succeeded is unknown. The following 1930 version by
Buster Carter and Preston Young softens the ending.
See: Anthology of American Folk Music, Volume I:
Ballads, Folkways FA 2951.

THE YOUNG MAN WHO WOULDN'T HOE CORN

1 I will sing a little song, but it ain't very long,
  'Bout a lazy farmer who wouldn't hoe his corn,
  And why it was I never could tell
  For that young man was always well,
    That young man was always well.

2 He planted his corn on June the last,
  In July it was up to his eye,
  In September there came a big frost
  And all that young man's corn was lost,
    All that young man's corn was lost.

3 He started to the field and he got there last,
  The grass and the weeds up to his chin,
  The grass and the weeds had grown so high
  It caused that poor man for to sigh,
    Caused that poor man for to sigh.

4 Now his courtship had just begun,
  Saying, "Young man have you hoed your corn?"
  "I've tried, I've tried, I've tried in vain
  But I don't believe I'll raise one grain,
    Don't believe I'll raise one grain."

5 "Why do you come to me to wed,
  If you can't raise your own corn bread?
  Single I am and will remain
  For a lazy man I won't maintain,
    A lazy man I won't maintain."

6 He hung his head and walked away,
  Saying, "Kind miss you'll rue the day,
  You'll rue the day that you were born,
  For giving me the devil 'cause I wouldn't hoe corn,
    Giving me the devil 'cause I wouldn't hoe
      corn."

7 Now his courtship was to an end,
  On his way he then begin,
  Saying, "Kind miss, I'll have another girl
  If I have to ramble this big, wide world,
    If I have to ramble this big, wide world."

BLACK

Black balladry in American folk music is significant for several reasons. (1) While only eight to ten
per cent of all native ballads are in the black tradi-

tion, they are as dramatic as their white counterparts
and generally far more poetic. (2) Unlike most white
ballads, the black ballads generally have been circu-
lated in oral form producing a more creative and varied
result. The numerous lines and stanzas that wander from
one song to another is reminiscent of the classic
British ballads in Chapter Two. (3) Black ballads
usually have hidden meanings scattered throughout their
stanzas. The ability to read between the lines is vital
for a complete understanding of their message. As a
minority group, first enslaved and then treated to
second class citizenship, blacks have had to sharpen
their skill at ambiguity. (4) The black singer stresses
the drama and realism of the ballad and makes few, if
any, moral judgements--another similarity to the classic
ballads. It may well be true that the black ballads, as
a group, surpass the native white ballads in overall
folk form.

Furthermore, the first black ballad in Laws, "John
Henry," I-l, is undoubtedly the finest native American
ballad of all. The story seems commonplace: a black
steel driver pits his muscles against a newly invented
steam drill. He wins the contest, but dies from his
exertions. However, there is a deeper implication to
"John Henry." It protests the dehumanizing nature of the
Industrial Revolution. In the late twentieth century,
the ballad retains its validity as the industrial
society yields to the rapidly expanding information
society producing yet another round of human suffering
and dislocation. In the early 1960's, a perceptive update of the ballad by Bob Gibson and Hamilton Camp,
"The Thinking Man, John Henry," heralded this new conflict between man and computer.

Researcher Guy B. Johnson believed that a black
man, John Henry, actually worked on the construction of
the Chesapeake and Ohio Railroad's Big Bend Tunnel near
Hinton, West Virginia, in the early 1870's. Yet it
really does not matter, for "John Henry," the ballad,
has transcended human form and stands as an American
folk epic symbolizing courage, defiance and even the
Puritan work-ethic. Traditional throughout much of the
United States, it has become a truly integrated musical
number, popular with both black and white singers and
audiences.

A black farmer in central Kentucky taught version
A to Bruce Buckley, who sings it on Ohio Valley Ballads,
Folkways FA 2025 (used by permission of Folkways
Records). B, from a 1927 recording by Henry Thomas, a

232

Texas songster and bluesman, is reissued on Henry Thomas, Herwin 209. "Spike Driver Blues," C, is a related work song recorded in 1928 by John Hurt, a rural black farmer with extraordinary musical ability; reissued on Mississippi John Hurt, Biograph BLP-C4. D, from a 1924 recording by two white rural Georgians, Gid Tanner and Riley Puckett, is reissued on Gid Tanner and His Skillet Lickers, Rounder 1005.

A - JOHN HENRY

1 Oh, some say he come from Cuba
  And some say he come from Spain,
  But I say he come from Hardrock levee camp
  Because steel driving John Henry was his name,
      name, name,
      Steel driving John Henry was his name.

2 When John Henry was a little infant baby
  Mama rocked him in the palm of her hand.
  It was early one morning that I heard the poor gal
      cry,
  "He's got a right to be a steel driving man, man,
      man,
      A right to be a steel driving man, man, man."

3 Well, John Henry growed to be a right smart sized
      boy;
  He was sittin' on his papa's knee.
  Spied number nine tunnel on that C and O road,
  Says, "It's bound to be the death of me, me, me,
      Bound to be the death of me."

4 Well, they took John Henry to the tunnel,
  Oh, they put him to headin' the drive.
  Well, the rock's being so high, John Henry being
      so low,
  He laid down his hammer and he cried, cried, cried,
      Laid down his hammer and he cried.

5 John Henry said to his captain,
  "You know I'm nothing but a man,
  But before I let that steam drill beat me down
  I'm gonna die with the hammer in my hand, hand,
      hand,
      Die with the hammer in my hand."

6 Well, they put John Henry on the right hand side,
  The steam drill on the left.
  John Henry says, "I'll beat that steam drill down

If I beat my fool self to death, death, death,
    Beat my fool self to death."

7 John Henry says to his captain,
"Lookie yonder what I see,
Your drills done broke and your holes done chocked,
And you can't drive steel like me, me, me,
    Can't drive steel like me."

8 Well, John Henry had a little woman,
And the dress that poor gal wore was red.
Well, she started down the track, she never did
    look back,
"I'm going where John Henry fell dead, dead, dead,
    Going where John Henry fell dead."

B - JOHN HENRY

1 Henry got a letter, said his mother was dead,
Put his children on a passenger train.
He gonna ride the blind, Lordy,
He gonna ride the blind.

2 Henry looked up the railroad track, spotted two
    ... coming down,
Before I let that steel driver beat me down,
Die with that hammer in my hand,
Gonna die with that hammer in my hand.

3 Henry went on the mountain top, give his horn a
    blow,
Last words the captain said,
"John Henry was a natural man,
John Henry was a natural man."

4 Henry had a woman, dress she wore was red.
Going on down that railroad track,
Going where John Henry fell dead,
Yes, I'm going where John Henry fell dead.

5 Henry had a baby boy, hold it in his palm of his
    hand.
Last words that poor boy said,
"I'm gonna learn to be a steel driving man,
Yes, I'll learn to be a steel driving man."

C - SPIKE DRIVER BLUES

1 Take this hammer and carry it to my captain,
Tell him I'm gone
Tell him I'm gone

Tell him I'm gone.
Take this hammer and carry it to my captain,
Tell him I'm gone
Tell him I'm gone
I'm sure he's gone.

[similarly]

2 This is the hammer that killed John Henry,
But it won't kill me . . .
Ain't goin' kill me.

3 It's been a long ways from east Colorado,
Honey, to my home . . .
That's why I'm gone.

4 John Henry he left his hammer
Layin' side the road . . .
All in rain
All in rain
That's why I'm gone.

5 John Henry's a steel drivin' boy
But he went down . . .
That's why I'm gone.

D - JOHN HENRY

1 John Henry was a little man
Sitting on his papa's knee.
Gave one long and lonesome cry,
"Hammer be the death of me, poor boy,
Hammer be the death of me."

2 John Henry told his captain,
"Lord, a man ain't nothing but a man,
But before I'll be governed by this old steam drill
Lord, I'll die with a hammer in my hand." (2)

3 John Henry had a little hammer
Handle was made of bone,
Everytime he hit the drill on the head,
Lord, his fireman reaches down and groan.

4 John Henry walked in the tunnel
Had his captain by his side,
But the rocks so tall, John Henry so small,
He laid down his hammer and he cried.

5 John Henry told his shaker,
"Shaker you better pray,

235

If I miss this piece of steel
Tomorrow'll be your burying day."

6 John Henry's captain stepped on a rock,
Said, "I believe this mountain's fallin' in."
John Henry turned around and said,
"That's my hammer falling in the wind."

7 John Henry had a little woman,
Her name was Polly Ann.
John Henry lay sick and on his bed,
Polly drove steel like a man.

8 John Henry had just one only son,
He could stand in the palm of your hand.
Last words that John Henry said,
"Son, gonna be a steel driving man."

9 Took John Henry to the White House,
Rolled him in the sand.
Three men from the east and a lady from the west
Came to see this old steel driving man.

John H. Cox in Folk-Songs of the South traced the
story of "John Hardy," 1-2, to McDowell County, West
Virginia, where Hardy was sentenced to death in 1894 for
killing a fellow C & O Railroad worker over a fifteen
cent gambling debt. Some versions confused the vil-
lain's name with that of the heroic John Henry (see Max
Hunter, Folk-Legacy FSA-11). Woody Guthrie sang
another variant, "Johnny Hard," and used the melody in
"Tom Joad," a protest song which was based on the central character in John Steinbeck's The Grapes of Wrath.
Sparky Rucker, a black interpreter, recorded a splendid
version on Heroes and Hard Times, Green Linnet SIF 1032,
in 1981, but the ballad appears to be more popular among
white singers. The text is from Frank Proffitt Sings
Folk Songs, Folkways FA 2360 (used by permission of
Folkways Records).

JOHN HARDY

1 John Hardy, he was a desperate little man
And he carried two pistols every day,
When he shot a man on the West Virginia line
You oughta saw John Hardy gettin' away, Lord, Lord,
You oughta saw John Hardy gettin' away.

2 John Hardy he went to the East Stone Bridge
And he vowed that he would be free;
Up stepped Ned Bawly and he took him by the arm,

236

"Johnny, walk along with me, Lord, Lord,
Johnny walk along with me."

3 John Hardy, he had a little girl
   And the dress that she wore was red;
   She followed him to his hangin' ground,
   "Papa, I would rather be dead, Lord, Lord,
   Papa, I would rather be dead."

4 John Hardy, he had another little girl
   And the dress that she wore was blue;
   She followed her daddy to his hangin' ground,
   "Papa, I've been good to you, Lord, Lord,
   Papa, I've been good to you."

5 Now I've been to the east and I've been to the west
   And I've been this whole world 'round;
   I've been to the river and I've been baptized,
   Now I'm on my hangin' ground, Lord, Lord,
   Now I'm on my hangin' ground.

"Frankie and Albert," I-3, best known as "Frankie
and Johnny," traces back to at least the 1890's. In
spite of its theme, it even has become a children's
song. Burl Ives helped popularize the song following
World War II, but it was widely recorded before then.
A priceless performance from 1928 was that of Mississippi John Hurt (reissued on Biograph BLP-C4).

FRANKIE AND ALBERT

1 Frankie was a good girl, everybody knows,
   She paid a hundred dollars
   For Albert's suit of clothes;
   He's her man and he done her wrong.

2 Frankie went down to the corner saloon
   Didn't gonna be so long;
   She peeped through the key hole in the door
   Spied Albert in Alice's arms,
   "He's my man and he done me wrong."

3 Frankie called Albert, Alice says "I didn't hear."
   "If you don't come to the woman you love
   Gonna haul you out of here,
   You're my man and you done me wrong."

4 Frankie shot Albert and she shot him three or four
        times,
   "Let's go back I've smoke in my gun,

237

Let me see if Albert's dyin'.
He's my man and he done me wrong."

5 Frankie and the judge walked down the stairs
And walked out side by side;
The judge said to Frankie,
"You're gonna be justified
Killin' your man and he done you wrong."

6 Dark was the night, cold was on the ground,
The last word I heard Frankie said,
"I laid old Albert down;
He was my man and he done me wrong."

7 I ain't gonna tell no story and I ain't gonna tell
      no lies,
Well Albert passed 'bout an hour ago
With a girl he called Alice Fry;
He's your man and he done you wrong.

"The Coon Can Game," I-4, is another black ballad
appropriated by white country singers including Dock
Boggs, who learned banjo technique from a black player
in Norton, Virginia, in the early twentieth century.
Boggs recorded "Poor Boy in Jail" on Folkways FA 2392,
Dock Boggs Volume 2 (used by permission of Folkways
Records).

POOR BOY IN JAIL

1 Oh, my mama's in the cold, cold ground,
My daddy, he went away;
My sister married a gamblin' man,
And now I'm gone astray.

2 I sit here in this old jail
And I do the best I can;
Get to thinking about the woman I loved,
She ran away with another man.

3 She ran away with another man, poor boy,
She ran away with another man;
Get to thinking about the woman I loved,
She ran away with another man.

4 I went out on the prairie
And I stopped the Katy train;
Took a bag of mail from standing there
And I walked away in the rain.

238

5 They got the bloodhounds on me,
  And they run me up a tree;
  Said, "Come down from there, my boy,
  And go to the penitentiary."

6 I said, "Mister judge, Mister judge,
  What you goin' to do to me?"
  Said, "If the jury finds you guilty, my boy,
  I'm goin' to send you to the penitentiary."

7 They took me to the railroad station,
  A train come rollin' by;
  I looked in the window, saw the woman I loved,
  And I hung my head and cried.

8 I hung my head in shame, poor boy,
  I hung my head and cried;
  I looked in the window, saw the woman I loved,
  And I hung my head and cried.

A long neglected and yet highly dramatic and
lyrical ballad is "Delia," I-5. Delia was shot by her
lover Coonie (or Johnny in our version) for unfaithful-
ness. The ballad concentrates on the events leading to
her funeral. Blind Willie McTell recorded a version for
the Library of Congress in 1940; pop artist David
Bromberg sang a touching version in the 1970's; and
Sparky Rucker added biting lines to his performance on
Green Linnet SIF 1032 ("The folks down in Atlanta/
They're busy tryin' to pass for whites"). The text is
from Paul Clayton's Riverside album Bloody Ballads, RLP
12-615.

DELIA

1 Now the reason Johnny shot Delia,
  She cursed him a wicked curse;
  And if he hadn't shot her
  She might have cursed him worse.
      She is gone, one more round, Delia's gone.
      [repeat after each stanza]

2 Now the first time Johnny shot Delia,
  He shot her in the side;
  The second time that he shot her,
  She curled right up and died.

3 Oh, roll me over easy,
  Roll me over slow,
  Roll me over one more time,
  Then never touch me no more.

239

4 So Delia's mother come running,
Come all dressed in white;
Did everything that a momma could do,
She cried both day and night.

5 Oh, Delia's doctor come running,
He come all dressed in black;
Did everything that a doctor could do,
But he couldn't bring Delia back.

6 Oh, some gave Delia a nickel,
Some gave Delia a dime;
But I didn't give her one darn cent,
'Cause she wasn't no gal of mine.

7 So it's goodbye, goodbye to Delia,
Goodbye one long time;
Taking her off to the graveyard,
But she taught me my last rhyme.

"Dupree," I-11, has many variations including a related white hillbilly ballad. The text is from the singing of a versatile folk and blues artist, Brownie McGhee, as recorded on Brownie McGhee Blues, Folkways FA 2030 (used by permission of Folkways Records).

DUPREE

1 Now Betty told Dupree
She wanted a diamond ring;
You know Betty, she told Dupree
She wanted a diamond ring;
He says, "Oh, yes, oh, yes, my love,
I'll get you most, most anything."
        [spoken] Wha'd he do? Wha'd he do?

2 He got himself a pistol
And it was a forty-four;
He got himself a pistol
And it was a forty-four;
Well, you know to get that diamond ring
He had to rob a jewelry store.

3 But he blind the passenger,
And he beat his way to Chicago;
You know, Dupree caught a passenger
Beat his way into Chicago;
Don't you know, little Betty, she hung her head
    and cried,
Said, "I won't see Dupree no more."

240

4 But the police they caught him,
  Carried him back to the Atlanta jail;
  The police they caught Dupree,
  Carried him back to the Atlanta jail;
  "Please send for my little Betty,"
  Sayin', "Please come and go my bail."

5 She went to the jailhouse,
  His face she could not see;
  She went to the jailhouse,
  His face she could not see;
  Well, she said, "Please Mister jailer,
  Won't you give him this note?"
    [spoken] This is how it read:

6 "I was there to see you
  But I could not see your face;
  I was there to see you
  But I could not see your face;
  Well, although you know that I love you,
  But I just can't take your place."

Few whites have been able to master the art of the blues. One who did was Frank Hutchison from Logan County, West Virginia. Around the year 1910, he learned blues material from Bill Hunt, a crippled black. Undoubtedly Hunt was the source of Hutchison's 1929 recording of "Railroad Bill," I-13, version A below, as reissued on Rounder 1007, The Train that Carried My Girl from Town. B is a more complete account as collected by Paul Clayton in Rockingham County, Virginia, and recorded on Folksongs and Ballads of Virginia, Folkways FA 2110 (used by permission of Folkways Records).

A - RAILROAD BILL

1 Railroad Bill, got so bad
  Stole all the chickens the poor farmer had,
  Wasn't he bad? Old Railroad Bill.

2 Railroad Bill went out west,
  Shot all the buttons off the brakeman's vest,
  Wasn't he bad, Railroad Bill?

3 Railroad Bill got so fine,
  Shot ninety nine holes in a killer shine,
  Ride, Railroad Bill.

4 Railroad Bill standing at the tanks
  Wait for the train they called Nancy Hanks,

Well, it's ride, Railroad Bill.

5 Railroad Bill standing at the curve,
Gonna rob a mail train, well, he didn't have the
     nerve,
Well, it's sad, Railroad Bill.

6 Railroad Bill he lived on a hill,
He never worked or he never will,
And it's ride, Railroad Bill.

7 Railroad Bill went out west,
Shot all the buttons off the brakeman's vest,
That's too bad, Railroad Bill.

B - RAILROAD BILL

1 Railroad Bill, Railroad Bill,
He never worked and he never will,
Well, it's bad Railroad Bill.

2 Railroad Bill, mighty bad,
Took everything that the farmer had,
That bad Railroad Bill.

3 Kill me a chicken, send me a wing,
Think I'm working but I ain't doin' a thing,
Then it's ride, ride, ride.

4 Railroad Bill, desperate and bad,
Take everything that your woman had,
Then it's ride, ride, ride.

5 I'm going home, tell my wife
Railroad Bill tried to take my life,
Well, it's bad Railroad Bill.

6 Railroad Bill, mighty bad man,
Killed McMillan with a gun in each hand,
Then it's ride, ride, ride.

7 Two policemen, dressed in blue,
Comin' down the street walkin' two by two,
Well, it's looking for Railroad Bill.

8 Everybody told him, better get back,
Bill was walkin' down the railroad track,
And it's ride, ride, ride.

"The Bully of the Town," I-14, also has crossed
over into the white tradition. The Georgia string band,

242

the Skillet Lickers, recorded an abridged version of the
ballad in 1926 (reissued on County Records 526). Paul
Clayton discovered the following variant in North
Carolina and recorded it on Wanted For Murder, Riverside
RLP 12-640.

THE BULLY OF THE TOWN

1 I'm lookin' for that bully, bully of the town,
  Lookin' for that bully, but that bully can't be
        found,
  Well, I'm lookin' for the bully of the town.

  chorus:
        I'm lookin' for that bully of the town,
        Every night I may be found,
        When I walk this levee around,
        Well, I'm lookin' for the bully of the town.

2 Now, have you seen that bully, bully of the town?
  I'm lookin' for that bully that shot his woman
        down,
  Well, I'm lookin' for the bully of the town.

3 Now, whiskey down at Mrs. Johnson's makes you dance
        a reel,
  Oh, Mrs. Johnson, how glad you make me feel
  When I'm lookin' for the bully of the town.

4 I went down to Miss Brother Jones' and I soon got
        high,
  Out come that bully and on him I cast an eye,
  Well, I'm lookin' for that bully and I got you
        found.

5 Walkin' down that alley with my axe in my hand,
  When I catch up to that bully I'm gonna wipe him
        off the land,
  I'm lookin' for the bully of the town.

6 Well, I met up with that bully just at four
        o'clock,
  Oughta hear that bully how he squealed and squawked,
  Well, I'm lookin' for that bully and I got you
        found.

7 I finished with that bully, they sent off for the
        hearse,
  I cut him up so bad Stackerlee couldn't cut him
        worse,

Well, I'm lookin' for that bully and I got him
found.

The reference to Stackerlee in the previous ballad
introduces a lasting character in black blues.
"Stagolee," or "Stackerlee," I-15, has been collected
throughout the South including Alan Lomax's version from
a prisoner at the Mississippi State Penitentiary at
Parchman in 1947. Lloyd Price recorded a hit pop version in 1959. This incomplete variant, "Stack O Lee
Blues," was recorded by songster John Hurt in 1928 (reissued on Biograph BLP-C4).

STACK O LEE BLUES

1 Police officer how can it be?
  You can arrest everybody
  But cruel Stack O Lee,
  That bad man, oh, cruel Stack O Lee [repeat at end
     of each stanza]

2 Mr. Lyons told Stack O Lee,
  "Please don't take my life,
  I've got two little babes and a darlin' lovin'
     wife."

3 "What do I care about your two little babes,
     darlin' lovin' wife?
  You done stole my Stetson hat,
  I'm bound to take your life."

4 [hums]
  Well, when I spied Billy Lyons
  He was lying down on the floor.

5 Gentlemen of the jury, what do you think of that?
  Stack O Lee killed Billy Lyons
  For a five dollar Stetson hat.

6 And on the gallows, head way up high,
  At twelve o'clock they killed him,
  They's all glad to see him die.

"The Boll Weevil," I-17, is a protest ballad disguised as an innocuous tale about an insect and its
struggle to survive. The story symbolizes the black
effort to gain equality in white America. The "little
black bug" is "just a-looking for a home" and succeeds;
persistence can conquer adversity. In 1929 the great
delta bluesman Charley Patton sang "Mississippi Bo
Weavil Blues" convincingly and with "growling earthi-

ness," as Paul Oliver wrote in <u>The Story of the Blues</u>.
Version A is from <u>Charley Patton: Founder of the Delta
Blues</u>, Yazoo L-1020. B is the more familar setting by
Cisco Houston, from <u>Cisco Sings</u>, Folkways FA 2346 (used
by permission of Folkways Records).

A - MISSISSIPPI BO WEAVIL BLUES

It's a little bo weavil she's movin' in the. . .
    lordie
You can plant your cotton and you won't get a half
    a cent, lordie
Bo weavil, bo weavil, where's your native home?
    lordie
"A-Louisiana leavin' Texas anywhere I'se bred and
    born," lordie
Well, I saw the bo weavil, lord, a circle, lordie,
    in the air, lordie
The next time I seed him, lord, he had his family
    there, lordie
Bo weavil left Texas, lord, he bid me, "Fare thee
    well," lordie
"Where you goin' now?" [spoken]
"I'm goin' down to the Mississippi, gonna give
    Louisiana hell," lordie
Bo weavil said to the farmer, "Ain't got ticket
    fare," lordie
"How is that, boy?" [spoken]
Sucks all the blossom and he leaves your hedges
    square, lordie
An' the next time I seed you, you know you had your
    family there, lordie
Bo weavil met his wife, "We can sit down on the
    hill," lordie
Bo weavil told his wife, "Let's take this forty
    here," lordie
Hold on, I'm gonna tell all about that [spoken]
"Let's live in Louisiana, we can go to Arkansas,"
    lordie
Well, I saw the bo weavil, lord, a circle, lord,
    in the air, lordie
Next time I seed him, lord, he had his family
    there, lordie
Bo weavil told the farmer that, "I ain't got ticket
    fare," lordie
Sucks all the blossom and leave your hedges square,
    lordie
Bo weavil, bo weavil, where your native home,
    lordie
"Most anywhere they raise cotton and corn," lordie

245

"Bo weavil, bo weavil, gonna treat me fair," lordie
"The next time I did you had your family there,"
    lordie.

B - THE BOLL WEEVIL

1 Well, the boll weevil is a little black bug
  Come from Mexico they say,
  Well, he come all the way to Texas,
  He was looking for a place to stay,
  Just looking for a home,
  He was looking for a home.

  chorus:
      He was looking for a home
      Looking for a home,
      He was looking for a home
      Well, looking for a home.

2 Well, the first time I seen the boll weevil
  He was sitting on the square,
  And the next time I seen the boll weevil
  He had his whole damn family there,
  They were looking for a home,
  Just a looking for a home.

3 Then the farmer took the boll weevil
  Put him in the hot sand,
  And the boll weevil said to the farmer,
  "Well, you're treating me like a man,
  It'll be my home, I'll have a home."

4 Then the farmer took the boll weevil
  Put him on the ice,
  And the boll weevil said to the farmer,
  "Well, it's mighty cool and nice,
  It'll be my home, it'll be my home,"

5 Well, the farmer said to his wife, "Honey
  What do you think about that?
  The old boll weevil done made a nest in my brand
      new Stetson hat,
  And it's full of holes, and its full of holes."

[repeat stanza 1]

MOSES ASCH
Photo by David Gahr Courtesy Folkways Records

SANDY and CAROLINE PATON with Editor in background
Photo by Jeanne Kukura

BLIND BLAKE

THE CARTER FAMILY

CHAPTER FIVE

SONGS: WHITE COUNTRY AND BLACK BLUES

Most of the songs in this chapter were first recorded in the 1920's and 1930's by rural southern musicians. While scholarly folk collectors searched for
new variants of "Barbara Allen" and "The Golden Vanity,"
pioneer record companies, such as Paramount, Vocalion,
Victor, Columbia and Gennett, were busily preserving a
newer folk tradition--even if their executives did not
realize it.

Dozens of talented rural entertainers were record-
ed. Among the white country musicians were: Grayson and
Whitter, Eck Robertson, Fiddlin' John Carson, Uncle Dave
Macon, Frank Hutchison, The Carter Family, Jimmie
Rodgers, Gid Tanner and His Skillet Lickers, and Charlie
Poole and the North Carolina Ramblers. Among the rural
black musicians were such legends as: Charlie Jackson,
Charley Patton, John Hurt, Henry Thomas, Lemon Jeffer-
son, Furry Lewis, Blind Blake, and Gus Cannon and His
Jug Stompers.

Many of these artists believed that the old time
musical traditions were worth preserving. They objected
to record company promoters who continually urged them
to update their material.[1] Among those who failed to
comply were The Carter Family: A. P., Sarah and May-
belle. From their first recording session in 1927,
through a depression and a world war, to their last
session in 1956, The Carter Family refused to compromise
their standards or alter their sound.

What follows is a sampling from the hundreds of
songs that have entered the folk tradition in the nineteenth and twentieth centuries. It is just a taste, a
sip, of the folk juices which have fermented in the
homes of both white and black rural Americans. The
music is divided arbitrarily into five sections and,
wherever possible, utilizes texts from either currently
available reissues or recent recordings.

---

[1]For a brief discussion on this point, see Tony
Russell, Old Time Music, No. 25, Summer, 1977, p. 39.

PLAY-PARTY AND DANCE

This country music survey begins with examples of play-party songs and those dance tunes to which lyrics have been added. The play-party, originating in the British Isles apparently as a children's game, was a popular form of American folk dance until about the 1930's. It differed from another American institution, the square dance, in that the play-party players sang their own songs as they danced. In spite of the origin and the name, play-parties were not for children, but rather for the entertainment of sexually mature adolescents as well as adults. They could be considered the staid forerunners of the discotheque. As the form developed, some play-party songs exhibited the signs of nascent balladry. "Old Joe Clark" is one such example. Hedy West's version is from the album Old Times and Hard Times, FSA-32 (used by permission of Hedy West).

OLD JOE CLARK

1 Old Joe Clark's mad at me
  And I'll tell you the reason why;
  I run through his cabbage patch
  And tore down all his rye.

  chorus:
      Walk, Joe Clark, talk, Joe Clark,
      Goodbye Billy Brown.
      Walk, Joe Clark, talk, Joe Clark,
      I'm going to leave this town.

2 I went down to old Joe Clark's
  To get me a glass of wine;
  He tied me to his whipping post
  And he give me ninety-nine.

3 I went back down to old Joe Clark's
  To get me a glass of gin;
  He charged me up for whipping his horse
  And he give me hell again.

4 I don't give a damn for old Joe Clark
  And I'll tell you the reason why;
  He blows his nose in old corn bread
  And calls it chicken pie.

5 Old Joe Clark come to my house,
  That lowdown filthy pup;
  He run the bulldog under the fence
  And drunk my liquor up.

250

6 Old Joe Clark's dead and gone,
  And I hope he's gone to hell;
  He made me wear the ball and chain
  And made my ankles swell.

Common form in play-party songs is to include lines
and stanzas borrowed from other songs. Witness "Old Doc
Jones," with lines from "Sail Away Ladies," as sung by
Logan English on Kentucky Folk Songs and Ballads, Folkways FA 2136 (used by permission of Folkways Records).

OLD DOC JONES

  Old Doc Jones was a fine old man,
  A fine old man, a fine old man;
  Old Doc Jones was a fine old man
  And he told ten thousand lies.

  chorus:
    Ladies and gentlemen sail away,
    Sail away, sail away;
    Ladies and gentlemen sail away,
    And chose just whom you please.

  If ever I get my new house done,
  If ever I get my new house done,
  If ever I get my new house done,
  I'll give it to my son.

Here is a composite version of "Sail Away Ladies"
based on Uncle Dave Macon's 1927 rendition (reissued on
County Records 521) and more recent sessions by Bob
Gibson and Guy Carawan. Uncle Bunt Stephens' fiddle
solo from the 1920's is available on Anthology of
American Folk Music, Volume II: Social Music, Folkways
FA 2952.

SAIL AWAY LADIES

1 Ain't no use to sit and cry,
  Sail away ladies, sail away,
  You'll be an angel by and by,
  Sail away ladies, sail away.

  chorus:
    Don't she rock him, die-di-o (repeat 3X)

2 Come along boys, and go with me,
  Sail away ladies, sail away,
  We'll go down to Tennessee,
  Sail away ladies, sail away.

3 If ever I get my new house done,
    Sail away ladies, sail away,
    I'll give the old one to my son,
    Sail away ladies, sail away.

4 Hush, little baby, don't you cry,
    Sail away ladies, sail away,
    You'll be an angel by and by,
    Sail away ladies, sail away.

Fiddlin' John Carson was among the first group of country artists to record. His initial release in 1923 featured this well-known fiddle tune (reissued on Rounder 1003).

THE OLD HEN CACKLED AND THE ROOSTER'S GOING TO CROW

Old hen cackled everybody knows,
The old hen cackled and the rooster's going to
    crow.

Old hen cackled, cackled mighty loud,
Ain't laid an egg, walked mighty proud.

Old hen cackled, cackled in the lot,
Last time she cackled, cackled in the pot.

"Waterbound" is a delightful play-party song from Grayson County, Virginia. The "Golden Ring" group perform it on Five Days Singing: Volume I, Folk-Legacy FSI-41 (used by permission of Folk-Legacy Records, Sharon, Conn.).

WATERBOUND

chorus:
    Waterbound, and I can't get home (3X)
    Way down in North Carolina.

1 Chickens crowing in the old plough field (3X)
    Way down in North Carolina.

2 Me and Tom and Dave goin' home (3X)
    Before the water rises.

3 The old man's mad and I don't care (3X)
    I'm going to get his daughter.

4 If he don't give her up, we're gonna run away (3X)
    Down to North Carolina.

5 I'm going home with the one I love (3X)
  Down to North Carolina.

"The Hound Dog Song" is a derivitive of the fiddle
tune "Sally Ann." The song's popularity in the early
twentieth century can be judged by the use of the chorus
in a cartoon by Herbert Johnson, "The War Chant," which
revealed the growing resentment toward President William
Howard Taft during his 1912 reelection campaign. The
cartoon depicted an abused hound, "Popular Government,"
and its master, "Common People," who was rolling up his
sleeve preparing to take action against the president.
Taft was defeated; whether or not the cartoon was re-
sponsible is unknown. The text is from Golden Ring,
Folk-Legacy FSI-16 (used by permission of Folk-Legacy
Records, Sharon, Conn.).

THE HOUND DOG SONG

chorus:
    Every time I go downtown,
    Somebody kicks my dog around;
    It makes no difference if he is a hound,
    They gotta quit kicking my dog around.

1 Me and Lem Briggs and old Bill Brown
  Took a load of corn to town;
  Old Jim-Dog, the ornery old cuss,
  He just naturally follered us.

2 As we drifted past Johnson's store,
  A passel of yaps come out the door;
  Jim he scooted behind a box
  With all them fellers a-throwing rocks.

3 They tied a can to old Jim's tail
  And run him past the county jail;
  That just naturally made us sore,
  Lem he cussed and Bill he swore.

4 Me and Lem Briggs and old Bill Brown
  Lost no time a-gettin' down;
  We rubbed them fellers on the ground
  For kicking my old Jim-Dog around.

5 Jim seen his duty there and then,
  He lit into them gentlemen;
  He sure mussed up the courthouse square
  With rags and meat and hide and hair.

In the late 1950's a youthful trio of urban "folk-niks" organized an old-timey musical group, The New Lost City Ramblers. They popularized this music for a new generation unaware of their heritage. Much of the NLCR material came from the play-party and dance tune genre. "Fly Around My Pretty Little Miss" was based on early recordings by such groups as the Georgia string band of Gid Tanner. Source: New Lost City Ramblers, Volume 3, Folkways FA 2398 (used by permission of Folkways Records).

FLY AROUND MY PRETTY LITTLE MISS

chorus:
    Fly around my pretty little miss,
    Fly around my daisy,
    Fly around my pretty little miss,
    You almost drive me crazy.

The higher up the cherry tree,
The riper grows the cherries;
The more you hug and kiss the girls,
The sooner they will marry.

Coffee grows on white oak trees,
The river flows with brandy;
If I had my pretty little miss,
I'd feed her sugar candy.

Going to get some weevily wheat,
I'm going to get some barley;
Going to get some weevily wheat,
And bake a cake for Charlie.

Another NLCR play-party number was "Hogeye," based on recordings by Pope's Arkansas Mountaineers and others. Text: New Lost City Ramblers, Volume 3, FA 2398 (used by permission of Folkways Records).

HOGEYE

Chicken in the bread pan kicking up dough,
Sally will your dog bite? No sir, no.

chorus 1:
    Sally in the garden sifting sand,
    Sally upstairs with a hog-eyed man.

Sally in the garden sifting, sifting,
Sally in the garden sifting sand.

254

chorus 2:
    Sally in the garden sifting, sifting,
    Sally upstairs with a hog-eyed man.

Sally will your dog bite? No sir, no,
Daddy cut his biter off a long time ago.

[repeat chorus 1]

    "Sally Goodin" was a popular dance and fiddle tune. The text is from The New Lost City Ramblers, Volume 2, Folkways FA 2397 (used by permission of Folkways Records).

SALLY GOODIN

A little piece of pie, a little piece of puddin;
Gonna give it all to my little Sally Goodin.

Going down the road, the road's mighty muddy,
So darn drunk, I can't stay steady.

    Uncle Dave Macon's rendition of "Whoop 'Em Up Cindy" is a country music gem from 1926. It was reissued on Vetco LP 105. The Ramblers' version is available on The New Lost City Ramblers, Volume 2, Folkways FA 2397 (used by permission of Folkways Records).

WHOOP 'EM UP CINDY

1 Went upon the mountain top, give my horn a blow,
  Thought I heard Cindy say, "Yonder comes my beau."

chorus:
    Whoop 'em up Cindy, Lord, Lord,
    I love Cindy, Lord, Lord,
    Whoop 'em up Cindy, Lord, Lord,
    Gone forever more.

2 Went upon the mountain top, cut my sugar cane,
  Every time I cut a stalk, thought about Cindy Jane.

3 Cindy she's a rattlin' girl, Cindy she's a rose,
  How I love Cindy girl, God almighty knows.

4 I got a girl in Baltimore, got one in Savannah,
  One in Baltimore name Lise, other little girl's
    named Hanna.

5 Higher up the mountain top, greener grow the
    cherries,

Sooner boys court the girls, sooner they get married.

6 Cindy in the summertime, Cindy in the fall,
   If I can't have Cindy all the time, don't want her at all.

Another lively tune with many variations is "Molly Put the Kettle On." It was recorded by numerous groups in the 1920's and 1930's including the Leake County Revelers, Ernest V. Stoneman and His Dixie Mountaineers, and the Skillet Lickers. The text is a collation of several versions including the one on The New Lost City Ramblers, Volume 2, Folkways FA 2397.

MOLLY PUT THE KETTLE ON

1 Molly put the kettle on,
  Sally blow the dinner horn;
  Molly put the kettle on
  We'll all take tea.

2 Swing Sal, swing that gal,
  Swing that gal with a run down shoe.

3 Swing maw, swing paw,
  Swing that gal from Arkansas;
  Take a piece of tobacco, swallow it all,
  Pull that calico from the wall.

4 Molly put the kettle on,
  Sally blow the dinner horn;
  Molly put the kettle on
  Daddy's come home.

An all-time favorite among the play-party and dance tunes is "Skip To My Lou." This is one I remember!

SKIP TO MY LOU

1 Lou, Lou, skip to my Lou,
  Lou, Lou, skip to my Lou,
  Lou, Lou, skip to my Lou,
  Skip to my Lou, my darlin'.

2 Lost my partner, what'll I do?
  Lost my partner, what'll I do?
  Lost my partner, what'll I do?
  Skip to my Lou, my darlin'.

3 Get me another one, pretty as you, (3X)
Skip to my Lou, my darlin'.

4 Little red wagon, painted blue, [!] (3X)
Skip to my Lou, my darlin'.

5 Flies in the buttermilk, shoo fly, shoo, (3X)
Skip to my Lou, my darlin'.

Another favorite is "Sourwood Mountain," with text
by North Carolina traditionalist Frank Proffitt from
Folk-Legacy FSA-1, Frank Proffitt (used by permission
of Folk-Legacy Records, Sharon, Conn.).

SOURWOOD MOUNTAIN

1 I've got a gal, she lives up in the holler,
    Ho de hum a doodle um a day;
She won't come and I ain't a-going to foller,
    Ho de hum a doodle um a day.

chorus:
    Chickens crowing on the Sourwood Mountain,
        Ho de hum a doodle um a day,
    Chickens crowing on the Sourwood Mountain,
        Ho de hum a doodle um a day.

2 The big girl'll court and the little girl'll
    slight you,
    Ho de hum a doodle um a day;
Big dog'll hunt and the little dog'll bite you,
    Ho de hum a doodle um a day.

3 Old man, old man, I want your daughter,
    Ho de hum a doodle um a day;
[spoken:] What do you want her for?
To bake my bread and to carry my water,
    Ho de hum a doodle um a day.

4 Get you a horse and put her up behind you,
    Ho de hum a doodle um a day;
Take her home and whip her till she minds you,
    Ho de hum a doodle um a day.

"The Old Soldier" is a fiddle tune with supple-
mental words that have little relationship to the dance.
Paul Clayton recorded an unusual variant that was traditional in his New England home. From Bay State
Ballads, Folkways FA 2106 (used by permission of Folkways Records).

257

THE OLD SOLDIER

1 Oh, there was an old soldier and he had a wooden
   leg,
   And he had no tobacco, no tobacco could he beg;
   Another old soldier just as sly as a fox,
   And he always had tobacco in his old tobacco box.

2 Said the one old soldier, "Won't you give me a
   chew?"
   Said the other old soldier, "I'll be derned if I
   do,
   Just save up your money and put away your rocks,
   And you'll always have tobacco in your old tobacco
   box."

3 So the one old soldier he was feeling might bad,
   He said, "I'll get even, I will begad."
   And so he grabbed a spike from out his wooden leg,
   And he grabbed the other soldier and he killed him
   dead.

4 Now there was an old hen and she had a wooden foot,
   And she made her nest by the mulberry root;
   She laid more eggs than any hen on the farm,
   And another wooden leg wouldn't do her any harm.

RELIGIOUS AND SPIRITUAL

In general, religious and spiritual folksongs ex-
hibit a vibrant emotionalism and a basic simplicity
rather than a complex philosophical narrative. They
range from unpretentious Shaker hymns to effervescent
revival music and black spirituals. Taken together the
music reflects the folk faith in the Judeo-Christian
concepts of love, understanding, compassion and salva-
tion.

One of the most expressive of the religious songs
was composed by a member of the Shaker faith around
1848. "Simple Gifts" has since entered the folk tradition and has been recorded by both folk and popular
artists. Text: The Golden Ring, Folk-Legacy FSI-16
(used by permission of Folk-Legacy Records, Sharon,
Conn.). For an authentic version by members of the
United Society of Shakers, Sabbathday Lake, Maine,
listen to Early Shaker Spirituals, Rounder Records 0078.

258

SIMPLE GIFTS

'Tis the gift to be simple,
'Tis the gift to be free,
'Tis the gift to come down
Where we ought to be.
And when we find ourselves
In the place just right,
It will be in the valley
Of love and delight.

When true simplicity is gained,
To bow and to bend
We will not be ashamed.
To turn, to turn
Will be our delight,
Till by turning, turning,
We come 'round right.

Howie Mitchell learned the words to "This Old World" from Bernie Lourie while attending Cornell University. Its message is universal. Text: Golden Ring, Folk-Legacy FSI-16 (used by permission of Folk-Legacy Records, Sharon, Conn.).

THIS OLD WORLD

This old world is full of sorrow,
Full of sickness, weak and sore.
If you love your neighbor truly,
Love will come to you the more.

We're all children of one Father,
We're all brothers and sisters too.
If you cherish one another,
Love and pity will come to you.

This old world is full of sorrow,
Full of sickness, weak and sore.
If you love your neighbor truly,
Love will come to you the more.

Frank Proffitt sang a secular song containing elements of the spiritual, "Man of Constant Sorrow." Source: Frank Proffitt, Folk-Legacy FSA-36 (used by permission of Folk-Legacy Records, Sharon, Conn.).

MAN OF CONSTANT SORROW

1 I am a man of constant sorrow,
  I've been in trouble all my days.

For six long years I've been a-rambling,
I don't have no parents left me now.

2 I'll take a trip on the northern railroad,
Perhaps I'll die upon that train.

3 Oh, I'm a man of constant sorrow,
Been in trouble all my days.
I bid farewell to my native country,
The place where I was borned and raised.

4 Oh, I bid farewell to my loved companions,
I know I'll never see you no more.
If in this world I never more see you,
I hope we'll meet on the beautiful shore.

5 Oh, I'm a man of constant sorrow,
Been in trouble all my days.

"Leaning On the Everlasting Arms" was sung by
Robert Mitchum in the 1955 motion picture The Night of
the Hunter, but it dates back to 1887. Text: Five Days
Singing, Volume I, Folk-Legacy FSI-41 (used by permission of Folk-Legacy Records, Sharon, Conn.).

LEANING ON THE EVERLASTING ARMS

What a fellowship, what a joy divine
Leaning on the everlasting arms.
What a blessedness, what a peace is mine,
Leaning on the everlasting arms.

chorus:
Leaning, leaning,
Safe and secure from all alarms,
Leaning, leaning,
Leaning on the everlasting arms.

What have I to dread, what have I to fear?
Leaning on the everlasting arms.
I have blessed peace with my Lord so near,
Leaning on the everlasting arms.

Oh, how sweet to walk in the pilgrim's way,
Leaning on the everlasting arms.
Oh, how bright the path grows from day to day,
Leaning on the everlasting arms.

The term "white spirituals" was coined by George
Pullen Jackson in his 1933 work, White Spirituals in
the Southern Uplands, to distinguish religious music in

260

the folk tradition from black spirituals. "Wondrous Love" is such a song. For the tune see: <u>Sing Out!</u>, Vol. 16, no. 1, Feb.-March, 1966, p. 33.

WONDROUS LOVE

What wondrous love is this, oh my soul, oh my soul;
What wondrous love is this, oh my soul!
What wondrous love is this,
That caused the Lord of bliss
To bear the dreadful curse for my soul, for my
soul.

When I was sinking down, sinking down, sinking
down;
When I was sinking down, sinking down;
When I was sinking down,
Beneath God's righteous frown,
Christ laid aside his crown for my soul, for my
soul,
Christ laid aside his crown for my soul.

And when from death I'm free, I'll sing on, I'll
sing on;
And when from death I'm free, I'll sing on;
And when from death I'm free,
I'll sing and joyful be,
And through eternity I'll sing on, I'll sing on,
And through eternity I'll sing on.

One technique used in early church singing was lining out: a church official would chant a line and the congregation would respond by singing it. The tradition probably originated during the American colonial period when the early hymnals, such as the <u>Bay Psalm Book</u> (1640), contained no printed musical score. New England Puritans deliberately omitted the music since they opposed instrumental music in church claiming that it was "popish" (Roman Catholic). Also, few people could read music anyway. For whatever reason, lining out became standard practice in most churches.

Betsy Rutherford provides a marvellous example of this technique on the primitive Baptist hymn "Amazing Grace." From <u>Traditional Country Music</u>, Biograph RC-6004.

AMAZING GRACE

1 Amazing grace how sweet the sound
  That saved a wretch like me;

I once was lost but now I'm found,
Was blind but now I see.

2 Was grace that taught my heart to fear
And grace my fears relieved;
How precious did that grace appear,
The hour I first believed.

3 Through many dangers, toils and snares,
I have already come;
Was grace that brought me safe thus far
And grace will lead me home.

4 When we think back ten thousand years,
Bright shining as the sun;
We know there's days to sing God's praise
Then when we first begun.

[repeat stanza one]

Lining out limited the artistic development of the congregation, so further techniques were required including the shape-note system of writing music. Each note in the scale was shaped differently for easy identification in the hymnals. The famous nineteenth century Sacred Harp hymnal used the following shapes:

| do | re | mi | fa | sol | la | ti | do |

For more information refer to the Sam Hinton article, "Folk Songs of Faith," in Sing Out! magazine.[1] The article prints an eighteenth century example of a shape-note hymn, "Windham." The best recorded collection of shape-note music is by George Pullen Jackson, Sacred Harp Singing, Library of Congress AAFSL11.

WINDHAM

Broad is the road that leads to death
And thousands walk together there;
But wisdom shows a narrow path
With here and there a traveller.

"The Hell Bound Train" has been collected in many different forms from bawdy to gospel, and from people

[1]Sing Out!, Vol. 16, no. 1, Feb.-March, 1966, pp. 31-37.

in various occupations from ranching to lumberjacking.
Frank Hutchison recorded a most unusual version in 1928
set to the tune of "Casey Jones." It was reissued on
Rounder 1007, Frank Hutchison.

THE HELL BOUND TRAIN

Come all you people if you want to hear
. A story about a bad engineer
Who run his train all down the road
And every car had a heavy load.

chorus:
 Jesus saves, glory hallelujah,
 Jesus saves, glory will come.
 Jesus saves, glory hallelujah,
 Mean to work for Jesus 'til my last work's done.

Boiler was loaded with whiskey and beer
And the Devil himself was the engineer;
Everybody seemed to be happy and gay
As the Hell bound train sped on its way.

Black and yaller, and red and white,
All mixed together, it was glorious sight;
Everybody seemed to be happy and gay
As the Hell bound train sped on her way.

"Sowing On the Mountain" is a traditional gospel
song in which the biblical warning of "fire next time"
takes on additional meaning in the nuclear age. The
text is similar to the singing of Woody Guthrie and
Cisco Houston on Lonesome Valley, Folkways FP 10 (FA
2010) (used by permission of Folkways Records).

SOWING ON THE MOUNTAIN

Sowing on the mountain,
Reaping in the valley;
Sowing on the mountain,
Reaping in the valley;
Sowing on the mountain,
Reaping in the valley,
You're gonna reap just what you sow.

God gave Noah the rainbow sign, (3X)
It won't be water, but fire next time.

Won't be water, but fire next time, (3X)
God gave Noah the rainbow sign.

Undoubtedly Texas-born Blind Willie Johnson was the finest of the black gospel singers of the late 1920's and early 1930's. Johnson developed a personal and vibrant style in his music. Three of his best songs follow, ending with "God Don't Never Change," his personal concept of Christianity. Texts: <u>Blind Willie Johnson</u>, Folkways RBF 10.

TROUBLE SOON BE OVER

chorus:
>Oh, trouble soon be over,
>Sorrow will have an end,
>Trouble soon be oh -
>Sorrow will have an end.

1 Well, Christ is my burden sharer,
He's ma only friend,
Early in my sorrow
He tole me be no end.

2 God is ma strong protection,
He's ma bosom friend,
Trouble rose around me
I know who'll take me in.

3 He proved a friend to David,
I heed him and I'll pray,
That same God that David save
Will yield me rest someday.

4 Well, though ma burden may be heavy
And almost crush me down,
Someday I'll rest with Jesus
And wear a starry crown.

5 I'll take this yoke upon me
And live a Christian life,
Take Jesus for ma saviour,
Ma burden will be light.

6 He proved a friend to David,
I heed him and I'll pray,
The same God that David save
Will yield me rest someday.

LORD, I JUST CAN'T KEEP FROM CRYING

chorus:
>Well, I just can't keep from cryin'
>Sometime,

264

Well, I just can't keep from cryin'
Sometime.
When my heart's full of sorrow
And my heart's filled with fear,
Lord, I just can't keep from cryin'
Sometime.

1 My mother often told me
Angels bonded your life away,
She said, "I wouldn't contemplate [?]
But trust in God and pray."
I'm on the King's highway,
I'm strugglin' every day.

2 My mother she's in her glory,
Thank God, I'm on my way,
Father he's gone too,
And sister she could not stay.
I'm trustin' Him every day
He will there my burden lay.

3 I thought when she first left me
I'd grieve a little while,
Soon it all would be over,
I'd join her with a smile.
But the thought as I grow older
I think of what I told her.

GOD DON'T NEVER CHANGE

chorus:
    Oh, God, God don't never change,
    He's God, always will be God.

1 God in the middle of the ocean,
God in the middle of the sea,
By the help of the great Creator
Truly been a God to me.

chorus:
    Oh, God, God don't never change,
    God, always will be God.

2 God in creation,
God when Adam fell,
God way up in Heaven,
God way down in Hell.

chorus:
    Praise God, God don't never change,
    Oh, always will be God.

3 Over to the mountain,
  Said how great I am,
  Want you to get up this mornin'
  Skip around like a lamb.

  chorus:
      God, God don't never change,
      Oh, always will be God.

4 God in the time of sickness,
  God is the doctor too,
  In the time of influenza
  He truly was a God to you.

  chorus:
      Well it's God, God don't never change,
      Praise God, always will be God.

5 God in the pulpit,
  God way down at the door,
  It's God in the amen corner,
  God's all over the floor.

  chorus:
      Well it's God, God don't never change,
      Oh, always will be God.

LOVE: TELLING IT LIKE IT IS

     Few traditional love songs express happiness and
contentment, rather they center around disillusionment,
loneliness and rejection. And that is what distinguish-
es them from the syrupy and hypocritical love songs
ground out by commercial composers. The folk know the
score in love as in so many other areas of life.

     This wisdom is apparent in "Black Is the Color,"
a masterpiece of the folk art. Betty Smith's version
is similar to the one Cecil Sharp collected in North
Carolina. From: Betty Smith, Folk-Legacy FSA-53 (used
by permission of Folk-Legacy Records, Sharon, Conn.).

BLACK IS THE COLOR

1 But black is the color of my true love's hair,
  His face is like some rosy fair.
  The prettiest face and the neatest hands,
  I love the ground whereon he stands.

266

2 I love my love and well he knows
  I love the ground whereon he goes.
  If you on earth no more I see,
  I can't serve you as you have me.

3 The winter's past and the leaves are green,
  The time is past that we have seen.
  And yet I hope the time will come
  When you and I shall be as one.

4 I'll go to the Clyde for to mourn and weep,
  But satisfied I never could sleep.
  I'll write to you in a few short lines,
  I'll suffer death ten thousand times.

5 My own true love, so fare you well,
  The time has past and I wish you well.
  And yet I hope the time will come
  When you and I shall be as one.

6 I love my love and well he knows
  I love the ground whereon he goes.
  The prettiest face and the neatest hands,
  I love the ground whereon he stands.

"Red Rosy Bush" is another example of plain old
loneliness. Guy Carawan recorded a fine version on his
Folkways album (FG 3548), but the text is from Betty
Smith, Folk-Legacy FSA-53 (used by permission of Folk-
Legacy Records, Sharon, Conn.).

RED ROSY BUSH

1 I wish I was some red rosy bush
  On a bank by the sea;
  And every time my true love passed by
  He would pick a rose off of me.

2 I wish I had a golden box
  To keep my true love in;
  I'd take him out and I'd kiss him twice,
  Then I'd put him right back again.

3 And if I lived in some lonesome holler
  Where the sun would never shine,
  And if my love loved another,
  Then he never would be mine.

4 Oh, don't you see yon lonesome dove?
  It flies from vine to vine;

267

He's mourning for his own true love,
Just as I do mourn for mine.

5 I wish I was some rosy bush
On a bank by the sea;
And every time my true love passed by
He would pick a rose off of me.

"Free a Little Bird" has a similar theme. It was recorded by the Allen Brothers in Atlanta, Georgia, in 1928, and reissued on Folk Variety Records FV 12501.

FREE A LITTLE BIRD

1 Just a free a little bird as I can be,
Just a free a little bird as I can be;
For I'm sitting on a hillside weeping all the day,
No sweetheart to grieve after me.

2 Oh, bring me a chair and I'll sit down,
Just a pen and ink I'll write it down;
And every line that I write down
I guess I'm going to the ground.

3 Oh, if I were a little bird
I would never build on the ground;
But I'd build my nest on my true lover's breast
Where the bad boys could not tear it down.

4 Oh, if I were a little fish
I would never swim in the sea;
But I'd swim in the brook where poor old Katy hung
her hook,
On the banks of the old Tennessee.

5 It is sweet to be drinking of ale,
It is sweet to be drinking of wine;
But the sweetest is to sit by that darling girl's
side
That stole away this tender heart of mine.

The female perspective is highlighted on "Single Girl." The Carter Family recorded the number in 1927 (reissued on Anthology of American Folk Music, Volume 3: Songs, Folkways FA 2953). The text by Frank Proffitt is more recent: Frank Proffitt, Folk-Legacy FSA-36 (used by permission of Folk-Legacy Records, Sharon, Conn.).

SINGLE GIRL

1 When I was single,
  Marriage I did crave;
  Now I am married,
  I'm troubled to my grave.
  Lord, I wish I was a single girl again.
  Lord, I wish I was a single girl again.

2 The dishes to wash,
  The spring to go to,
  Got nobody to help me,
  I've got it all to do.
  Lord, I wish I was a single girl again. (2X)

3 I took in some washing,
  I made a dollar or two;
  My husband went and stole it,
  I don't know what to do.
  Lord, I wish I was a single girl again. (2X)

4 Two little children
  Laying in the bed,
  Both of them so hungry
  They can't raise up their heads.
  Lord, I wish I was a single girl again. (2X)

Complaints by both sexes could be eliminated by simply taking the advice offered in "Bachelor's Hall." Learned by Paul Clayton from his great aunt, Mrs. William Tillson, he sings it on Bay State Ballads, Folkways FA 2106 (used by permission of Folkways Records).

BACHELOR'S HALL

1 A bachelor's hall is one of the best,
  Be drunk or be sober you're always at rest,
  No wife for to scold you, no children to squall,
  So happy's the man that keeps Bachelor's Hall.

  chorus:
      Singing, ho, row, row,
      Row, diddy oh.

2 A maid when she's single can live at her ease,
  Get up when she likes and sit down when she please,
  Get up when she likes and sit down on her throne,
  And eat her own cake be it raw or be done.

269

3 Needles and pins, needles and pins,
  When a man's married his troubles begin,
  His troubles and trials and that isn't all,
  It makes the gay spirit grow weary and small.

"Baldheaded End of the Broom" is another humorous
warning obviously written by an experienced husband.
Monroe Presnell recorded it for Sandy Paton on The Tra-
ditional Music of Beech Mountain, North Carolina,
Volume II, FSA-23 (used by permission of Folk-Legacy
Records, Sharon, Conn.).

BALDHEADED END OF THE BROOM

1 Oh, love is such a very funny thing,
  It catches the young and old.
  It's just like a plate of boarding [house] hash,
  And of a many a man it has sold.

2 It makes you feel like a fresh water eel,
  Causes your head to swell.
  You'll lose your mind, for love is blind,
  It empties your pocketbook as well.

  chorus:
      Oh, boys, stay away from the girls, I say,
      Oh, give them lots of room.
      They'll find you and you'll wed and they'll
          bang you till you're dead
      With the baldheaded end of the broom.

3 When a man is a-going on a pretty little girl,
  His love is firm and strong,
  But when he has to feed on hash,
  His love don't last so long.

4 With a wife and seven half-starved kids,
  Boys, I'll tell you it is no fun,
  When the butcher comes around to collect his debts
  With a dog and a double-barreled gun.

  chorus:

5 When your money is gone and your clothing in hock,
  You'll find the old saying it is true:
  That a mole on the arm's worth two on the legs,
  But [what is] he going to do?

6 With a cross-eyed baby on each knee
  And a wife with a plaster on her nose,

270

You'll find true love don't run so smooth
When you have to wear your second-hand clothes.

"I Wish I Was Single Again" should be the theme
song for complaining husbands. Paul Clayton sings it
on his album Unholy Matrimony, but the text is from
Carl Sandburg, The American Songbag (New York: Harcourt
Brace Jovanovich, Inc., 1955), p. 47.

I WISH I WAS SINGLE AGAIN

1 When I was single, O then, O then,
   When I was single, O then,
   When I was single, my money did jingle,
   I wish I was single again, again,
   And I wish I was single again.

2 I married me a wife, O then, O then,
   I married me a wife, O then,
   I married me a wife, she's the plague of my life,
   And I wish I was single again, again,
   And I wish I was single again.

3 My wife she died, O then, O then,
   My wife she died, O then,
   My wife she died, and then I cried,
   To think I was single again, again,
   To think I was single again.

4 I married another, the devil's grandmother,
   I wish I was single again,
   For when I was single, my money did jingle,
   I wish I was single again, again,
   I wish I was single again.

Through humor the folk cautioned young persons to
expect trouble in love and marriage. "East Virginia"
warns of unrequited love in a more tender way. The
text is from Logan English's Kentucky Folk Songs and
Ballads, Folkways FA 2136 (used by permission of Folkways Records).

EAST VIRGINIA

1 I was born in East Virginny,
   North Carolina I did go;
   Courted there a pretty fair maiden
   And her name I did not know.

2 Her hair it was of a light brown color,
   And her lips were rosy red;

On her breast she wore a white lily,
Many's the tears for her I've shed.

3 For in my heart I love her dearly,
At my door you're welcome in;
At my gate I'll run to meet you,
If your heart I could only win.

4 For I'd rather be in some lone holler
Where the sun don't never shine,
Than to think you're another man's darling
And to know that you'll never be mine.

5 For I'm going away to Alabamy,
Oh, it's for your sake must I go;
Must I go all broken-hearted
Like some poor little soldier boy?

[repeat stanza one]

"Little Rosewood Casket" carries the unrequited love theme to an extreme. Highly popular in North Carolina, the song was learned by a native, Betty Smith, from her father. Hear it on <u>Betty Smith</u>, Folk-Legacy FSA-53 (used by permission of Folk-Legacy Records, Sharon, Conn.).

LITTLE ROSEWOOD CASKET

1 There's a little rosewood casket
Setting on a marble stand,
And a packet of love letters
Written by a cherished hand.

2 Will you go and get them, sister?
Read them o'er and o'er to me,
For oft times I've tried to read them,
But for tears I could not see.

3 Last Sunday I saw him walking
With a lady by his side,
And I thought I heard him tell her
She could never be his bride.

4 When I'm dead and in my coffin,
And my shroud's around me bound,
And my narrow grave is waiting
In some lonesome churchyard ground.

5 Take his letters and his locket
Place together o'er my heart,

272

But the golden ring he gave me
From my finger never part.

"Little Maggie" claims the distinction of being
both a banjo tune and a drinking song, yet it is also
a farewell song. Monroe Presnell's version is from The
Traditional Music of Beech Mountain, North Carolina,
Volume II, Folk-Legacy FSA-23 (used by permission of
Folk-Legacy Records, Sharon, Conn.).

LITTLE MAGGIE

1 Wake up, wake up little Maggie,
  Why do you sleep so sound
  When the highway robbers are raging
  And the sun is almost down?

2 I wrote my love a letter,
  And this is the way it read:
  "My darling, I know you'll see trouble,
  But never hang down your head.
  Little Maggie, I know you'll see trouble,
  But never hang down your head."

3 The last time I seen little Maggie,
  She were a-standing in the door.
  Said, "Fare you well, loving Jimmy,
  I'll never see you any more.
  Oh, fare you well, little Jimmy,
  I'll never see you any more."

4 When I were crossing the cold, icy mountain,
  It was so chilly and cold.
  Fare you well, little Maggie,
  I'll never see you any more.

When love causes conflicts with parents, one
solution for the lovers is to leave home. This theme
is found in many love songs. Monroe Presnell had one
in his repertoire: "Johnny, Oh, Johnny." From The Traditional Music of Beech Mountain, Volume I, Folk-Legacy
FSA-22 (used by permission of Folk-Legacy Records,
Sharon, Conn.).

JOHNNY, OH, JOHNNY

1 Johnny, oh, Johnny, you are my darling,
  Like a red rose that grows in the garden.
  I'd rather have Johnny without one thing
  As to have any other with a thousand scarling.
    [sterling?]

2 It ain't the wind that blows so high,
  Nor neither rain that makes me cry.
  The whitest frost that ever fell,
  I love you, Johnny, but I dare not to tell.

2 My father he offers me a house and land,
  If I'll stay at home and do his command.
  But his command I will disobey,
  I'll follow you, Johnny, where you go or stay.

4 My mother she scorns both night and day,
  But she can scorn and scorn at leisure,
  The side of Johnny, I'll take my pleasure.

5 So fare you well, father, like-well, mother,
  Fare you well, sisters, fear no danger.
  I'll forsaken you all and go with a stranger.

The concluding song in this section is set to one
of the most exquisite melodies in all of folk music.
"Spanish Is a Loving Tongue" was written long ago by
cowboy Charles B. Clark. One version was popularized
by the polished art singer Richard Dyer-Bennett in the
1940's, and even Bob Dylan has recorded it. Bill
Staines sings the following variant on his Folk-Legacy
recording Just Play One Tune More, FSI-66 (used by permission of Folk-Legacy Records, Sharon, Conn.).

SPANISH IS A LOVING TONGUE

1 Spanish is a loving tongue,
  Soft as music, light as spray;
  'Twas a girl I learned it from,
  Living down Sonora way.

2 I don't look much like a lover,
  Yet I say her love words over
  Often when I'm all alone:
  "Mi amor, mi corazon."

3 On the nights that I would ride,
  She would listen for my spurs,
  Throw the big doors open wide,
  Raise those loving arms of hers.

4 How those hours would go a-flying,
  And, too soon, I'd hear her sighing
  In her little sorry tone:
  "Mi amor, mi corazon."

5 I ain't seen her since that night,
  I can't cross the line, you know;
  I'm wanted for a gambling fight,
  But, like as not, it's better so.

6 But I've always sort of missed her
  Since the last sad night when I kissed her,
  Left her heart and lost my own:
  "Adios, mi corazon,"
  Left her heart and lost my own:
  "Adios, mi corazon."

RAMBLING, GAMBLING AND DRINKING

An unusually large number of folksongs concern
themselves with rambling, gambling and drinking themes.
Why would sensible, hard working, god-fearing people be
attracted to such subjects and why would they admire, or
at least commiserate with, the central characters in
these songs? Is it because the songs offer escape from
the dull, routine life of the listeners? Is it because
the songs glamourize anti-establishment life styles?
Is it sympathy for the problems facing the central
characters in the songs and the realization that "there
but for the grace of God go I?" Undoubtedly all of
these factors are involved in the continuing popularity
of these songs.

From the first permanent settlement at Jamestown
to the present, the inhabitants of English-speaking
North America have been on the move. Rambling is an
American institution. Cisco Houston, an authentic roam-
er from the 1930's and 1940's, captured this essence in
"The Rambler." From 900 Miles and Other R. R. Songs,
Folkways FP 13 (used by permission of Folkways Records).
In 1972 Ry Cooder recorded it under the title "Boomer's
Story."

THE RAMBLER

1 Come and gather all around me,
  Listen to my tale of woe,
  Got some good advice to give you,
  Lots of things you ought to know.

2 Take a tip from one whose traveled
  And never stopped from rambling round,
  'Cause once you get the roaming fever
  Why, you never want to settle down,
  You never want to settle down.

3 I met a little gal in 'Frisco,
   Asked her if she'd be my wife,
   I told her I was tired of roaming,
   Goin' to settle down for life.

4 Then I heard the whistle blowin'
   And I knew it was a Red Ball train,
   And I left that gal beside the railroad
   And I never saw that gal again,
   I never saw that gal again.

5 Well, I travelled all over the country,
   I travelled everywhere,
   I've been on every branch line railroad,
   And I never paid a nickel fare.

6 I've been from Maine to Californy,
   And from Canada to Mexico,
   And I never tried to save no money,
   And now I've got no place to go,
   Now I've got no place to go.

7 Well, listen to a boomer's story,
   Pay attention to what I say,
   Well, I hear another train a-comin'
   And I guess I'll be on my way.

8 If you want to do me a favor
   When I lay me down and die,
   Just dig my grave beside the railroad
   So I can hear the trains go by,
   So I can hear the trains go by.

One of the most plaintive and beautiful folksongs
is "Wandering." Carl Sandburg printed two versions in
The American Songbag. Walt Robertson learned the
following from a worker in an Omaha meat-packing plant.
Source: American Northwest Ballads, Folkways FA 2046
(used by permission of Folkways Records)

WANDERING

1 I've been a-wandering early and late,
   New York City to the Golden Gate,
   And it looks like ain't never going to cease my
      wandering.

2 Been working in the army, working on a farm,
   All I got to show for it's just this muscle in my
      arm,

And it looks like ain't never going to cease my
   wandering.

3 There's snakes on the mountain, there's eels in the
      sea,
   Red-headed woman made this wreck out of me,
   And it looks like ain't never going to cease my
      wandering.

4 My daddy is an engineer, my brother drives a hack,
   Sister takes in washing and the baby balls the
      jack,
   And it looks like ain't never going to cease my
      wandering.

   Joe Hill was a songwriter for the radical labor
union, the Industrial Workers of the World, or Wobblies.
Active in the United States prior to World War I, the
union championed the cause of migratory workers, those
at the bottom of the work force. Hill's "The Tramp"
focused attention on the plight of these workers. Text:
The Songs of Joe Hill, sung by Joe Glazer, Folkways FP
39 (used by permission of Folkways Records).

                      THE TRAMP

1 If you will shut your trap
   I will tell you 'bout a chap
   That was broke and up against it and threadbare;
   He was not the kind that shirks,
   He was looking hard for work,
   But he heard the same old story everywhere.

   chorus:
       Tramp, tramp, tramp keep on a-tramping,
       Nothing doing here for you;
       If I catch you 'round again
       You will wear the ball and chain,
       Keep on tramping, that's the best thing you
           can do.

2 He walked up and down the street
   'Till the shoes fell off his feet;
   In a house he spied a lady cooking stew,
   And he said, "How do you do,
   May I chop some wood for you?"
   What the lady told him made him feel so blue.

3 Down the street he met a cop
   And the copper made him stop;
   And he asked him, "When did you blow into town?

Come with me up to the judge."
But the judge he said, "Oh, fudge,
Bums that have no money needn't come around."

4 Finally came the happy day
When his life did pass away,
He was sure he'd go to heaven when he died;
When he reached the Pearly Gate
Saint Peter, mean old skate,
Slammed the gate right in his face and loudly
    cried:

Appropriately enough, The New Lost City Ramblers
recorded "Rambler's Blues" on their Folkways album
Gone to the Country, FA 2491 (used by permission of
Folkways Records).

RAMBLER'S BLUES

chorus:
    I'm just a roaming rambler
    I'm always on the roam;
    I do my sleeping in an old haystack
    And a boxcar is my home.

1 Some folks they love their pleasure,
What pleasure do I see?
The only girl I ever loved
She's turned her back on me.

2 My mother she's in heaven
And daddy has gone there too,
And the reason that I ramble
Is because I'm lonesome and blue.

3 My rambling days are over,
I have no place to go
Until the angels call me
Over on the other shore.

"Acres of Clams" was written in the nineteenth
century by Judge Francis D. Henry, who titled it "The
Old Settler." Even though the hero of the song settles
down in the Puget Sound area of Washington, his philosophy, expressed in the last stanza, remains essentially that of a rambler. The tune is from the old
Irish song "Rosin the Beau," also used for the protest
songs "Hayseed Like Me" and "Lincoln and Liberty, Too"
(see protest section in Chapter Six). More recently
the theme and music of "Acres of Clams" was employed for
the anti-nuclear reactor song "It's the Nukes That Must

Go and Not Me." Walt Robertson sings "Acres of Clams" on <u>American Northwest Ballads</u>, Folkways FA 2046 (used by permission of Folkways Records).

ACRES OF CLAMS

1 I've travelled all over this country
  Prospecting and digging for gold,
  Tunneled, hydrauliced and cradled
  And I have been frequently sold.

2 For one who makes riches at mining
  Perceiving that hundreds grow poor,
  I made up my mind to try farming
  The only pursuit that is sure.

3 So I packed all my grub in a blanket
  And I left all my tools on the ground,
  Started right off for to shank it
  To the country they call Puget Sound.

4 Arriving dead broke in mid-winter,
  I found it enveloped in fog
  And covered all over with timber,
  Thick as hair on the back of a dog.

5 I tried to get out of that country
  Till poverty forced me to stay,
  Then I became an old settler,
  Now, nothing could drive me away.

6 So I staked out a claim in the forest
  And settled right down to hard toil,
  For two years I chopped and I labored
  But I never got close to the soil.

7 But now that I'm used to the climate
  I think that if man ever found
  A place to be peaceful and quiet,
  Then that place is on Puget Sound.

8 No longer a slave of ambition
  I laugh at the world and its shams,
  As I think of my happy condition
  Surrounded by acres of clams.

Charlie Poole's 1927 number "If I Lose, I Don't Care" combines rambling with a gambling theme (reissued on County Records 509). The text is from <u>The New Lost City Ramblers</u>, <u>Volume 5</u>, Folkways FA 2395 (used by permission of Folkways records).

IF I LOSE, I DON'T CARE

1 I can't walk, neither can I talk,
Just getting back from the state of old New York
One morning, before day.

   chorus:
      If I lose, let me lose,
      I don't care how much I lose,
      If I lose a hundred dollars while I'm trying to
         win a dime,
      For my baby she needs money all the time.

2 Now Flossie, oh, Flossie,
Now what is the matter?
I walked all the way from ol' Cincinnati
One morning, before day.

3 The blood it was a-running, and I was a-running
   too,
I give my feet good exercise, had nothing else to
   do
One morning, before day.

4 Now, see those girls, standing at the tanks,
Watching to catch the freight train they call Ol'
   Nancy Hanks
One morning, before day.

Charlie Poole's songs closely followed his life
style. His band was well named, The North Carolina
Ramblers, for Poole had a restless spirit and occasionally disappeared for as long as six weeks at a time.
He liked a good fight, hard liquor and cards. At their
first recording session in 1925, the Ramblers recorded
"Don't Let Your Deal Go Down." It became their best
seller (reissued on County Records 505). The text is
from The New Lost City Ramblers (Vol. 1), Folkways FA
2396 (used by permission of Folkways Records).

DON'T LET YOUR DEAL GO DOWN

1 Well, I've been all around this whole round world,
I've done most everything;
I've played cards with the king and the queen,
The ace, the deuce and the trey.

   chorus:
      Don't let your deal go down (3X)
      For my last gold dollar is gone.

2 Well, I left my little girl a-crying
   Standing in the door;
   She threw her arms around my neck
   Saying, "Honey, don't you go."

3 "Where did you get your high-top shoes
   And the dress that you wear so fine?"
   "I got my shoes from an engineer
   And my dress from a driver in the mines."

"The Prisoner's Dream" combines rambling, gambling and drinking themes. Originally recorded by the Allen Brothers in Atlanta in 1928, it was reissued on Folk Variety 12501.

THE PRISONER'S DREAM

1 Last night as I lay sleeping, I had a solemn dream;
   I dreamed I was in Michigan rolled out on Collins
       Street.
   I dreamed that my little darling had risen to my
       bail.
   I woke up broken hearted in a Hamilton County jail.

2 I used to be a pretty boy, I worked upon the
       square.
   I used to pocket money, but I did not pick it
       there.
   I travelled on my journey, I learned to rob and
       steal,
   And when I'd make a big haul, how happy I would
       feel.

3 My father was a gambler, he taught me how to play,
   To always have a hand with the aces, jacks and
       treys.
   The ace and deuce are high, low; the jack it stands
       for gain.
   Before I lose my money, I'll squabble in this game.

4 I used to wear a white hat, I rode a horse so fine.
   I used to court a pretty little girl and I always
       called her mine.
   I courted her for beauty 'till I found it was in
       vain.
   She sent me around to Nashville to wear the ball
       and chain.

5 Around came the jailer about nine o'clock,
   A bunch of keys was in his hand my cell door to
       unlock.

"Now hold up your hands, prisoner," I heard the
    jailer say;
"You're bound for the penintentiary for ten long
    years to stay."

6 Now, of all my mama's people, I love myself the
    best.
Well, lay off of life for me and the devil take
    the rest.
One pocket for corn whiskey, the other for rye,
Let's have a drink of high time before I go to die.

"Jack o' Diamonds" has been reported in both southern and western tradition and generally incorporates
floating stanzas from other songs. The following text
is an abridgment of a western version from Harry Jackson, The Cowboy, Folkways FH 5723 (used by permission
of Folkways Records).

                    JACK O' DIAMONDS

1 Jack o' Diamonds, Jack o' Diamonds,
  I know you of old,
  You robbed my poor pockets
  Of silver and gold.

2 For the work I'm too lazy
  And beggin's too low,
  Train robbin's too dangerous
  So to gamblin' I'll go.

3 My foot's in my stirrup
  My bridle in my hand,
  Farewell redhead Molly
  Your the damnedest in the land.

4 Your parents don't like me
  They say I'm too poor,
  They say I'm unworthy
  To enter your door.

5 They say I drinks whiskey,
  My money's my own,
  And them that don't like me
  Can leave me along.

6 Well, if the ocean was whiskey
  And I was a duck,
  I'd dive to the bottom
  And never come up.

                         282

But the ocean ain't whiskey
And I ain't no duck,
So I'll play Jack o' Diamonds
And then will get drunk.

8 Well, boast of your knowledge
And talk of your sense,
'Twill all be forgotten
A hundred years hence.

"Rye Whiskey" may be the best known drinking song
of all. Like "Jack o' Diamonds," it incorporates verses
from other songs. Compare stanza seven in the following
version with stanza six in the last song. The tune of
Frank Proffitt's variant is employed in other songs including "The Wagoner's Lad" and "At the Foot of Yonders
Mountain." From Frank Proffitt, Folk-Legacy FSA-1 (used
by permission of Folk-Legacy Records, Sharon, Conn.).

RYE WHISKEY

1 On top of yon mountain
I wandered alone,
Drunk as the devil
And a long ways from home

2 Rye whiskey, rye whiskey,
Rye whiskey I cry;
If I don't get rye whiskey
I surely will die.

3 I went on yon mountain,
I set on a log,
My liquor jug beside me
And sicker than a dog.

4 Poor drunkard, poor drunkard,
How bad I do feel;
Poor drunkard, poor drunkard,
How bad I do feel.

5 I'm a-going on yon mountain,
I'll build me a still;
I'll make you a gallon
For a two dollar bill.

6 [repeat stanza 4]

7 If the ocean was whiskey
And I was a duck,

283

I'd dive to the bottom
And drink my way up.

8 [repeat stanza 2]

The following two excerpts celebrate the making of
illegal liquor, or moonshine. "Real Old Mountain Dew"
is Irish, and "Good Old Mountain Dew" is the Southern
Appalachian equivalent. Complete versions can be heard
on Sam Hinton's The Wandering Folk Song, Folkways FA
2401 (used by permission of Folkways Records).

A - REAL OLD MOUNTAIN DEW

Let waters flow and breezes blow
In a free and easy way,
But give me enough of the real old stuff
That's made near Galway Bay.

And the peelers [police] all, from Donegal,
From Sligo and Leitrim too--
We'll give 'em the slip and take a sip
Of the real old mountain dew.

B - GOOD OLD MOUNTAIN DEW

There's an old hollow tree
Down the road here from me,
Where you lay down a dollar or two.
When you go round the bend,
Then you come back again,
There's a bucket of that good old mountain dew.

They call it that good old mountain dew,
And them that refuse it are few.
Shut up your mug
And they'll fill up your jug
With that good old mountain dew!

"Take a Drink On Me" is the low powered alcohol-
oriented variant of the high powered ode to cocaine
"Take a Whiff On Me." Mike Seeger, John Cohen and Tom
Paley sing it on The New Lost City Ramblers (Volume I),
Folkways FA 2396 (by permission of Folkways Records).

TAKE A DRINK ON ME

1 Now, what did you do with the gun in your hand?
  You give it to a rounder and he shot a good man.
  Oh, Lord, honey take a drink on me.

284

chorus:
>Take a drink on me, take a drink on me,
>All you rounders take a drink on me.
>Oh, Lord, honey take a drink on me.

2 If you keep on stalling, you'll make me think
Your daddy was a monkey and your mother was an ape.
Oh, Lord, honey take a drink on me.

3 You see that gal with a hobble on,
She's good looking as sure as sure's your born.
Oh, Lord, honey take a drink on me.

4 [repeat stanza 1]

When Frank Proffitt died in 1965 Sandy Paton wrote: "America lost one of her truly great traditional singers." Part of the Proffitt legacy is this tongue-in-cheek lament about the dangers of home-made "Blackberry Wine." From Frank Proffitt Memorial Album, Folk-Legacy FSA-36 (used by permission of Folk-Legacy Records, Sharon, Conn.).

BLACKBERRY WINE

1 Come all you young fellows and a story I'll tell
Of how the law caught me and put me in jail,
Then on to the chain gang to serve out my time,
Just 'cause I'd been making blackberry wine.

chorus:
>Blackberry wine, boys, was the cause of it all,
>>Oh, my Lord,
>Making blackberry wine was my downfall.
>They caught me on the mountain, on the Tennes-
>>see line.
>They took me to the chain gang for making
>>blackberry wine.

2 Now, when I was a young feller, I felt oh, so gay.
I went to the parties, to dances and plays.
I thought I could have me a lot better time,
So I got out and I made some blackberry wine.

3 I courted a little girl with hair golden brown.
I used to go see her when the sun was going down.
We'd take us a walk on the Tennessee line.
I'd sip me a sup of blackberry wine.

4 They held court one morning, my trial did begin.
I vainly looked around me for the face of a friend.

The judge he told me, "You've done a bad crime."
So he sent me to the chain gang for making black-
    berry wine.

5 Now them there rock piles they were piled up so
    high,
And I swore to my Lord I surely would die.
I hammered in that hot sun serving my time,
Just 'cause I'd been making blackberry wine.

6 I come back home, then to the church I did go.
The way people done me it hurt my heart so.
I could hear 'em a-whispering, "He went and done
    time.
He's the one they sent off for making blackberry
    wine."

7 I'm a-getting old now, my hair's turning grey.
It won't be too long till I'll be on my way.
They'll bury me on the mountain in a coffin of
    pine.
They'll say, "He's quit making that blackberry
    wine."

COUNTRY BLUES

The blues is a uniquely American art form. When
and where the blues began will never be pinpointed. All
that can be affirmed about the blues is that it was
created somewhere in the South sometime between the end
of the Civil War and the beginning of the Spanish-Ameri-
can War. It combines field hollers, slave and work
songs, and religious music into a twelve bar, three line
structure with flattened "blue" notes which gives the
blues its melancholy. What exactly is the blues? Paul
Oliver answers: "Seen from any point of view, the blues
is both a state of mind and a music which gives voice
to it. Blues is the wail of the foresaken, the cry of
independence, the passion of the lusty, the anger of the
frustrated and the laughter of the fatalist. It's the
agony of indecision, the despair of the jobless, the
anguish of the bereaved and the dry wit of the cynic."[1]
These traits have made the blues a universal music without regard to race, age, national origin or sex.

---

[1]From THE STORY OF THE BLUES by Paul Oliver; Copyright 1982, 1969. Reprinted with the permission of the
publisher, Chilton Book Company, Radnor, Pa., p. 6.

This study is restricted to the country blues: the music of blacks living in the rural southern United States. Much of it was recorded in the 1920's and 1930's by pioneer record companies seeking a market for what they eventually labeled "race records." In Chapter One I advised that folk music is not meant to be read, but heard. That comment is even more true for the blues. How can anyone read the hidden meanings and feelings in the songs of someone like Charley Patton or Henry Thomas? And how can anyone transcribe these melodies to the printed page? Fortunately, numerous re-issues of old blues discs are available to hear, through all the surface noise and distortion, just what the blues is all about.

Let those who experienced the blues define it for us. Four short examples from Alabama, 1915-16, were printed in Newman I. White, American Negro Folk-Songs (Cambridge: Harvard University Press, 1928), pp. 393-396.

A - BLUES AIN'T NOTHIN' BUT

De blues ain't nothing
But a poor man's heart disease.

B

When a man gets the blues, when a man gets the
    blues,
He jes' catches a train and rides;
When a man gets the blues, he catches a train and
    rides.
But when a woman gets the blues, she lays her
    little head and cries.

A blond woman, a blond woman,
Make a tadpole hug a whale,
A blond woman make a tadpole hug a whale;
But a dark-haired woman make you go right straight
    to jail.

C

Blues ain't nothin' but a good man feeling bad.

D

I got de blues
But I'm too damn mean to cry.

The music of Henry Thomas exemplifies the personal
nature of the blues. Thomas was born on a farm in Up-
shur County, Texas, in 1874. But farming was not for
him; he preferred a roving and rambling life style.
And wherever he went he sang blues, reels and rags,
accompanying himself on guitar and pan pipes. His music
bridges the gap between the blues and the pre-Civil War
field hollers and play-party songs. With Thomas, you
are listening to the beginning of the blues--almost.
In the first decade of the twentieth century most black
songs were one-verse songs: one verse repeated again
and again. Thomas' "Lovin' Babe" expands this concept
by fusing together a series of one-verse songs to pro-
duce a single unified mood. Henry Thomas, Herwin 209,
reissues all twenty-three songs recorded by Thomas
during 1927-29 and includes a fascinating account of the
search for information about the singer by Mack
McCormick.

LOVIN' BABE

1 Oh, lovin' babe I'm all out and down,
Lovin' babe I'm all out and down, (2X)
I'm laying close to the ground.

2 Look where the evening sun is gone,
Look where the evening sun's gone,
Look where that evening sun done gone,
Gone, God knows where.

3 It's the longest day, darling, ever I seen,
Yes, the longest day, honey ever I've seen,
Well, the longest day, honey, ever I seen,
The day Roberta died.

4 Just make me one pallet on your floor (2X)
Ah, make me a pallet on your floor,
Oh, make it so your husband never know.

5 That east-bound train come and gone, (3X)
Going to come no more.

6 Got the blues, darling, feeling bad,
Yeah, I got the worried blues feeling bad,
I got the blues, I'm feeling bad,
Feeling bad, God knows where.

7 Babe, I'm all out and down,
Ah, lovin' babe, I'm all out and down,
Lovin' babe I'm all out and down,
I'm laying to the ground.

8 St. Louis "Sun" come and gone, [a railroad train]
   Lord, east-bound "Sun" come and gone,
   Yes, the east-bound "Sun's" come and gone,
   Lovin' babe I'm all out and down.

9 Roberta baby's gone away,
   Yes, Roberta honey's gone away,
   Yes, Roberta babe gone away,
   She's going to come no more.

10 Rub me down on your floor,
   Yes, rub me down on your floor, (2X)
   Rub as though your man never know.

11 Mmmm, what have I done?
   Oh, lovin' babe what have I done?
   Lovin' babe what have I done?
   Honey babe you treating me wrong.

12 I'm going to come no more,
   Yes, I'm going away to come no more,
   I'm going away to come no more,
   Make me one more on your floor.

Henry Thomas' "Don't Ease Me In" contains a phrase
from a black work gang song dating to 1892 in Fayette
County, Texas. Again, Thomas takes us tantalizingly
close to the roots of the blues. Source: Henry Thomas,
Herwin 209.

DON'T EASE ME IN

1 Don't ease, don't you ease,
   Ah, don't you ease me in,
   It's all night, Cunningham, don't ease me in.
   Sometimes I walk, sometimes I talk,
   I never get drunk, thank God, til my bluebirds
      talk.

2 Don't ease, don't you ease,
   Don't you ease me in,
   It's all night long, Cunningham, don't ease me in.
   I beat my girl with a singletree,
   She heist up the window, sweet mama hollered,
      "Watch over me."

3 Don't ease, don't you ease,
   Ah, don't you ease me in,
   It's all night long, Cunningham, don't ease me in.
   I've got a girl, she's little and short,
   She leave here walking, lovin' babe, talking true
      love talk.

4 Don't ease, don't you ease,
  Ah, don't you ease me in,
  It's all night long, Cunningham, don't you ease me
      in.
  I was standing on the corner, talking to my brown,
  I turned around, sweet mama, I was workhouse bound.

5 Don't ease, don't you ease,
  Ah, don't you ease me in,
  It's all night long, Cunningham, don't you ease me
      in.
  Says, "I've got a girl and she working hard,"
  Says, "The dress she's wearing, sweet mama," says,
      "It's pink and blue."
  She brings me coffee and she brings me tea,
  She brings me everything 'cept the jailhouse key.

6 Don't ease, don't you ease,
  Ah, don't you ease me in,
  It's all night long, Cunningham, don't ease me in.
  Got these Texas blues, I got the Texas blues,
  It's all night long, Cunningham, don't leave me
      here.
  Says, "I looked down Main, old Ellum too,"
  Says, "All the women coming down Main had them
      Texas blues."

"Bull Doze Blues" by Thomas recalls the harsh days
following the Civil War. Southern whites, opposing the
nation's reconstruction policies, literally whipped
blacks into voting for the "correct" candidates. The
whipping was called a "bull-doze" ("dooze"). The tune
for the song was borrowed by the group Canned Heat for
their 1971 hit single "Going Up the Country." Source:
<u>Henry</u> <u>Thomas</u>, Herwin 209.

BULL DOZE BLUES

  I'm going away, babe, and it won't be long,
  I'm going away and it won't be long. (2X)
  Just as sure as that train leaves out of that
      Mobile yard. (3X)
  Come shake your hand, tell your papa goodbye. (3X)
  I'm going back to Tennessee,
  I'm going back to Memphis, Tennessee,
  I'm going back, Memphis, Tennessee.
  I'm going where I never get bulldozed,
  I'm going where never get the bulldoze,
  I'm going where I never get bulldozed.
  If you don't believe I'm sinking, look what a hole
      I'm in. (2X)

If you don't believe I'm sinking, look what a fool
    I've been.
Oh, my babe, take me back,
How in the world, Lord, take me back.

Charley Patton was born in the late 1880's near
Edwards, Mississippi. He sang the blues in juke joints
and influenced other delta bluesmen, including Willie
Brown and Son House. But try as hard as they could, no
one could capture successfully the rhythmic technique
of Patton. His guitar work and low, growling voice made
Patton truly a unique bluesman. "Down the Dirt Road
Blues" contains a commentary on life for blacks in the
Mississippi delta that rings true, at least for 1929
when Patton recorded it, "Every day seems like murder
here." Reissued on Charley Patton, Founder of the Delta
Blues, Yazoo L-1020.

DOWN THE DIRT ROAD BLUES

1 I'm goin' away to where I don't know, (2X)
  I'm worried now, but I won't be worried long.

2 My rider got somethin', she's tryin' to keep it
      hid,
  My rider got somethin', she try to keep it hid,
  Lord I got somethin' to find that somethin' with.

3 I feel like choppin' it, chips flyin' everywhere,
      (2X)
  I been to the Nation, Lord, but I couldn't stay
      there.

4 Some people say them overseas blues ain't bad,
  [spoken] My God, they aren't.
  Some people say them overseas blues ain't bad,
  [spoken] What was a-matter with 'em?
  It must not a-been them overseas blues I had.

5 Every day seem like murder here,
  [spoken] My God, I'm gonna stay around.
  Every day seem like murder here,
  I'm gonna leave tomorrow, I know you don't bid my
      care.

6 Can't go down this dirt road by myself,
  Can't go down the dirt road by myself,
  [spoken] My God, who you gonna carry?
  I don't carry my rider, gonna carry me someone
      else.

"A Spoonful Blues" is an example of erotic music
based on a tradition pre-dating the blues. On his 1929
recording Patton does not sing the word "spoonful" after
the first line, but instead utilizes the slide guitar
method to form the syllables. (Slide guitar is a playing technique using a bottleneck or ring of metal on one
finger which is slid along the strings creating a sort
of moveable fret.) Patton's style must be heard to be
appreciated on <u>Charley Patton</u>, Yazoo L-1020, a two record set.

A SPOONFUL BLUES

[spoken words in brackets]
[I'm got to jail about this spoonful]
An' all a spoon, aw that spoonful
Women goin' crazy every day in their life 'bout
    a...
It's all I want in this creation is a...
I go home [wanna fight] 'bout a...
Doctors dyin' [way in Hot Springs] just 'bout a...
These women goin' crazy every day in their life
    'bout a...
Will you kill my mandy?
["Yes, I will"] just 'bout a...
Oh babe, I'm a fool about my...
Hey baby, you know I need my...
It's mens on Parchman [done lifetime] just 'bout
    a...
Hey baby [you know I ain't long] about my...
All I want [honey in this creation] is a...
I go to bed, get up and wanna fight 'bout a...
["Looka here baby, would you slap me?" "Yes I
    will"] just 'bout a...
Hey baby [you know I'm a fool a...] 'bout my...
"Would you kill my man?" ["Yes I would, you know
    I'd kill him"] just 'bout a...
Most every man [that you see is] fool about his...
[You know baby, I need] that ol'...
Hey baby [I wanna hit the jug [judge?] on a] 'bout
    a...
["Baby, you gonna quit me?" "Yeah honey"] just
    'bout a...
It's all I want baby, this creation is a...
[Lookey here baby, I'm leavin' town] just 'bout
    a...
Hey baby [you know I need] that ol'...
[Don't make me mad baby] 'cause I want my...
Hey baby, I'm a fool about that...
[Lookey here honey] I need that...
Most every man lives without a...

[Some these days, you know I know they are] 'bout
     a...
Hey baby [I'm sneakin' around here] ain't got me
     a...
Oh that spoon..., hey baby, you know I need my...

The minstrel show and ragtime banjo player Papa
Charlie Jackson created a market for the country blues
with his 1924 recording of "Papa's Lawdy Lawdy Blues"
on Paramount Records. Four years before Patton's
session, Jackson recorded his variation of "Spoonful"
titled "All I Want Is a Spoonful." Reissued on Papa
Charlie Jackson, Biograph BLP-12042.

ALL I WANT IS A SPOONFUL

1 You can brown your gravy, fry your steak,
   Sweet mama, don't make no mistake,
   'Cause all I want, honey baby, just a spoonful,
      spoonful.

2 Just as sure as the winter follows the fall,
   There ain't no one woman got it all,
   'Cause all I want, honey baby, just a spoonful,
      spoonful.

3 When you've made a woman, you cain't understand
   If she's lookin' for you or a monkey man,
   'Cause all I want, honey baby, just a spoonful,
      spoonful.

4 Now t'you kind mama, say you needn't stall,
   Throw it out the winder, I'll catch it before it
      falls,
   'Cause all I want, honey babe, is a spoonful,
      spoonful.

5 I got the blues so bad I couldn't sleep at night,
   My cool kind mama want to fuss and fight,
   'Cause all I want, honey babe, is a spoonful,
      spoonful.

John Hurt was born in Teoc, Mississippi, in 1892.
He was known as a songster. A songster is someone who
does not restrict himself to a particular idiom, but
rather draws his music from many sources including dance
tunes and ballads as well as blues. Occasionally Hurt
recorded double-entendre blues such as "Candy Man
Blues," which can be heard on the Biograph reissue of
his 1928 recordings, Mississippi John Hurt, BLP-C4, as

293

well as on the bawdy anthology Party Blues, Melodeon
MLP-7324.

CANDY MAN BLUES

1 All you ladies all gather round,
That good big candy man's in town.

   chorus:
        It's the candy man,
        It's the candy man.

2 He's got stick candy just nine inches long;
He sells it fast [like] a hog'll chew his corn.

3 Overheard Mrs. Johnson say,
She always takes her candy stick to bed.

4 Don't stand close to the candy man;
He'll leave a big candy stick in your hand.

5 He sold the candy to sister Bad;
The very next day she took all he had.

6 If you tried candy with a friend of mine,
Sure will want it for a long, long time.

7 This stick candy don't melt away,
It just gets better so the ladies say.

   Hurt's double-entendre approach on "Candy Man
Blues" contrasts with the franker sexual verses employed by another Mississippian, Bo Carter (Bo Chatmon),
who delighted in recording "blue" blues. His sizzling
lyrics on "All Around Man" must have strained the limits
of censorship when the song was released in 1936. Reissued on Party Blues, Melodeon MLP-7324.

ALL AROUND MAN

1 Now I ain't no butcher, no butcher's son,
I can do your cuttin' until the butcher-man comes.

   chorus:
        'Cause I'm an all around man, oh I'm an all
            around man;
        I mean I'm a all around man,
        I can do 'most anything that comes to hand.

2 Now I ain't no plumber, no plumber's son,
I can do your screwin' 'till the plumber-man comes.

294

3 Now I ain't no miller, no miller's son,
  I can do your grindin' 'til the miller-man comes.

[spoken] Oh baby, you know I'm a all around man.

4 Now I ain't no milkman, no milkman's son,
  I can pull your titties 'til the milkman comes.

5 Now I ain't no spring-man, no spring-man's son,
  I can bounce your springs 'til the spring-man
      comes.

6 Now I ain't no auger-man, no auger-man's son,
  I can blow your hole 'til the auger-man comes.

An impressive Mississippi bluesman was Nehemiah
"Skip" James. His "Cypress Grove Blues" deals with
another major theme in the blues: rejected love. Ori-
inally recorded in 1931 on Paramount, the song was reissued on Skip James: Early Blues Recordings, 1931,
Biograph BLP-12029.

CYPRESS GROVE BLUES

1 I would rather be buried in some sack of gold (2X)
  To have some woman, Lord that I can't control.

2 And I'm goin' away now, goin' away to stay, (2X)
  I'll be all right pretty mama . . . .

3 When the sun go down you know what you brought on
      me? (2X)
  And what's the matter baby? I can't see.

4 I would rather be dead and six feet in my grave,
      (2X)
  Than to be way up here honey, treated this a-way.

5 And the old people told me baby, but I never did
      know, (2X)
  "The Good Book declare you got to reap just what
  you sow."

6 When your knee bone achin' and your body cold, (2X)
  Means you just gettin' ready honey, for the cypress
  grove.

The titan of the Texas bluesmen was Blind Lemon
Jefferson, born eighty miles south of Dallas in the mid-
1890's. He played for nickels and dimes on street cor-
ners, in bars, in bawdy houses, in railroad stations and

on passenger trains. His sensitive and wide ranging
vocal style, coupled with his poetical lyrics, was a
perfect match for his exquisite guitar technique. Many
have tried to copy his art form, but no one has been completely successful. Probably his best known number is
"See That My Grave Is Kept Clean." Reissues are plenti-
ful, including Blind Lemon Jefferson, 1926-1929,
Biograph BLP-12000.

SEE THAT MY GRAVE IS KEPT CLEAN

1 Well it's one kind favor I ask of you, (2X)
  Lord, it's one kind favor I ask of you,
  See that my grave is kept clean.

2 It's a long lane that's got no end, (3X)
  It's so bad when the devil came.

3 Lord, it's two white horses in a line, (3X)
  Gonna take me to my burying ground.

4 My heart stopped beating and my hands got cold,(3X)
  It was a long journey I been told.

5 Have you ever heard a coffin sound? (3X)
  Then you know that the poor boy's in the ground.

6 Oh, dig my grave with a silver spade, (3X)
  You may leave me down with a golden chain.

7 Have you ever heard a church bell tone? [toll] (3X)
  Then you know that the poor boy's dead and gone.

Jefferson's "War Time Blues" contains classic blues
lines. From Son House--Blind Lemon Jefferson, Biograph
BLP-12040.

WAR TIME BLUES

1 What you gonna do when they send your man to war?
  What you gonna do--send your man to war?
  What you gonna do when they send your man to war?
  I'm gonna drink muddy water, gonna sleep in a
    hollow log.

2 I ain't got nobody, I'm all here by myself,
  Got nobody, all here by myself. (2X)
  Oh, these women don't care, but the men don't need
    me here.

3 Well I'm going to the river gonna walk it up and
      down,
   Going to the river, walk it up and down. (2X)
   If I don't find Corinna, I'm gonna jump overboard
      and drown.

4 If I could shine my light like a headlight on some
      train,
   If I could shine like a headlight on some train,
      (2X)
   I would shine my light and call a real train.

5 Well they tell me that southbound train had a wreck
      last night,
   Lord, that southbound train had a wreck last night.
      (2X)
   Listen here section foreman, they ain't treating
      your railroad right.

6 Well the gal I love and the one I crave to see,
   Woman I love, one I crave to see,
   Woman I love, and the one I crave to see.
   Well she's living in Memphis and the fool won't
      write to me.

7 I said, "Little woman what have I said and done?
   Hey, mama, what I said and done?
   Hey, mama, what have I said and done?
   You treat me like my trouble has just begun."

Ramblin' Thomas was another Texan with an intense-
ly personal delivery as well as a superb slide guitar
technique which he displayed on "No Job Blues," recorded in 1928 and reissued on Ramblin' Thomas, Biograph
BLP-12004.

                    NO JOB BLUES

1 I've been walkin' all day and all night too, (2X)
   'Cause my meal ticket woman have quit me and I
      can't find no work to do.

2 I's pickin' up the newspaper and I lookin' in the
      ads, (2X)
   And the policeman came along and arrested me for
      vag. [vagrancy]

3 Now boys you ought to see me in my black and white
      suit, (2X)
   It won't do.

                       297

4 I asked the judge, "Judge what may be my fine?"(2X)
   He said, "Get your pick and shovel and get down in
      mine."

5 I'm a poor black prisoner working in the ice and
      snow, (2X)
   I got to get me another meal ticket woman so I
      won't have to work no mo'.

Blind Blake was the Paramount label's most commer-
cially successful blues and ragtime virtuoso of the
1920's and early 1930's. His recorded legacy of over
seventy sides has influenced black and white musicians
ever since. Blake's relaxed, yet sophisticated, musical style is in sharp contrast to the primitive Missis-
ippi sound of that same era. His two-part "Rope
Stretchin' Blues" from 1931 combines humor and satire
within the framework of a rejected love theme.

ROPE STRETCHIN' BLUES

1 I caught a stranger in my house and I busted his
      head with a club. (2X)
   I lay 'm in my coal with his heels in a tub.

2 I seen the sheriff comin' and I jumped for the
      door. (2X)
   But I jumped too late, the sheriff had done jumped
      before.

3 They buried the man Thursday, just two short days
      you see. (2X)
   And it makes me wonder what they gonna do to me.

4 I killed a man and that's the how and how. (2X)
   I'm sittin' here wonderin' if a woman's worth it
      now.

5 Mmmmm, rope stretchin' all day long, (2X)
   In just a few more days I won't be able to sing my
      song.

6 Don't trust no woman who mistreats a man. (2X)
   When you think she's in your kitchen cookin', she's
      got a stranger by the hand.

7 Ain't no need of you chasin' women, brother, if you
      really haven't got the cash. (2X)
   Other men get all the chicken and all you get is
      ham.

8 I have a lot of women, but I sure don't want none
      now. (2X)
   She always milk me dry, [babe have you] ever milk-
   ed a cow?

9 Mmmmm, rope stretchin' all day long. (2X)
   I'm singin' now mama, because it won't be long.

10 It wouldn't be so bad, if the rope would just get
      slack. (2X)
   I wouldn't mind at all but I just got a crick in
   my back.

11 When it's all over mama, and you're all alone by
      my side, (2X)
   Just keep the flies from buzzin' by me and then I
   will be satisfied.

Blake's "Georgia Bound" mixes black and white
country lyrics together in a musical arrangement of a
traditional blues tune. The last two blues were reissued on Rope Stretchin' Blues--Blind Blake, Volume 4,
Biograph BLP-12037.

GEORGIA BOUND

1 Packin' up my duffle, gonna leave this town. (2X)
   And I'm gonna hustle to catch that train southbound.

2 I got the Georgia blues for the plow and hoe. (2X)
   Walked out my shoes over this ice and snow.

3 Tune up the fiddle, dust the cat 'n bow. (2X)
   Put on the griddle, and open the cabin door.

4 I thought I was goin' to the northland to stay.(2X)
   South is on my mind, my blues won't go away.

5 Potatoes in the ashes, possum on the stove, (2X)
   You can have the hash but please leave me the claw.

6 Chicken on the roofin', melon on the vine,
   Chicken on the roofin', big watermelon on the vine,
   I'll be glad to get back to that Georgia gal of
      mine.

Peg Leg Howell was a bootlegger and ex-convict who
was discovered singing in a street band in Atlanta by a
recording company scout. Like Blind Blake, Howell's
repertoire included various musical forms, but his blues

best exposed his innermost feelings. "Low Down Rounder Blues" from 1928 is an autobiographical gem. Reissued on The Country Blues, RBF, RF-1.

LOW DOWN ROUNDER BLUES

1 Just a worried old rounder, just a troublesome
    mind, (2X)
  All bundled up from hardship, fate has to me been
    unkind.

2 I wouldn't listen to my mother, wouldn't listen to
    my dad. (2X)
  By my reckless livin' I put myself in bad.

  [spoken:] I wouldn't listen to nobody. . . . Did-
  n't hear what nobody said. Mama talked to me all
  the time, but I just wouldn't have listened to her.

3 I ain't trustin' nobody, I'm 'fraid of myself. (2X)
  I've been too low down like'a put on the shelf.

4 My friends has turned against me, smilin' in my
    face, (2X)
  Since I been so disobedient I must travel in
    disgrace.

5 I cannot shun the devil, he stays right by my
    side. (2X)
  There is no way to cheat him, I'm so dissatisfied.

6 Ain't nobody wants me, they wouldn't be in my
    shoes. (2X)
  I feel so disgusted, I got those low down rambler
    blues.

BLIND LEMON JEFFERSON

NEW GOLDEN RING
Photo by Ann Mitchell   Courtesy Folk-Legacy Records

PETE SEEGER
Photo by Marty Gallanter   Courtesy Harold Leventhal Management

302

CHAPTER SIX

SONGS: WORK AND STRUGGLE

Two important areas in the study of folk music conclude this survey: work songs and songs of struggle or protest. Both subjects generally have been neglected by collectors and scholars who believed the songs were of little importance, or were offensive, or lacked literary merit. Yet to the social historian the music provides an opportunity to study the thoughts and attitudes of people who otherwise have had little input into the traditional histories of a nation.

Sea shanties and black work gang songs comprise a surprising proportion of North American work songs. Both types are truly the music of the people and by the people, for they were sung "on location" by groups of workers as they performed their back-breaking chores in the days prior to the introduction of labor-saving machinery. Sailors hoisting heavy sails on whaling ships and gandy dancers laying track for railroads required some kind of a rhythmic pattern or beat in order to perform their task in unison with a minimum of effort and a maximum of force. Work songs provided that beat and the shantymen on ships and the rhyming leaders of work gangs were essential to revive spirits, restore energy and ensure laughter in spite of the tedious tasks and harsh surroundings.

WORK: SEA SHANTIES

Sea shanties, or chanteys, date back in print to the eighteenth century and evidence exists that they are much older. Shanties can be divided roughly into three categories: short-haul, halyard and capstan. Each one refers to a specific type of motion or action needed to perform a shipboard task. Short-haul shanties were sung when just a few short pulls or hauls on the rope were needed to take in or set sails. Halyard shanties were sung when prolonged pulling on the ropes or halyards was necessary to hoist the main sails or when casting the anchor. Capstan, or windlass, shanties were longer and more elaborate in order to meet the time requirements for hoisting anchors or manning pumps.

Songs of another kind, forecastle or mainhatch, were sung when the sailors were off-duty and needed a diversion. These songs included some of the same type

as non-seafaring folk sang, as well as nautical compo-
sitions, such as homeward-bound songs.

"Boney," a condensed history lesson describing the
career of Napoleon Bonaparte, was a favorite short-haul
shanty sung on board both British and American merchant-
men. Sam Eskin collected the following version and included it on Loggers' Songs and Sea Shanties, Folkways
FA 2019 (used by permission of Folkways Records).

BONEY

1 [shantyman] Boney was a warrior
  [chorus]   Away who ya!
  [shantyman] A warrior, a tarrier,
  [chorus]   John Franswar.

[repeat chorus as above on following stanzas]

2 Boney beat the Prooshians
  And then he fought the Rooshians,

3 Moscow was a blazing
  And Boney was a-raging,

4 Boney went to Waterloo
  And there old Boney's chance was through,

5 Boney broke his heart they say
  Down in St. Helena way,

"Haul On the Bowlin'" is an ancient short-haul
shanty. The pull comes on the word "haul" at the end
of each verse. This version is from several sources including an out-of-print recording by A. L. Lloyd and
Ewan MacColl.

HAUL ON THE BOWLIN'

1 Haul on the bowlin', the bully ships a-rollin',
  Haul on the bowlin', the bowlin', haul. [repeat at
    end of each stanza]

2 Haul on the bowlin', Kitty is my darlin',

3 Haul on the bowlin', Kitty comes from Liverpool,

4 Haul on the bowlin', it's a far cry to paradise,

5 Haul on the bowlin', we'll hang for finer weather,

"Blow the Man Down" is one of the oldest and best examples of a halyard shanty. It has many variations, some bawdy, and was composed originally by Irish sailors working on packet ships of New York's Black Ball Line which began regularly scheduled passenger and mail service to England in 1818. Paul Clayton sings this version on Bay State Ballads, Folkways FA 2106 (used by permission of Folkways Records).

BLOW THE MAN DOWN

chorus:
> Oh, blow the man down, bullies, blow the man
> down,
> To me way, hey, blow the man down,
> When Captain O'Bigsby commands the Black Ball,
> Give me some time to blow the man down.

1 Come all you young fellows that follow the sea,
To me way, hey, blow the man down,
Please pay attention and listen to me,
Give me some time to blow the man down.

2 As I was a-walking down Paradise Street,
To me way, hey, blow the man down,
A saucy young maiden I chanced for to see,
Give me some time to blow the man down.

3 I hailed her in English, I hailed her all 'round,
To me way, hey, blow the man down,
Ship ahoy, ship ahoy, Lass, where are you bound?
Give me some time to blow the man down.

4 I'm a Flying Fish sailor just home from Hong Kong,
To me way, hey, blow the man down,
Give me some whiskey, I'll sing you a song,
Give me some time to blow the man down.

5 On a trim Black Ball liner I first served my time,
To me way, hey, blow the man down,
On a trim Black Ball Liner I wasted my prime,
Give me some time to blow the man down.

6 It's attention to orders to you one and all,
To me way, hey, blow the man down,
For there right above you there flies the Black
Ball,
Give me some time to blow the man down.

7 Come quickly aloft to the break of the poop,
To me way, hey, blow the man down,

Or I'll help you along with the toe of my boot,
Give me some time to blow the man down.

Although sailors preferred "the demon rum" to other
beverages, "Whiskey Johnny" was a popular halyard
shanty. The sailors generally sang it while hoisting
the mizen topsail. It was clearly an "apple-polishing"
shanty designed to extract a ration of rum from the
captain. Text: Bay State Ballads, Folkways FA 2106
(used by permission of Folkways Records).

WHISKEY JOHNNY

1 Oh, whiskey is the life of man,
  Whiskey Johnny;
  Oh, whiskey is the life of man,
  Whiskey for me Johnny.

2 Oh, whiskey killed me poor old dad,
  Whiskey Johnny;
  And whiskey drove me mother mad,
  Whiskey for me Johnny.

3 Oh, whiskey made me tear my clothes,
  Whiskey Johnny;
  And whiskey gave me this red nose,
  Whiskey for me Johnny.

4 Oh, I drink whiskey when I can,
  Whiskey Johnny;
  And whiskey from an old tin can,
  Whiskey for me Johnny.

5 Oh, whiskey straight, and whiskey strong,
  Whiskey Johnny;
  You give me grog, I'll give you a song,
  Whiskey for me Johnny.

6 I thought I heard the old man say,
  Whiskey Johnny;
  I'll treat my crew in a decent way,
  Whiskey for my Johnny.

7 A glass of grog for every man,
  Whiskey Johnny;
  And a bottle for the shantyman,
  Whiskey for my Johnny.

8 Oh, whiskey is the life of man,
  Whiskey Johnny;

Oh, I drink whiskey when I can,
Whiskey for my Johnny.

"Reuben Ranzo," sung when hauling the topsail haly-
yards, was one of the few work songs used aboard
whalers. The text is from the excellent seafaring album
Heart of Oak!, Folkways FTS 32419, as sung with gusto
by the X Seamens Institute (used by permission of Folkways Records).

REUBEN RANZO

1 Poor old Reuben Ranzo,
  Ranzo, me boys, Ranzo,
  Poor old Reuben Ranzo,
  Ranzo, me boys, Ranzo.

[repeat lines 2 and 3 in the following stanzas]

2 Oh, Ranzo was no sailor,
  He was a New York tailor.

3 Oh, Ranzo was no sailor,
  But they shipped him aboard of a whaler.

4 Now Ranzo was no beauty,
  And he would not do his duty.

5 So they give him lashes thirty,
  Because he was so dirty.

6 But the captain's daughter Suzy,
  She begged her dad for mercy.

7 Well she give him wine and water,
  And a bit more that she oughter.

8 She give him an education,
  And she taught him navigation.

"Shenandoah" may well be the most popular of the
capstan shanties in the United States. It originated
as a land ballad among frontiersmen in North America
and traveled down the rivers to the waterfronts of Mo-
bile and New Orleans where blacks adapted the music for
their work of servicing ships. Gulf port sailors, by
emphasizing the chorus lines, transformed it into a slow
capstan shanty. In the late 1960's Jack Stanesco learned a version from West Indian whalers which he included
on Five Days Singing, Volume I, Folk-Legacy FSI-41. The
text is by Allan Mills from Songs of the Sea, Folkways

307

FA 2312 (used by permission of Folkways Records).

SHENANDOAH

1 Oh, Shenandoah, I long to hear you,
Away, you rolling river,
Oh, Shenandoah, I long to hear you,
Away we're bound to go, 'cross the wide Missouri.

[repeat lines 2 and 4 in the following stanzas]

2 Oh, Shenandoah, I love your daughter,
Oh, Shenandoah, I love your daughter,

3 Oh, Shenandoah, I took a notion,
To sail across the stormy ocean,

4 'Tis seven long years since last I see thee,
'Tis seven long years since last I see thee,

5 Oh, Shenandoah, I long to hear you,
Oh, Shenandoah, I long to hear you,

The capstan shanty "Santy Anna" has turned history upside down. In the first place, the United States force under General Zachary Taylor easily captured Monterrey while General Santa Anna was still an exile in Cuba. When Santa Anna returned to regain the Mexican presidency, he led a superior force against Taylor at Buena Vista, but was repulsed by "Old Rough and Ready." Nevertheless, most versions of the shanty emphatically declare the Mexican leader as the victor, including the following from Songs of the Sea, FA 2312 (used by permission of Folkways Records).

SANTA ANNA

1 Oh, Santy Anna gained the day,
Hooray, Santy Anna!
Oh, Santy Anna gained the day,
All on the plains of Mexico!

[repeat lines 2 and 4 in the following stanzas]

2 Oh, Gen'ral Taylor ran away,
He ran away at Monterrey,

3 Oh, Santy Anna fought for fame,
And that's where Santy gained his name,

308

4 Oh, Santy Anna fought for gold,
  And the deeds he done have oft been told,

5 Oh, Santy Anna's day is o'er,
  And Santy Anna will fight no more,

6 Oh, Santy Anna won the day,
  And Gen'ral Taylor ran away,

"South Australia" probably originated as a California gold rush song. It was transformed into a shanty on board clipper ships plying the waters between Britain and Australia in the 1870's. The text is from Heart of Oak!, Folkways FTS 32419 (used by permission of Folkways Records).

SOUTH AUSTRALIA

1 In South Australia I was born,
  To me heave away, to me haul away.
  In South Australia round Cape Horn,
  We're bound for South Australia.

[repeat lines 2 and 4 in the following stanzas]

chorus:
    Haul away your rolling king,
    Haul away you'll hear me sing.

2 As I walked out one morning fair,
  T'was there I met Miss Nancy Blair,

3 I shook her up, I shook her down,
  I shook her round and round and round,

4 I run her all night, I run her all day,
  I run her before we sailed away,

5 There ain't but one thing grieves me mind,
  To leave Miss Nancy Blair's behind,

6 And as we walloped around Cape Horn,
  I wished to Christ I was never born,

7 I wish I was on Australia's strand,
  With a bottle of whiskey in me hand,

"Cape Cod Girls" is a derivitive of "South Australia," thus making it a late entry in the capstan shanty category. Paul Clayton learned the song while growing up in the former whaling town of New Bedford,

309

Massachusetts. He sings it on Bay State Ballads, Folkways FA 2106 (used by permission of Folkways Records).

CAPE COD GIRLS

1 Cape Cod girls they have no combs,
  Heave away, heave away;
  They comb their hair with codfish bones,
  We are bound for Australia.

  [repeat lines 2 and 4 in the following stanzas]

  chorus (1):
      Heave away my bully, bully boys,
      Heave away and make a lot of noise.

2 Cape Cod boys they have no sleds,
  They slide down hill on codfish heads,

  chorus (2):
      Heave away my bully, bully boys,
      Heave away and don't you make a noise.

  [alternate choruses with remaining stanzas]

3 Cape Cod cats they have no tails,
  They blew away in heavy gales,

4 Australia is a very fine place,
  To come from there is no disgrace,

5 Australian girls are very fine girls,
  No codfish bones tucked in their curls,

"Clear the Track and Let the Bulgine Run" was of
Irish-Negro origin. The lyrics were from black sources:
"bulgine" meant "engine" among blacks. The tune was
from the Irish song "Shule Agra." The lively shanty was
recorded by Sam Eskin on Loggers' Songs and Sea
Shanties, Folkways FA 2019 (used by permission of Folkways Records).

CLEAR THE TRACK AND LET THE BULGINE RUN

1 Oh, the smartest clipper you can find,
  Oh, ho, way ho, are you most done?
  Is the Marg'et Evans of the Blue Cross Line,
  So clear the track let the bulgine run.

  [repeat lines 2 and 4 in the following stanzas]

chorus:
      To me hey rig-a-jig in a jaunting car,
      With Liza Lee all on my knee.

2 Oh, the Marg'et Evans of the Blue Cross Line,
  She's never a day behind her time,

3 Oh, when I come home across the sea,
  It's Liza you will marry me,

Forecastle (fo'c's'le) or mainhatch songs were sung
by sailors in their off-duty hours. They sang both
landlubber and seafaring songs and ballads. One of
their favorites was "The Flying Cloud" (see Chapter
Three). Both whalers and merchant seamen also enjoyed
"Blow Ye Winds" ("The New Bedford Whalers"). Text:
Songs of the Sea, Folkways FA 2312 (used by permission
of Folkways Records).

BLOW YE WINDS

1 'Tis advertised in Boston
  New York and Buffalo,
  Five hundred brave Americans
  A-whaling for to go.

chorus:
      Singing blow ye winds in the morning,
      Blow ye winds heigh-ho,
      Clear away your running gear
      And blow ye winds heigh-ho.

2 They send you to New Bedford
  That famous whaling port,
  And give you to some land-sharks
  To board and fit you out.

3 They tell you of the clipper ships
  A-going in and out,
  And say you'll catch five hundred whales
  Before you're six months out.

4 It's now we're out to sea, my boys,
  The wind comes on to blow,
  One half the watch is sick on deck
  The other half below.

5 The skipper's on the quarter deck
  A-squinting at the sails,
  When up aloft the lookout sights
  A mighty school of wales.

311

6 Now clear away the boats, my boys,
  And after him we'll travel,
  But if you get too near his tail
  He'll kick you to the devil.

7 Oh, first we turn him over
  Then we tow him alongside,
  Then over with our blubber-hooks
  And rob him of his hide.

8 Then comes the stowing down, my boys,
  We work both night and day,
  And we'll get fifty cents apiece,
  Ain't that a handsome pay!

9 Our ship is full, we're homeward bound
  And soon we're through with sailing,
  A friendly glass around we'll pass
  And blast this blubber whaling!

The whaling ship "The Diamond" put out to sea in 1825; five years later it sank, along with twenty other vessels, crushed by ice in the Arctic Ocean. Did the composer of the following forecastle song perish with his ship? It is sheer speculation. From Heart of Oak! Folkways FTS 32419 (used by permission of Folkways Records).

THE DIAMOND

1 The Diamond is a ship me lads,
  For the Davis straits she's bound.
  And the pier it is all garnished
  With bonnie lasses round.

2 Captain Thompson gives the order
  To sail the ocean wide.
  Where the sun it never sets me lad,
  Nor darkness dims the skies.

  chorus:
        So its cheer up me lads
        Let your hearts never fail,
        For the bonnie ship the Diamond
        Goes a-fishin' for the whale.

3 It's on the quay at Peterhead
  The lassies stand around.
  Shawls all wrapped around their head,
  And salt tears runnin' down.

312

4 Don't you weep me bonnie lass
  Though you be left behind.
  For the rose will grow on Greenland's shore
  Before we change our mind.

5 Here's a health to the Resolution,
  Likewise the Eliza Swan.
  Here's a health to the Battler of Montrose
  And the Diamond ship of fame.

6 We wear the jackets of the white
  The trousers of the blue.
  When we get back to Peterhead
  We'll have sweethearts enoo.

7 It'll be bright both day and night
  When the bonnie lads come home,
  With a ship that's full of oil me boys,
  And money to their name.

8 They'll make the cradles for to rock,
  The blankets for to tear.
  And all the girls in Peterhead
  Sing hush a bye my dear.

Two favorite homeward-bound songs were "Rolling
Home" and "Goodbye, Fare You Well." English sailors
preferred the first song; Americans, the second.
"Rolling Home" uses an old Irish air generally associ-
ated with rebel songs such as "Kevin Barry." "Goodbye,
Fare You Well" is both a capstan shanty and a forecastle
song; the version which follows is from the singing of
West Indian whalers in the 1960's. Both texts are from
Five Days Singing, Volume II, Folk-Legacy (used by per-
mission of Folk-Legacy Records, Sharon, Conn.).

ROLLING HOME

1 Call all hands to man the capstan,
  See the cable running clear;
  Heave away and with a will, boys,
  For New England we will steer.

    chorus:
        Rolling home, rolling home,
        Rolling home across the sea,
        Rolling home to old New England,
        Rolling home, dear land, to thee.

2 Fare you well, you Spanish maidens,
  It is time to say adieu.

Happy times we've spent together,
Happy times we've spent with you.

3 'Round Cape Horn one frosty morning,
And our sails were full of snow,
Clear your sheets and sway your halyards,
Swing her out and let her go.

4 Up aloft amid the rigging
Blows a wild and rushing gale,
Like a monsoon in the springtime,
Filling out each well-known sail.

5 And the waves we leave behind us,
Seem to murmur as they flow,
There's a hearty welcome waiting
In the land to which you go.

6 Many thousand miles behind us,
Many thousand miles before,
Ocean lifts her winds to bring us
To that well-remembered shore.

GOODBYE, FARE YOU WELL

1 Fare you well, Julianna, you know,
Hoo row, row, row my boys,
To the westward we row and we now coming home,
Goodbye, fare you well, goodbye, fare you well.

[repeat lines 2 and 4 in the following stanzas]

2 Fare you well to the fish in the sea,
To the westward we row and we now coming home,

3 Fare you well, let us leave and go home,
And here we coming with blackfish and men,

4 Fare you well is the fisherman's song,
And here we coming with cock, cow and men,

5 Fare you well and our sails they are set,
And the whales that we leave, well, we leave with
    regret,

6 Fare you well, Julianna, you know,
To the westward we row and we now coming home,

WORK: BLACK WORK GANG

Blacks sang work songs on African waterways long before their forced emigration to North America occurred. Many of their songs were linked rhythmically to the work at hand. This was especially true of boat songs. One early nineteenth century collector discovered the close parallel between rowing songs of slaves at Port Royal, in the Georgia Sea Islands, and boatmen's songs from the Nile River in Egypt. Through the efforts of pioneer folk collectors, a few examples of boat and rowing songs of slaves were preserved.

A variant of "Lay This Body Down" was sung by black oarsmen transporting guests to a Sea Island home. William Allen, Charles Ware and Lucy Garrison reported another variant in Slave Songs of the United States, 1867, number 26, p. 19. (Dialect on this and the following three songs has been removed.)

LAY THIS BODY DOWN

O graveyard, O graveyard,
I'm walkin' through the graveyard;
Lay this body down.

I know moonlight, I know starlight,
I'm walkin' through the starlight'
Lay this body down.

"Heaven Bell A-Ring" was described as "a favorite rowing tune" by the same collectors. From Slave Songs, number 27, pp. 20-21.

HEAVEN BELL A-RING

1 My Lord, my Lord, what shall I do?
And a heaven bell a-ring and praise God.

2 What shall I do for a hiding place?
And a heaven, etc. [similarly in stanzas 3-17]

3 I run to sea, but the sea run dry.

4 I run to the gate, but the gate shut fast.

5 No hiding place for sinner there.

6 Say you when you get to heaven say you 'member me.

7 Remember me, poor fallen soul.

315

8 Say when you get to heaven say your work shall
   prove.

9 Your righteous Lord shall prove 'em well.

10 Your righteous Lord shall find you out.

11 He cast out none that come by faith.

12 You look to the Lord with a tender heart.

13 I wonder where poor Monday there.

14 For I am gone and sent to hell.

15 We must harkee what the worldy say.

16 Say Christmas come but once a year.

17 Say Sunday come but once a week.

Another common rowing song was "Bound To Go." From
Slave Songs, number 30, p. 22.

BOUND TO GO

1 I build my house on the rock, O yes, Lord!
  No wind, no storm can blow 'em down, O yes, Lord!

chorus:
        March on, member,
        Bound to go;
        Been to the ferry,
        Bound to go;
        Left St. Helena,
        Bound to go;
        Brother, fare you well.

2 I build my house on shiftin' sand, O yes, Lord!
  The first wind come he blow him down, O yes, Lord!

3 I am not like the foolish man, O yes, Lord!
  He build his house upon the sand, O yes, Lord!

4 One mornin' as I was a walkin' along, O yes, Lord!
  I saw the berries a-hanging down, O yes, Lord!

5 I pick the berries and I suck the juice, O yes,
    Lord!
  He sweeter than the honey comb, O yes, Lord!

On several occasions when the authors of Slave Songs were being transported to the Sea Islands, they observed that the ship's black crew would sing "Michael Row the Boat Ashore," "when the load was heavy or the tide was against us." Slave Songs, no. 31, pp. 23-24.

MICHAEL ROW THE BOAT ASHORE

1 Michael row the boat ashore, Hallelujah!

2 Michael boat a gospel boat, Hallelujah!

3 I wonder where my mother there, Hallelujah!

4 See my mother on the rock goin' home, Hallelujah!

5 On the rock goin' home in Jesus' name, Hallelujah!

6 Michael boat a music boat, Hallelujah!

7 Gabriel blow the trumpet horn, Hallelujah!

8 O you mind you boastin' talk, Hallelujah!

9 Boastin' talk will sink your soul, Hallelujah!

10 Brother, lend a helpin' hand, Hallelujah!

11 Sister, help for trim that boat, Hallelujah!

12 Jordan stream is wide and deep, Hallelujah!

13 Jesus stand on the other side, Hallelujah!

14 I wonder if my massa there, Hallelujah!

15 My father gone to unknown land, Hallelujah!

16 O the Lord he plant his garden there, Hallelujah!

Closely related to the rowing songs is "Heave Away," a Savannah firemen's song sung by slaves who belonged to one of the engine companies in that city. See Slave Songs, number 82, p. 61.

HEAVE AWAY

Heave away, heave away!
I'd rather court a yellow gal than work for Henry
    Clay.
Heave away, heave away!
Yellow gal, I want to go,

317

I'd rather court a yellow gal than work for Henry
    Clay.
Heave away! Yellow gal I want to go.

"Corn Shucking Song" was printed in Putnam's
Monthly, January, 1855, p. 78. It was sung by slaves
while shucking corn (dialect modified by compiler).

CORN SHUCKING SONG

1 Cowboy on middle the island,
   Ho, meleety, ho!
   Cowboy on middle the island,
   Ho, meleety, ho!

   [similarly]

2 Missus eat the green persimmon,
   Ho, meleety, ho!

3 Mouth all drawed up in a pucker,
   Ho, meleety, ho!

4 Stayed so till she went to supper,
   Ho, meleety, ho!

A wheat cutting song of black field workers was
collected in Auburn, Alabama, in 1915-16. The cradle
was swung to the holler "O! Alle! O!" Printed in Newman
I. White, American Negro Folk-Songs (Cambridge: Harvard
University Press, 1928), p. 286.

O! ALLE! O!

Watch me whet my cradle, O! Alle! O!
I'll make it beat de beater, O! Alle! O!
Watch me throw my cradle, O! Alle! O!
I'se been all over Georgia, O! Alle! O!
I never saw but one man, O! Alle! O!
Who could cut it better'n I can, O! Alle! Oh!
Watch'er lie before me, O! Alle! O!
Come on my binder, O! Alle! O!
Watch the bundles behind her, O! Alle! O!
The storm clouds arising, O! Alle! O!
The dinner'll soon be here, O! Alle! O!
The rain it am a coming, O! Alle! O!
Better save the grain, O! Alle! O!

This black lumberjack's song from Alabama, circa
1915-16, was printed in White, Negro Folk-Songs, p. 265.

Hey, Bull and Ben tally--wham!
How long, how long--wham!
Fo' the sun goes down--wham!
Poor boy cryin', all day long--wham!
Can't hear no train--wham!

Can't hear no whistle blow--wham!
All I can hear--wham!
The Boss man say--wham!
"Let the chips fly"--wham!

A black construction gang was heard singing "Old
Skubald" in Jackson, Mississippi in 1906. White, in Negro
Folk-Songs, p. 267, claimed the work song was an out-
growth of the ballad "Skewball," Q-22 (see Chapter
Three).

OLD SKUBALD

I don't mind race riding,
If 't wa'n't for my wife,
Old Skubald might stumble
And away goes my life.

Following the Civil War, black prisoners were
leased out to private sugar cane plantations in Mississippi and Texas. A cane-cutting song from Texas, "No
More Cane On This Brazos," details the human depriva-
tions on these plantations. For a variant, hear Alan
Lomax on Texas Folksongs, Tradition TLP-1029.

NO MORE CANE ON THIS BRAZOS

1 There ain't no more cane on this Brazos, Ohhh!
  You done drive that bully till he went stone blind,
      Ohhh!

2 Oughta come on the river in 1904, Ohhh!
  You could find a dead man on every turn row, Ohhh!

3 Oughta come on the river in 1910, Ohhh!
  They was drivin' the women just like the men, Ohhh!

4 Now, wake up dead man, help me drive my row, Ohhh!
  Wake up dead man, help me drive my row, Ohhh!

5 Wake up lifer, hold up your head, Ohhh!
  You may get a pardon, and you may drop dead, Ohhh!

6 Go down old Hannah, don'cha rise no more, Ohhh!
  If you come back, bring the Judgement Day, Ohhh!

7 There ain't no more cane on this Brazos, Ohhh!
  They done grind it all in molasses, Ohhh!

8 Some in the prison and some on the farm, Ohhh!
  Some in the fields and some goin' home, Ohhh!

One of the favorite work songs of blacks was "John
Henry" and its variant "This Old Hammer" (see Chapter
Four, "John Henry," I-1, especially version C). Version
A was sung by a chain gang working on road construction
in North Carolina in 1911. B, from Pickens County,
Alabama, circa 1915-16, was reported as a "railroad work
song." From White, Negro Folk-Songs, pp. 260-261.

A - JOHN HENRY

Poor John Henry--hic
Was a steel-driving man--hic,
Old John Henry--hic
Was a steel-driving man--hic.
Drove that steel--hic
Steel wouldn't stand--hic.

B - THIS OLD HAMMER

1 This old hammer killed John Henry,
  But it can't kill me.
  Take this old hammer, take it to the Captain,
  Tell him I'm gone, babe, tell him I'm gone.

2 If he asks you what wuz the matter,
  Tell him you don't know, babe,
  Tell him you don't know.

3 If he asks you wuz I running,
  Tell him no, tell him no.

An authentic railroad work song was collected in
Jefferson County, Alabama, from a crew of black gandy
dancers as they aligned track with iron bars. Printed
in White, Negro Folk-Songs, pp. 263-264.

JACK THE RABBIT

Jack the rabbit! Jack the bear!
Can't you line him just a hair,
Just a hair, just a hair?
Annie Weaver and her daughter
Ran a boarding house on the water.
She's got chicken, she's got ham,
She's got everything I'll be damned.

320

Old Joe Logan he's gone north
To get the money for to pay us off.

BUNK HOUSE AND CAMPFIRE

Many of the songs and ballads in this entire collection could have been sung by off-duty workers as they
relaxed in their bunk houses or gathered around their
campfires. Yet these same workers also could draw from
a stock of songs linked more closely to their occupations. A few examples follow.

H. M. Kilpatrick collected this untitled folksong
in Pickens County, Alabama, shortly before World War I,
from black field hands while they were taking a work
break. See White, Negro Folk-Songs, pp. 301-302. Leadbelly included similar lyrics in his song "We Shall Be
Free," Folkways FA 2488, Leadbelly Sings Folk Songs.

> Ain't no use of my workin' so hard, darlin',
> Ain't no use of my workin' so hard, darlin';
> I got a gal in the white folk's yard.
> > She kill a chicken
> > She bring me the wing;
> > Ain't I livin' on an easy thing,
> > > Honey Babe?
> Ain't no use in working so hard,
> I got a woman in the white folk's yard,
> She totes me meat, she totes me lard,
> Ain't no use in working so hard.

The various immigrant crews who built America's
rail network in the nineteenth century had their own
special songs. "Drill, Ye Tarriers, Drill" was a tribute to an Irish blasting crew who risked their lives
dynamiting stubborn rock in the path of the railroad
line. One of the most authentic renditions of the song
was by Cisco Houston on his Folkways album, Cisco Sings,
FA 2346 (used by permission of Folkways Records).

DRILL, YE TARRIERS, DRILL

> 1 Early in the morning at seven o'clock
> There are twenty tarriers drilling at the rock.
> And the boss comes around and he says, "Keep still,
> And come down heavy on your cast iron drill!"

> chorus:
> > And drill, ye tarriers, drill; drill, ye
> > tarriers, drill.

Well you work all day for the sugar in your
    tea,
Down behind the railway, and drill, you tar-
    riers, drill.
And blast, and fire.

2 Now our new foreman was Jim McGann,
By golly, he was a blinken man.
Last week a premature blast went off,
And a mile in the sky went big Jim Goff.

3 Now when next payday comes around,
Jim Goff a dollar short was found.
When asked the reason, came this reply,
"You were docked for the time you were up in the
    sky."

4 Now the boss was a fine man down to the ground,
And he married a lady six feet round.
She baked good bread and she baked it well,
But she baked it as hard as the holes in hell.

"Pat Works On the Railway" salutes a special Irish
railroad worker. Also from Cisco Sings, Folkways FA
2346 (used by permission of Folkways Records).

PAT WORKS ON THE RAILWAY

1 In 1841 I put my corduroy britches on,
I put my corduroy britches on
To work upon the railway.

    chorus:
        Filli-mee-oo-ri-oo-ri-ee, filli-mee-oo-ri-oo-
            ri-ee,
        Filli-mee-oo-ri-oo-ri-ee, to work upon the
            railway.

2 In 1842 I left the old world for the new,
Bad cess to the luck that brought me through
To work upon the railway.

3 Well it's "Pat do this!" and "Pat do that!"
Without a stocking or cravat,
And nothing for an old straw hat,
While working on the railway.

4 In 1843 twas then I met sweet Bitty McGhee,
Ah, an elegant wife she's been to me,
While working on the railway.

322

5 In 1847 sweet Bitty McGhee she went to heaven,
  If she left one child she left eleven
  To work upon the railway.

6 In 1848 I learned to drink me whiskey straight,
  It's an elegant drink that can't be beat
  For working on the railway.

Cowboys led lonely and unromantic lives, especially
while herding cattle along the trails from Texas to the
railheads in Kansas. Harry Jackson, who as a young man
punched cattle in Wyoming, claims "Roll On, Little
Dogies" was sung at night to quiet the cattle. The
song also reveals the introspective nature of the cowboy. Jackson sings it on The Cowboy: His Songs, Ballads
and Brag Talk, Folkways FH 5723 (used by permission of
Folkways Records).

ROLL ON, LITTLE DOGIES

1 Last night as I lay on my pillow
  And looked at the stars in the sky,
  I wondered if ever a cowboy
  Will drift to the home in the sky.

  chorus:
      Roll on, oh roll on,
      Roll on, little dogies, roll on, roll on,
      Roll on, oh roll on,
      Roll on, little dogies, roll on.

2 When I think of the last great round-up
  On the eve of eternity's dawn,
  I think of the host of cowboys
  That have been here and rode on.

3 Well, I wonder if any will greet me
  When finally I reach that far shore
  With a hearty, God welcome, old cowboy,
  That I've met so many times before.

4 Well, I often look upward and wonder
  If the green fields will seem half so fair,
  If any the wrong trail have taken
  And will fail to turn up right there.

5 Well, the trail that leads to perdition
  Is posted and blazed all the way,
  But the one that leads up to heaven
  Is a dim narrow trail, so they say.

Canadian collector Edith Fowke described "Blood On
the Saddle" succinctly: "Seldom have so few words
painted such a gory picture with so much relish." Tony
Kraber recorded the definitive version of it on
Hootenanny At Carnegie Hall, Folkways FN 2512 (used by
permission of Folkways Records).

BLOOD ON THE SADDLE

There was blood on the saddle, and blood all
    around,
And a great big puddle of blood on the ground.

The cowboy lay in it, all covered with gore,
And he won't go riding no bronchos no more.

Oh, pity the cowboy all bloody and red,
For his broncho fell on him and mashed in his head.

[repeat first stanza]

Pioneer farmers, moving into the high grass regions
of the Great Plains where water and wood were at a pre-
mium, satirized their problems in the lyrics of "Little
Old Sod Shanty." It is a first cousin to the eastern
song, "The Little Old Log Cabin In the Lane," popularized by Fiddlin' John Carson in the 1920's. The text is
a variant of the one printed in Carl Sandburg's The
American Songbag, pp. 89-91.

LITTLE OLD SOD SHANTY

1 I'm looking rather seedy now
  While holding down my claim,
  My vittles are not always of the best,
  And the mice play shyly 'round me,
  As I nestle down to rest
  In my little old sod shanty on my claim.

2 Yes I rather like the novelty
  Of living in this way,
  Though my bill of fare is always rather tame;
  But I'm happy as a clam
  On the land of Uncle Sam,
  In my little old sod shanty on my claim.

chorus:
    Oh, the hinges are of leather
    And the windows have no glass,
    The board roof lets the howling blizzards in;
    And I hear the hungry coyote

As he sneaks up through the grass
'Round my little old sod shanty on my claim.

3 Oh, when I left my eastern home,
A bachelor so gay,
To try to win my way to wealth and fame,
I little thought that I'd come down
To burning twisted hay
In my little old sod shanty on my claim.

4 My clothes are plastered o'er with dough,
I'm looking like a fright,
And everything is scattered 'round the room;
But I wouldn't give the freedom
That I have out in the West,
For the table of the eastern man's old home.

5 Still I wish that some kind hearted gal
Would pity on me take
And relieve me from the mess that I'm in.
Oh, the angel how I'd bless her,
If this her home she'd make,
In this little old sod shanty on my claim.

6 And we would make our fortunes
On the prairies of the West,
Just as happy as two lovers we'd remain;
We'd forget the trials and troubles
We endured at the first
In that little sod shanty on my claim.

7 And if kindly fate should bless us
With now and then an heir,
To cheer our hearts with honest pride of fame,
Oh, then we'd be contented
For the toil we had spent
In that little old sod shanty on our claim.

8 When time enough had lapsed,
And all those little brats,
To noble man and womanhood had grown,
It wouldn't seem so lonely
As around us we would look
And see the little old sod shanty on our claim.

Whether or not "The Erie Canal" was sung in bunk houses or campfires, it satirizes the trials and tribulations of the "canalers" as they plied their trade between Albany and Buffalo on the "big ditch"--forty feet wide and four feet deep. This important link between the East and the West was built by Irish immigrants.

When it opened in 1825, the canal was hailed as the eighth wonder of the world by European engineers. The text is from _Frontier Ballads_, Folkways FP 5003 (used by permission of Folkways Records). For other delightful odes to that pioneer public works project, listen to _Oh! That Low Bridge: Songs of the Erie Canal_ by George Ward, Front Hall Records, FHR-028.

THE ERIE CANAL

chorus:
    O the Erie was a-rising
    And the gin was a-gettin' low,
    And I scarcely think we'll get a drink
    Till we get to Buffalo,
    Till we get to Buffalo.

1 We were forty miles from Albany,
    Forget it I never shall;
    What a terrible storm we had one night
    On the Erie Canal.

2 We were loaded down with barley,
    We were chock-up full of rye;
    The captain he looked down on me
    With his gol-durn wicked eye.

3 Two days out from Syracuse
    The vessel struck a shoal,
    We like to all be foundered
    On a chunk o' Lackawanna coal.

4 We hollered to the captain
    On the towpath, treadin' dirt;
    He jumped on board and stopped the leak
    With his old red flannel shirt.

5 The cook she was a grand old gal,
    She wore a ragged dress;
    We heisted her upon the pole
    As a signal of distress.

6 The wind begin to whistle
    The waves begin to roll,
    We had to reef our royals [!]
    On that raging canal.

7 When we got to Syracuse
    Off-mule he was dead,
    The nigh mule he got blind staggers,
    We cracked him on the head.

8 The captain he got married,
   The cook she went to jail,
   And I'm the only sea-cook son
   That's left to tell the tale.

"The Shanty Boys" is a nascent ballad widely collected in the lumbering regions of North America. Sandy
Ives sings a Penobscot lumberjack's variation on Folksongs of Maine, Folkways FH 5323 (used by permission of
Folkways Records).

THE SHANTY BOYS

1 Come all ye good jolly fellows, come listen to my
      song,
   It's all about the shanty boys and how they get
      along;
   We're all good jolly fellows as you will ever find,
   To wear away the winter months a whaling down the
      pine.

2 The chopper and the sawyer, they lay the timber
      low,
   The swamper and the teamster, they haul it to and
      fro;
   You'd ought to hear our foreman soon after the
      break of day,
   "Load up your team two thousand feet--to the river
      you'll steer away."

3 Crack! Snap! goes my whip, I whistle and I sing,
   I sit upon my timber load as happy as a king;
   My horses they are ready and I am never sad,
   There's no one now so happy as the jolly shanty
      lad.

4 Noon will soon be over, to us the foreman will say,
   "Put down your saws and ax my boys, for here's
      your pork and beans."
   Arriving at the shanty, 'tis then the fun begins,
   A'dippelin' in the water pail and dinglin' of the
      tin.

5 And then to us the cook will say, "Come fella,
      come fly, come Joe;
   Come pass around the water pail as far as the water
      goes."
   As soon as lunch is over, to us the foreman will
      say,
   "Put on your coat and cap, my boys, to the woods
      we'll bear away."

327

6 We all go out with a cheerful heart and a well
      contented mind,
   The days don't seem so long among the wavy pine;
   You ought to hear our foreman, soon after the sun
      goes down,
   "Put down your saws and ax, my boys, to the shanty
      we are bound."

7 Arriving at the shanty with wet and damp cold feet,
   We all pull off our larrigans, our suppers for to
      eat;
   We all play cards till nine o'clock, then into our
      bunks we climb,
   To wear away the winter months a-whaling down the
      pine.

PROTEST

   Ignored by mainstream folk collectors for years,
protest music finally was taken seriously in the United
States, first, during the depression of the 1930's, and
then, more recently, during the civil rights movement of
the 1950's and 1960's and the anti-Vietnam War movement
of the 1960's and 1970's.

   But protest music is not new. During the Peasant
Revolt of 1381 in England, "quiet rhymes" protesting
intolerable social, political and economic conditions
appeared throughout the countryside. One was attributed
to the "mad priest," John Ball:

   When Adam delved and Eve span
   Who was then the gentleman?

   Medieval folk idealized the legendary Robin Hood;
"The Cutty Wren" was a symbol of defiance in fourteenth
century England; "Lilliburlero" served the same purpose
during the reign of King James II (see Chapter Two for
these examples). In North America, Jesse James, Billy
the Kid and Pretty Boy Floyd were transformed into anti-
establishment heroes.

   However, the vast bulk of early protest songs have
disappeared from the literature for several reasons.
(1) Most people tolerate the intolerable too long and
then, once change occurs, past grievances are forgotten.
Most struggle songs die quickly in such circumstances.
(2) Protest songs are usually spontaneous outbursts of
resentments and, therefore, are cruder and less artistic
than traditional folk music causing many singers and

collectors to ignore the songs. (3) Early folk com-
pilers were downright hostile towards protest themes
directed against the establishment of which they themselves were members. Thus it has been only recently
that folk enthusiasts, spurred on by pioneers in the
Woody Guthrie-Pete Seeger mold, have recognized the significance of this historically important music.

But what exactly is protest music? Much of it is
not strictly folk music, although some of it has entered
the folk tradition. John Greenway in his pioneer work
American Folksongs of Protest defines it best: "These
are the struggle songs of the people. They are outbursts of bitterness, of hatred for the oppressor, of
determination to endure hardships together and to fight
for a better life."[1] To classify a song as protest depends upon the ideology of the classifier, for one person's dissent is another's assent. In 1776 the British
regarded "Free America(y)" as a vulgar and traitorous
song, while American revolutionaries considered it as
a patriotic masterpiece. Similarly, Joe Hill's "The
Preacher and the Slave" was thought of as a terrorist
battle cry by American industrialists and financiers,
while members of a radical union, the Industrial Workers
of the World, valued it as an exhilarating call to freedom.

Here then are "the struggle songs of the people,"
subdivided into eight historical and topical categories
for easy identification. Many of those chosen have become true folksongs reflecting their appeal above and
beyond the relatively narrow group of people for whom
they were written.

I. AMERICAN REVOLUTION-WAR OF 1812

Shortly before the battle of Bunker Hill in 1775,
a member of the Sons of Liberty, perhaps Dr. Joseph
Warren, wrote "Free America(y)" to the tune of "The
British Grenadiers." The song was a powerful stimulant
for the growing national consciousness of the United
States, especially with its prophecy: "Some future day
shall crown us/The masters of the main." From Ballads
of the Revolution, Folkways FP 5001 (used by permission
of Folkways Records). See also Revolutionary Tea, Old

---

[1]John Greenway, AMERICAN FOLKSONGS OF PROTEST,
University of Pennsylvania Press, Philadelphia, Pa.,
1953, p. 10.

North Bridge Records, ONB 1776, and <u>American</u> <u>Revolution-</u>
<u>ary</u> <u>War</u> <u>Songs</u> <u>to</u> <u>Cultivate</u> <u>the</u> <u>Sensation</u> <u>of</u> <u>Freedom</u>,
<u>Folkways FH 5279</u>.

FREE AMERICA(Y)

1 That Seat of Science, Athens,
   And earth's proud mistress, Rome;
   Where now are all their glories?
   You scarce can find a tomb;
   Then guard your rights, Americans,
   Nor stoop to lawless sway,
   Oppose, oppose, oppose,
   For North America.

2 Torn from a world of tyrants,
   Beneath this western sky,
   We formed a new dominion,
   A land of liberty;
   The world shall own we're masters here,
   Then hasten on the day,
   Huzza, huzza, huzza,
   For free America.

3 Proud Albion bowed to Caesar,
   And numerous lords before;
   To picts, to Danes, to Normans,
   And many masters more;
   But we can boast, Americans,
   We've never fallen a prey;
   Huzza, huzza, huzza,
   For free America.

4 Lift up your hands, ye heroes,
   And swear with proud disdain,
   The wretch that would ensnare you,
   Shall lay his snares in vain;
   Should Europe empty all her force,
   We'll meet her in array,
   And fight and shout, and fight
   For North America.

5 Some future day shall crown us,
   The masters of the main,
   Our fleet shall speak in thunder
   To England, France and Spain;
   And the nations over the ocean spread
   Shall tremble and obey,
   The sons, the sons, the sons,
   Of brave America.

"Yankee Doodle" first appeared as a British song satirizing the lack of soldiership among colonial militiamen during the French and Indian War. But as sometimes happens, the "satirees" turned the music to their own advantage and it quickly became the most popular marching song of the Continental Army. Text: <u>Ballads of the Revolution</u>, Folkways FP 5001 (used by permission of Folkways Records).

YANKEE DOODLE

1 Father and I went down to camp,
   Along with Captain Gooding;
   There we see the men and boys,
   As thick as hasty pudding.

   chorus:
      Yankee Doodle keep it up,
      Yankee Doodle dandy;
      Mind the music and the step,
      And with the girls be handy.

2 And there we see a thousand men,
   As rich as Squire David;
   And what they wasted every day,
   I wish it could be sav-ed.

3 And there we see a swamping gun,
   Large as a log of maple,
   Upon a duced little cart,
   A load for father's cattle.

4 And every time they shoot it off,
   It takes a horn of powder;
   It makes a noise like father's gun,
   Only a nation louder.

5 I see a little barrel too,
   The heads were made of leather,
   They knocked upon't with little clubs,
   And called the folks together.

6 And there was Captain Washington,
   And gentlefolks about him;
   They say he's grown so tarnal proud,
   He will not ride without 'em.

7 The flaming ribbons in their hats,
   They looked so tearing fine, ah,
   I wanted plaguily to get,
   To give to my Jemima.

8 I see another snarl of men,
  A digging graves, they told me,
  So tarnal long, so tarnal deep,
  They 'tended they should hold me.

9 It scar'd me so, I hook'd it off,
  Nor stopp'd, as I remember;
  Nor turn'd about 'till I got home,
  Lock'd up in mother's chamber.

President John Adams enraged many Americans by his
support for the Alien and Sedition Acts, especially one
provision that made it a crime to engage in "false,
scandalous and malicious" criticism of Congress and the
President. As a result of the outcry, Thomas Jefferson's party defeated Adams' Federalists in the election
of 1800. "Jefferson and Liberty" was written to signal
the end of "the reign of terror." Source: Election
Songs, Folkways FH 5280 (used by permission of Folkways
Records).

JEFFERSON AND LIBERTY

1 The gloomy night before us flies
  The reign of terror now is o'er;
  No gags, inquisitors and spies,
  The herds of harpies are no more.

2 Rejoice, Columbia's sons, rejoice,
  To tyrants never bend the knee,
  But join with heart, with soul and voice,
  For Jefferson and liberty.

3 No lordlings here with gorging jaws
  Shall wring from industry the food;
  No bigots with their holy laws
  Lay waste our fields and streets in blood.

4 Here strangers from a thousand shores,
  Compelled by tyranny to roam
  Shall find amidst abundant stores,
  A nobler and a happier home.

Yet Jefferson was soon to have his own problems.
In order to counteract the restrictive trade practices
of the two warring European powers, Britain and France,
Jefferson instituted the Embargo Act of 1806 cutting off
overseas trade. This action upset New England merchants
and shipping interests who expressed their sentiments in
such songs as "The Embargo," sung to the tune of "Yankee
Doodle." Incidentally, "Brother Jonathan" was the col-

lective term for the people of the United States. From
Bay State Ballads, Folkways FA 2106 (used by permission
of Folkways Records).

THE EMBARGO

1 Attention pay, you bonny lads,
  And listen to my Fargo,
  About a nation deuced thing
  Which people called Embargo.

  chorus:
      Yankee Doodle, keep it up,
      Yankee Doodle Dandy,
      We'll soak our hide in home made rum
      If we can't get French brandy.

2 In Boston town the other day,
  The people were all blustering,
  And sailors, too, as thick as hail
  Away to sea were mustering.

3 I asked the reason of the stir
  And why they made such pother,
  But deuce a word they answered me
  Or Jonathan, my brother.

4 At last a man with powdered hair
  Come up and said to me, Sir,
  Why stand you gaping here you rogue,
  Come list and go to sea, Sir.

5 I've got a vessel at the wharf,
  Well loaded with a cargo,
  And want a few more hands to help
  To clear the cursed embargo.

6 I told him then he need not think
  I was so great a goat, Sir,
  As to throw off for clothes all tarred
  My go-to-meeting coat, Sir.

7 Then he turned upon his heel
  And called me country bumpkin,
  And said I hadn't got more brains
  Than an old rotten pumpkin.

8 Then Jonathan and I went down
  To look around the wharf, Sir,
  And there we see a hundred men
  Shoving a big boat, Sir.

333

9 Then Jonathan a fellow asked,
   How men in that thing dare go,
   The fellow said why damn your eyes
   You lubber, that's the Embargo.

10 Lord, how it was a monstrous thing,
   Big as a meeting house, Sir,
   And on the top, by gracious, there
   We see both hogs and cows, Sir.

11 And in the middle of it grew
   Three trees high in the air, Sir,
   And as the people climbed them up,
   Lord, how the men did swear, Sir.

12 Now, Jonathan, says I, when we
   Get home and tell to Nancy
   And Sal and Paul and Jack and Joe,
   They'll say it was our fancy.

13 But I can vow 'tis all as true
   As two and two make four, Sir,
   And if you don't believe it now
   I'll tell a great deal more, Sir.

14 Now let ye caper, dance and sing,
   And drink and merry be, Sir,
   Because as sure as death and rates
   The Embargo's gone to sea, Sir!

The War of 1812 with Great Britain raised the national consciousness of the young republic to a new high. Poets and song writers helped. Francis Scott Key's "The Star Spangled Banner" was a renowned example. It was set to the tune of the British drinking song "To Anacreon in Heaven," published in 1779-80 and already a vehicle for numerous American parodies. (See Vera Brodsky Lawrence, Music for Patriots, Politicians, and Presidents, pp. 128-9, 204-9.)

Joseph Hutton's "Perry's Victory" celebrated Commodore Oliver Hazard Perry's triumph on Lake Erie and helped create a new folk hero. The text is from War of 1812, Folkways FP 5002 (used by permission of Folkways Records).

PERRY'S VICTORY

1 O'er the bosom of Erie, in fanciful pride,
  Did the fleet of Old England exultingly ride,

334

Till the flag of Columbia her Perry unfurled,
The boast of the west and the pride of the world.

chorus:
  And still should the foe dare the fight to
    sustain
  Gallant Perry shall lead on to conquest again,
  Gallant Perry shall lead on to conquest again,
  For freedom of trade and a right to the main!

2 The spirit of Lawrence his influence sheds,
To the van of the fight while the <u>Lawrence</u> he
  leads;
There death dealt around, though such numbers
  oppose,
And leveled the gun at fair Liberty's foes.

3 When covered with slain, from his deck he withdrew,
And led the <u>Niagara</u>, the fight to renew;
Where, undaunted in danger, our sea-beaten tars
O'er the cross of St. George waved the stripes and
  the stars.

4 Six ships, while our banners triumphantly flew,
Submitted to tars who were born to subdue,
When they rushed to the battle resolved to maintain
The freedom of trade and our right to the main.

5 With the glory of conquest our heroes are crowned,
Let their brows with the bright naval chaplet be
  bound!
For still should the foe dare the fight to sustain,
Gallant Perry shall lead them to conquest again!

II. CIVIL WAR AND RECONSTRUCTION

Tragic themes in music are quite common and it is
no wonder that the most calamitous episode in the history of the United States, the Civil War, produced hundreds of such songs, many of which entered the folk tradition.

Jesse Hutchinson, a member of the renowned mid-
nineteenth century musical group, the Hutchinson Family
Singers, fitted new lyrics to the Irish fiddle tune
"Rosin the Beau." The result was "Lincoln and Liberty,
Too," an election campaign song for 1860. An updated
version helped reelect Lincoln four years later and that
is the one sung on <u>Ballads of the Civil War</u>, Folkways
FP 5004 (used by permission of Folkways Records). For
other songs employing the same tune see "Acres of Clams"

in Chapter Five and "Hayseed Like Me" in this chapter.

LINCOLN AND LIBERTY, TOO

1 Hurrah for the choice of the nation!
Our chieftain so brave and so true;
We'll go for the great reformation,
For Lincoln and Liberty, too.

2 We'll go for the son of Kentucky,
The hero of Hoosierdom through;
The pride of the Suckers so lucky,
For Lincoln and Liberty, too.

3 They'll find what by felling and mauling,
Our rail-maker statesman can do;
For the people are ev'rywhere calling,
For Lincoln and Liberty, too.

4 Then up with the banner so glorious,
The star-spangled, red white and blue,
We'll fight till our banner's victorious,
For Lincoln and Liberty, too.

5 Our David's good sling is unerring,
The Slavocrat's giant he slew,
Then shout for the freedom preferring,
For Lincoln and Liberty, too.

6 [repeat stanza 2]

Every northern Unionist knew "The Battle Hymn of
the Republic," but equally popular was George F. Root's
"Battle Cry of Freedom." In fact, when Fort Sumter in
Charleston harbor was recaptured by Union troops in
1865, Root's melody was chosen for the formal surrender
ceremonies. Text: Songs of the Civil War, Folkways FH
5717 (used by permission of Folkways Records).

BATTLE CRY OF FREEDOM

1 Oh, we'll rally round the flag, boys,
We'll rally once again,
Shouting the battle cry of freedom;
We will rally from the hillside,
We'll gather from the plain,
Shouting the battle cry of freedom

chorus:
The Union forever, hurrah, boys, hurrah!
Down with the traitor, up with the star;

336

While we rally round the flag, boys,
Rally once again,
Shouting the battle cry of freedom.

2 We are springing to the call of our brothers gone
        before,
Shouting the battle cry of freedom,
And we'll fill the vacant ranks with a million
        freedmen more,
Shouting the battle cry of freedom.

3 We will welcome to our numbers the loyal, true and
        brave,
Shouting the battle cry of freedom,
And although they may be poor, not a man shall be
        a slave,
Shouting the battle cry of freedom.

4 So we're springing to the call, from the East and
        from the West,
Shouting the battle cry of freedom,
And we'll hurl the Rebel crew from the land we
        love the best,
Shouting the battle cry of freedom.

For Southerners, "Dixie" and "Bonnie Blue Flag"
were favorites. Harry MacCarthy, an Irish vaudevillian
known as "The Arkansas Comedian," wrote the lyrics for
"Bonnie Blue Flag" to the tune "The Irish Jaunting Car."
A smash hit following its premier performance in New
Orleans in the spring of 1861, the song was updated with
new verses as additional states seceded from the union.
Text: Ballads of the Civil War, Folkways FP 5004 (used
by permission of Folkways Records).

BONNIE BLUE FLAG

1 We are a band of brothers, and native to the soil,
Fighting for the property we gained by honest toil;
And when our rights were threatened, the cry rose
        near and far,
"Hurrah for the Bonnie Blue Flag that bears a
        single star!"

chorus:
        Hurrah! Hurrah! for southern rights, hurrah!
        Hurrah for the Bonnie Blue Flag that bears a
                single star.

2 As long as the Union was faithful to her trust,
Like friends and like brethren kind were we, and
        just;

But now, when northern treachery attempts our
   rights to mar,
We hoist on high the Bonnie Blue Flag that bears a
   single star.

3 First gallant South Carolina nobly made the stand,
Then came Alabama and took her by the hand;
Next, quickly, Mississippi, Georgia, and Florida,
All raised on high the Bonnie Blue Flag that bears
   a single star.

4 Ye men of valor gather round the banner of the
   right,
Texas and fair Louisiana join us in the fight;
With Davis, our loved President, and Stephens,
   statesmen rare,
We'll rally round the Bonnie Blue Flag that bears
   a single star.

5 And here's to brave Virginia, the Old Dominion
   State,
With the young Confederacy at length has linked her
   fate;
Impelled by her example, now other states prepare
To hoist on high the Bonnie Blue Flag that bears a
   single star.

6 Then here's to our Confederacy, strong we are and
   brave,
Like patriots of old we'll fight, our heritage to
   save;
And rather than submit to shame, to die we would
   prefer,
So cheer for the Bonnie Blue Flag that bears a
   single star.

7 Then cheer, boys, cheer, and raise a joyous shout,
For Arkansas and North Carolina, now have both gone
   out,
And let another rousing cheer for Tennessee be
   given,
The single star of the Bonnie Blue Flag has grown
   to be eleven.

War leaves bitter memories, especially for the
losers. Several protest songs were composed following
the Civil War by unreconstructed Southerners. "I'm a
Good Old Rebel" was one. It entered the folk tradition
and was collected in Texas, the Carolinas and Virginia.
The text is essentially the same as the Hermes Nye
variant in Ballads of the Civil War, Folkways FP 5004

(used by permission of Folkways Records). See also
Vance Randolph, <u>Ozark</u> <u>Folksongs</u>, Volume II, pp. 291-
295.

I'M A GOOD OLD REBEL

1 Oh, I'm a good old rebel!
  Now that's just what I am;
  For this "Fair Land of Freedom"
  I do not care a damn.
  I'm glad I fit against it,
  I only wish we'd won,
  And I don't want no pardon
  For anything I've done.

2 I hate the Constitution,
  This great Republic, too;
  I hate the Freedman's Bureau,
  In uniforms of blue.
  I hate the nasty eagle,
  With all his brag and fuss,
  The lying, thieving Yankees,
  I hate them wuss and wuss.

3 I hate the Yankee Nation
  And everything they do;
  I hate the Declaration
  Of Independence, too;
  I hate this glorious Union,
  'Tis dripping with our blood;
  I hate this striped banner,
  I fit it all I could.

4 I followed old Marse Robert
  For four years, near about,
  Got wounded in three places,
  And starved at P'int Lookout.
  I cotched the roomatism
  A-camping in the snow;
  But I killed a chance of Yankees,
  I'd like to kill some mo'.

5 Three hundred thousand Yankees
  Lie stiff in southern dust;
  We got three hundred thousand
  Before they conquered us.
  They died of southern fever
  And southern steel and shot;
  I wish it was three million,
  Instead of what we got.

6 I can't take up my musket
And fight 'em now no more;
But I ain't a-going to love 'em,
Now that is certain sure.
And I don't want no pardon,
For what I was and am;
I won't be reconstructed,
And I don't care a damn.

III. EARLY BLACK PROTEST

For Northerners the Civil War was fought to save
the Union; for Southerners, to preserve the heritage of
the Old South. An important part of that heritage was
slavery. Union armies freed slaves as they marched into
the South, an action that was expanded and legalized by
the Thirteenth Amendment to the Constitution of the
United States. Yet even before the slaves were freed
they were singing songs of defiance not only among themselves, but also in the presence of whites. "Many
Thousand Go" or "No More Auction Block For Me" was sung
by Sea Island slaves while building Confederate fortifi-
cations at Hilton Head and Bay Point for General Beau-
regard. Later the song was sung by black Union soldiers.
Text: Allen, et al, Slave Songs, p. 48. Also see Songs
of the Civil War, Folkways FH 5717.

MANY THOUSAND GO

1 No more peck o' corn for me,
No more, no more;
No more peck o' corn for me,
Many thousand go.

[similarly]

2 No more driver's lash for me.

3 No more pint o' salt for me.

4 No more hundred lash for me.

5 No more mistress' call for me.

By adding new verses, the spiritual "O Freedom" was
transformed into a marching song for black soldiers. A
version similar to the text was sung by Odetta as part
of a medley entitled "Spiritual Trilogy" (Tradition TLP
1010).

O FREEDOM

1 No more moaning, no more moaning,
  No more moaning, Lord, for me;
  And before I'd be a slave, I'd be buried in my
      grave,
  And go home to my Lord and be free.

2 No more crying, no more crying,
  No more crying, Lord, for me;
  And before I'd be a slave, I'd be buried in my
      grave,
  And go home to my Lord and be free.

3 Free to be me, free to be me,
  Free to be me, Lord, for me;
  And before I'd be a slave, I'd be buried in my
      grave,
  And go home to my Lord and be free.

4 O freedom! O freedom!
  O freedom, Lord, for me!
  And before I'd be a slave, I'd be buried in my
      grave,
  And go home to my Lord and be free.

Such early expressions of jubilation gave way to a
bleaker mood as segregation became established throughout the South following the end of Reconstruction in
1877.   Restrictions separating blacks and whites multi-
plied and became known as Jim Crow laws (named after an
early minstrel song "Jump Jim Crow").   Segregation even
involved transportation facilities.   Passenger trains
had their "Jim Crow" cars as this untitled song indicates.   It was collected near Louisville, Kentucky,
during World War I.   Still, a defiant spirit prevailed
as the last line in each stanza indicates.   Source:
White, Negro Folk-Songs, p. 319.

The white girl smells like Castile soap,
The yaller gal try to do the same,
The poor black gal smell like little billy goat,
But she gets there just the same.

The white gal rides in the Pullman car,
Yaller gal try to do the same,
The poor black girl rides in the old Jim Crow car,
But she gets there just the same.

Economic disparity between the races is the theme
of the next song from a North Carolina plantation in

341

1914; printed in White, <u>Negro Folk-Songs</u>, p. 382.

>The old bee makes the honey-comb,
>The young bee makes the honey;
>Colored folks plant the cotton and corn,
>And the white folks gets the money.

Unequal justice in the courts was expressed in this succinct two-liner from Alabama; also from White, <u>Negro Folk-Songs</u>, p. 382.

>If a white man kills a Negro, they hardly carry
>   it to court,
>If a Negro kills a white man, they hang him like
>   a goat.

IV. TEMPERANCE AND SUFFRAGE

There is a close relationship between the temperance and the women's suffrage movements of the nineteenth and early twentieth centuries. Many of the women, and men too, in one organization were active in the other. The crusade against the evils of liquor was championed by women for a sound reason. Discrimination against a married woman in the job market made her dependent upon her husband, and if he had a drinking problem both she and the children suffered the most.

Probably the most famous temperance song was written by Henry Clay Work in 1864, "Father, Dear Father, Come Home With Me Now." The 1913 text was printed in Vance Randolph, <u>Ozark Folksongs</u>, Volume II, pp. 396-397.

FATHER, DEAR FATHER, COME HOME WITH ME NOW

1 Father, dear father, come home with me now,
   The clock in the steeple strikes one,
   You said you were comin' right home from the shop,
   As soon as your day's work was done.

2 Our fire has went out, our home is all dark,
   An' mother's a-watchin' for thee,
   With pore little Jenny so sick in her arms
   An' no one to help her but me.

3 Father, dear father, come home with me now,
   The clock in the steeple strikes two,
   The weather is colder an' Jenny is worse,
   An' always a-callin' for you.

4 Jenny is worse an' maw says she will die
  Perhaps before mornin' shall dawn,
  An' this is the word that she sent me to bring,
  Come home quick or she will be gone.

5 Father, dear father, come home with me now,
  The clock in the steeple strikes three,
  The house is so lonesome an' time is so long
  For pore weepin' mother an' me.

6 We're all alone now, for Jenny is gone,
  She went with the angels so bright,
  An' those was the very last words that she said,
  I want to kiss papa goodnight.

The suffrage movement gathered momentum following the Seneca Falls Convention of 1848 where Lucretia Mott and Elizabeth Cady Stanton proclaimed the equality of the sexes and demanded the "inalienable right to the elective franchise" for women. But the slavery controversy and the Civil War sidetracked the issue for over two decades. And while the Territory of Wyoming granted the vote to women in 1869, the struggle had hardly begun. Suffragettes employed songs, such as Harriet H. Robinson's "Columbia's Daughters," to spread the message. It was written to the melody of the widely sung gospel hymn "Hold the Fort." (For another parody of "Hold the Fort" see the worker protest section, VI, in this chapter.) From Songs of the Suffragettes, Folkways FH 5281 (used by permission of Folkways Records).

COLUMBIA'S DAUGHTERS

1 Hark the sound of myriad voices
  Rising in their might!
  'Tis the daughters of Columbia
  Pleading for the right.

  chorus:
      Raise the flag and plant the standard,
      Wave the signal still;
      Brothers, we must share your freedom,
      Help us, and we will.

2 Think it not an idle murmur,
  You who hear the cry;
  'Tis a plea for human freedom
  Hallowed liberty!

3 O our country, glorious nation,
  Greatest of them all!

343

Give unto thy daughters justice,
Or thy pride will fall.

4 Great Republic! to thy watchword
Wouldst thou faithful be,
All beneath thy starry banner
Must alike be free.

Elizabeth Boynton Herbert's "The New America" was
a parody of "America." Its singing was warmly applauded
at the National American Woman's Suffrage Convention of
1891. Also from Songs of the Suffragettes, Folkways FH
5281 (used by permission of Folkways Records).

THE NEW AMERICA

1 Our country, now from thee
Claim we our liberty,
In freedom's name.
Guarding home's altar fires,
Daughters of patriot sires,
Their zeal our own inspires
Justice to claim.

2 Women in every age
For this great heritage
Tribute have paid.
Our birth-right claim we now--
Longer refuse to bow;
On freedom's altar now
Our hand is laid.

3 Sons, will you longer see,
Mothers on bended knee
For justice pray?
Rise now, in manhood's might,
With earth's great souls unite
To speed the dawning light
Of freedom's day.

V. FARMER PROTEST

While women were agitating for temperance and suffrage, farmers were suffering from the dual effects of
inflation and declining farm prices following the Civil
War. Their political power base also was eroding as
urban areas experienced rapid growth as a result of a
developing industrial and financial capitalism. Finding
little solace in the actions of the Republicans and the
Democrats, the farmers turned towards farm-oriented
political organizations such as the Grange, the Green-

back party and, especially the Populist party. Protest
music became an important propaganda weapon in their
crusade. In the 1890's two Populist songs were composed: "Hayseed Like Me" and "The Farmer Is the Man."
The first was written to the tune of "Rosin the Beau,"
already a much parodied song (see "Acres of Clams" in
Chapter Five and "Lincoln and Liberty, Too" in this
chapter). Pete Seeger sings "Hayseed Like Me" on American Industrial Ballads, Folkways FH 5251, an important
research tool (used by permission of Folkways Records).

HAYSEED LIKE ME

1 I once was a tool of oppression
And as green as a sucker could be;
And monopolies banded together
To beat a poor hayseed like me.

2 The railroads and the old party bosses
Together did sweetly agree;
They thought there would be little trouble
In working a hayseed like me.

3 In working a hayseed like me,
In working a hayseed like me,
They thought there would be little trouble
In working a hayseed like me.

4 But now I've roused up a little,
Their greed and corruption I see;
And the ticket we vote next November
Will be made up of hayseeds like me.

5 Will be made up of hayseeds like me,
Will be made up of hayseeds like me,
And the ticket we vote next November
Will be made up of hayseeds like me.

"The Farmer Is the Man" has entered the folk tradition reflecting both its musical quality and its
accurate portrayal of the farmer's perennial problems.
From American Industrial Ballads, Folkways FH 5251 (used
by permission of Folkways Records).

THE FARMER IS THE MAN

1 When the farmer comes to town
With his wagon broken down,
Oh, the farmer is the man who feeds them all.
If you'll only look and see,

I think you will agree
That the farmer is the man who feeds them all.

2 Oh, the farmer is the man,
  The farmer is the man,
  Lives on credit till the fall;
  Then they take him by the hand,
  And they lead him from the land,
  And the middleman's the one who gets it all.

3 When the lawyer hangs around
  And the butcher cuts a pound,
  Oh, the farmer is the man who feeds them all.
  And the preacher and the cook
  Go a-strolling by the brook,
  But the farmer is the man who feeds them all.

4 Oh, the farmer is the man,
  The farmer is the man,
  Lives on credit till the fall.
  With the interest rate so high,
  It's a wonder he don't die,
  For the mortgage man's the one that gets it all.

5 When the banker says he's broke
  And the merchant's up in smoke,
  They forget that it's the farmer who feeds them
      all.
  It would put them to the test
  If the farmer took a rest,
  Then they'd know that it's the farmer feeds them
      all.

6 Oh, the farmer is the man,
  The farmer is the man,
  Lives on credit till the fall.
  And his pants are wearing thin,
  His condition it's a sin,
  He's forgot that he's the man who feeds them all.

Of all the farmers, the sharecroppers suffered the
most. These tenants were continually in debt to either
their landlords or their merchants. "Down On Penny's
Farm" and its many variants describe these conditions of
economic slavery perfectly. The Bentley Boys recorded
a version in 1929 that was reissued on Anthology of
American Folk Music, Volume One: Ballads, Folkways FA
2951.

DOWN ON PENNY'S FARM

1 Come you ladies and gentlemen, listen to my song,
  Sing it to you right, but you might think it's
      wrong;
  May make you mad, but I mean no harm,
  It's just about the renters on Penny's farm.

   chorus:
      It's hard times in the country
      Out on Penny's farm.

2 You move out on Penny's farm
  Plant a little crop of 'bacco and a little crop of
      corn;
  Come around to see you, gonna flip and flop,
  Till you get yourself a mortgage on everything you
      got.

3 Hasn't George Penny got a flattering mouth?
  Move you to the country and a little log house;
  Got no windows but the cracks in the wall,
  He'll work you all the summer and rob you in the
      fall.

4 You go in the fields, you'll work all day,
  Way after night, but you get no pay;
  Promise some meat or a little bucket of lard,
  It's hard to be a renter on Penny's farm.

5 Here's George Penny, he'll come into town
  With a wagonload of peaches, not a one of 'em
      sound;
  Got to have his money or somebody's check,
  Pay him for a bushel and you don't get a peck.

6 George Penny's renters they'll come into town
  With their hands in their pockets and their head
      hanging down;
  Go in the store and the merchant will say,
  "Your mortgage is due and I'm looking for my pay."

7 Down in his pocket with a tremblin' hand,
  "Can't pay you all, but I'll pay you what I can."
  Then to the telephone the merchant make a call,
  He'll put you on the chain gang don't pay it all.

VI.   WORKER PROTEST

   Technological unemployment was one of the by-pro-
ducts of the mechanization of industry in the nineteenth

century. American workers were hard pressed to challenge this situation, but they tried. Unions were formed, political strategies were charted, and protest songs were written. "Peg and Awl" describes the impact of the machine age upon a skilled craftsman in the shoe-making industry. Despite the dates in the lyrics, the song was composed near the middle of the century. From American Industrial Ballads, Folkways FH 5251 (used by permission of Folkways Records). See also Anthology of American Folk Music, Volume One: Ballads, Folkways FA 2951, for a 1929 version by the Carolina Tar Heels.

PEG AND AWL

1 In the days of eighteen and one, peg and awl,
  In the days of eighteen and one, peg and awl,
  In the days of eighteen and one
  Peggin' shoes was all I done,
  Hand me down my pegs, my pegs, my awl.

[similarly]

2 In days of eighteen and two, peg and awl,
  Peggin' shoes was all I'd do,

3 In the days of eighteen and three, peg and awl,
  Peggin' shoes was all you'd see,

4 In the days of eighteen and four, peg and awl,
  I said I'd peg those shoes no more,
  Throw away my pegs, my pegs, my pegs, my awl.

5 They've invented a new machine, peg and awl,
  Prettiest little thing you ever seen,
  Throw away my pegs, my pegs, my pegs, my awl.

6 Makes one hundred pairs to my one, peg and awl,
  Peggin' shoes it ain't no fun,
  Throw away my pegs, my pegs, my pegs, my awl.

"The Blind Fiddler" portrays the tragedy of a work-er blinded in a railroad blacksmith shop and was a hid-den plea for state workmen's compensation laws in the late 1850's. Pete Seeger sings it on American Indus-trial Ballads, Folkways FH 5251 (used by permission of Folkways Records).

THE BLIND FIDDLER

1 I lost my eyes in a blacksmith shop
  In the year of fifty-six,

While dusting out a T-planch
Which was out of fix.
It bounded from the tongs
And there concealed my doom.
I am a blind fiddler and
Far from my home.

2 I've been to San Francisco,
I've been to Doctor Lane.
He operated on one of my eyes,
But nothing could he gain.
He told me that I'd never see,
And it's no use to mourn.
I am a blind fiddler and
Far from my home.

3 I have a wife and three little ones
Depending now on me.
To share all my troubles,
Whatever they may be.
I hope that they'll be careful
While I'm compelled to roam.
I am a blind fiddler and
Far from my home.

As hundreds of thousands of Irish Catholics fled
their homeland for the United States in the aftermath
of the potato famine of 1845-46, native Americans first
became frightened, and then angry, at the growing numbers. Organizations such as the Know Nothing party were
determined to restrict the flow of foreigners. Many
laborers allied themselves with the nativists since the
immigrants contributed directly to the unemployment
problem. The song "No Irish Need Apply" illustrates the
widespread discrimination against the Irish and offers
one possible response. Source: <u>Frontier Ballads</u>, Folkways FP 5003, (used by permission of Folkways Records).

NO IRISH NEED APPLY

1 I'm a decent boy just landed
From the town of Balyfad;
I want a situation yes,
And want it very bad.

2 I seen employment advertised,
It's just the thing says I;
But the dirty Spalpeen ended with:
"No Irish need apply."

349

3 O, says I, but that's an insult,
O, to get the place I'll try;
So I went to see the blackguard
With his no Irish need apply.

chorus:
Some do think it is a misfortune
To be christened Pat or Dan,
But to me it is an honor
To be born an Irishman.

4 I started out to find the house,
I got it mighty soon;
There I found the old chap seated,
He was reading the <u>Tribune</u>.

5 I told him what I came for
When he in a rage did fly;
"No," he says, "you are a Paddy and
No Irish need apply."

6 Well, I gets my dander rising,
I would like to black his eye;
To tell an Irish gentleman
No Irish need apply.

7 I couldn't stand it longer
So a-hold of him I took;
I gave him such a whelting
As he'd get at Donnybrook.

8 He hollered, "Milia Murther,"
And to get away did try;
And swore he'd never write again
No Irish need apply.

9 O, he makes a big apology
I bid him then goodby;
Saying, "When next you want a beating, you write
No Irish need apply."

Many of the best struggle songs were written by
coal miners. The very nature of the work--isolated and
hazardous--may explain the quality and the quantity of
their songs. By the late nineteenth century, miners began organizing in an effort to improve intolerable working conditions and low wages. Strikes were frequent and
the owners retaliated in various ways. In the South
they even employed convict labor to break strikes.
"Buddy Won't You Roll Down the Line" is a well known
Tennessee miner's song from the 1890's that, ironically,

350

was based on a song composed by black convicts working the mines as strikebreakers. Uncle Dave Macon of "Grand Ole Opry" fame recorded a version in 1928 similar to the text from American Industrial Ballads, Folkways FH 5251 (used by permission of Folkways Records).

BUDDY WON'T YOU ROLL DOWN THE LINE

1 Way back yonder in Tennessee they leased the con-
    victs out.
  Sent them working in the mines against free labor
    stout.
  Free labor rebelled against it, to win it took
    some time.
  But when the lease was in effect, they made 'em
    rise and shine.

  chorus:
      Buddy, won't you roll down the line,
      Buddy, won't you roll down the line,
      Yonder comes my darling,
      Coming down the line.

2 Early Monday morning they get 'em up on time,
  Send you down to Lone Rock just to look into that
    mine.
  Send you down to Lone Rock just to look into that
    hole,
  Very next thing the captain says, "You better get
    your pole."

3 The beans they are half done, the bread is not so
    well.
  The meat it is all burnt up and the coffee's black
    as heck.
  But when you get your task done, and on the floor
    you fall,
  Anything you get to eat it'd taste good, done or
    raw.

4 The bank boss he's a hard man, a man you all know
    well.
  And if you don't get your task done, he's gonna
    give you hallelujah.
  And when you get your task done and on the floor
    you fall,
  Very next thing the captain says, "You better get
    your pole."

"Come All You Hardy Miners" was written in the 1900's to rally workers behind President John White and

his union, the United Mine Workers of America. From
American Industrial Ballads, Folkways FH 5251 (used by
permission of Folkways Records).

COME ALL YOU HARDY MINERS

1 Come all you hardy miners and help us sing this
        song,
    Sung by some union men, four hundred thousand
        strong.
    With John White, our general, we'll fight without
        a gun,
    He'll lead us on to victory and sixty cents a ton.

2 Come all you hardy miners and help us sing this
        song,
    On the twenty-first day of April we struck for
        sixty cents a ton.
    The operators laughed at us and said we'd never
        come
    All out in one body and demand that sixty cents a
        ton.

3 Come out, you scabs and blacklegs, and join the
        men like one,
    Tell them that you're in the fight for sixty cents
        a ton.
    They're now in old Virginny, they're scabbing right
        along,
    But when we win they're sure to try for the sixty
        cents a ton.

4 Come all you hardy miners, let's try to do our
        best,
    We'll first get old Virginny, Kentucky, and then
        we'll get a rest.
    There's going to be a meeting, right here in this
        land,
    When we reach across the river and take them by the
        hand.

"Shut Up In the Mines of Coal Creek" was written
by Norman Gilford in 1935 to memorialize the Coal Creek
mine disaster of 1902 in which 217 miners perished. Hedy
West learned it from her father, a union organizer, who
obtained the song from Gilford. West sings it on _Old
Times and Hard Times_, Folk-Legacy FSA-32 (used by permission of Hedy West).

SHUT UP IN THE MINES OF COAL CREEK

1 Shut up in the mines at Coal Creek
  And I know I will have to die.
  Go tell my wife and children
  That I'm prepared to die.

2 The birds are gaily singing
  Upon the mountain high.
  Go tell my dear old mother
  I'll meet her in the sky.

3 Shut up in the mines at Coal Creek
  And I know I will have to die.
  Go tell my miner friends
  I'll meet them in the sky.

"The Coal Miner's Child" betrays it origin as a
re-working of a popular song by its overly sentimental
lyrics. Nevertheless, it does not exaggerate the misery
and starvation-like conditions the miners faced during
the depression of the 1930's, nor the worker's hostility
towards the rich and powerful. Text: Old Times and
Hard Times, Folk-Legacy FSA-32 (used by permission of
Hedy West).

THE COAL MINER'S CHILD

1 "I have no home," said the coal miner's child
  At the door of a rich man's hall,
  As she trembling stood on the marble steps
  And leaned on the polished wall.

2 "My father was killed in the coal mines," she said,
  As the tears dimmed her eyes so bright,
  "And last of all, my mother is dead;
  I'm an orphan alone tonight."

3 The night was cold and the snow fell fast,
  But the rich man closed his door.
  His proud lips spurned with scorn as he said,
  "No bread, no room for the poor."

4 The rich man slept on his velvet couch
  And dreamed of his silver and gold,
  While the orphan laid on a bed of snow,
  Dying of hunger and cold.

5 This is the story of a coal miner's child,
  A little girl only nine years old.

She was found dead by a rich man's door;
She died of hunger and cold.

Deplorable working conditions, low wage rates, and
the bitter hostility of the owners towards unionism contributed to unrest in the southern textile industry.
The textile workers, like their counterparts in coal
mining, expressed their thoughts in song. "Hard Times
In the Mill" was written in the 1890's by workers in the
knitting mills of Columbia, South Carolina. The final
stanza sums up their frustration in the days before the
eight hour work shift was achieved. From American Industrial Ballads, Folkways FH 5251 (used by permission
of Folkways Records).

HARD TIMES IN THE MILL

1 Every morning at half-past four,
You hear the cook hop on the floor.

chorus:
It's hard times in the mill, my love,
Hard times in the mill.

2 Every morning just at five,
Gotta get up dead or alive.

3 Every morning right at six,
Don't that old bell make you sick?

4 The pulley got hot, the belt jumped off,
Knocked Mr. Guyon's derby off.

5 Old Pat Goble thinks he's a hon,
He puts me in mind of a doodle in the sun.

6 The section hand he thinks he's a man,
He ain't got sense to pay off his hands.

7 They steal his ring, they steal his knife,
Steal everything but his big fat wife.

8 My bobbin's all out, my end's all down,
The doffer's in my alley and I can't get around.

9 The section hand's standing at the door,
Ordering the sweepers to sweep up the floor.

10 Every night when I go home,
A piece of corn bread and an old jaw bone.

11 Ain't it enough to break your heart?
   Have to work all day and at night it's dark.

"Let Them Wear Their Watches Fine" is a straightforward description of life without dignity in a southern textile town in the 1910's. From American Industrial Ballads, Folkways FH 5251 (used by permission of
Folkways Records).

LET THEM WEAR THEIR WATCHES FINE

1 I lived in a town away down south by the name of
     Buffalo;
  And worked in the mill with the rest of the trash
     as we're often called, you know.

2 You factory folks who sing this rhyme will surely
     understand
  The reason why I love you so is I'm a factory hand.

3 While standing here between my looms, you know I
     lose no time
  To keep my shuttles in a whiz and write this little
     rhyme.

4 We rise up early in the morn and work all day real
     hard,
  To buy our little meat and bread and sugar, tea and
     lard.

5 We work from weekend to weekend, and never lose a
     day;
  And when that awful payday comes, we draw our
     little pay.

6 We then go home on payday night and sit down in a
     chair;
  The merchant raps upon the door--he's come to get
     his share.

7 When all our little debts are paid and nothing left
     behind,
  We turn our pockets wrong side out but not a cent
     can we find.

8 We rise up early in the morn and toil from soon to
     late;
  We have no time to primp or fix and dress right up
     to date.

9 Our children they grow up unlearned, no time to go
    to school;
  Almost before they have learned to walk, they have
    learned to spin or spool.

10 The boss man jerks them round and round and
      whistles very keen;
   I'll tell you what, the factory kids are really
     treated mean.

11 The folks in town who dress so fine and spend their
      money free
   Will hardly look at a factory hand who dresses like
     you and me.

12 As we go walking down the street all wrapped in
      lint and strings,
   They call us fools and factory trash and other low-
     down things.

13 Well, let them wear their watches fine, their rings
      and pearly strings;
   When the day of judgement comes we'll make 'em shed
     their pretty things.

Written during the depths of the 1930's depression,
"Winnsboro Cotton Mill Blues" is a slashing piece of
satire from North Carolina. Source: American Industrial Ballads, FH 5251 (used by permission of Folkways
Records).

        WINNSBORO COTTON MILL BLUES

    Old man Sargent, sitting at the desk,
    The damned old fool won't give us no rest.
    He'd take the nickels off a dead man's eyes
    To buy a Coca-Cola and an Eskimo Pie.

    chorus:
        I got the blues, I got the blues,
        I got the Winnsboro cotton mill blues.
        Lordy, Lordy, spoolin's hard;
        You work for Tom Watson, got to work like hell.
        I got the blues, I got the blues,
        I got the Winnsboro cotton mill blues.

    When I die, don't you bury me at all,
    Hang me up on the spool room wall.
    Place a bobbin in my hand
    So I can keep on a-workin' in the Promised Land.

                    356

The successful early labor unions, such as the American Federation of Labor, appealed to the working class elite--skilled craftsmen. Less successful were the industrial unions that opened their ranks to all workers, but especially welcomed the unskilled. However, one industrial union, the Knights of Labor, appeared headed for a long life. At its height in 1886, it approached the one million mark in membership, yet, as we shall see, that achievement was short-lived. The union's rallying cry was "Storm the Fort, Ye Knights of Labor" which was based on the Hymn "Hold the Fort." (see "Columbia's Daughters," section IV in this chapter, for another parody.)

STORM THE FORT, YE KNIGHTS OF LABOR

Toiling millions now are waking,
See them marching on.
All the tyrants now are shaking,
Ere their power is gone.

chorus:
    Storm the fort, ye Knights of Labor,
    Battle for your cause.
    Equal rights for every neighbor,
    Down with tyrant laws!

Who will dare to shun the conflict?
Who would be a slave?
Better die within the trenches,
Forward, then ye brave.

"Storm the Fort" has an involved history of trans-Atlantic crossings. It spread to Great Britain where a transportation union rewrote the lyrics and changed the title back to the original. After World War I a remodeled "Hold the Fort" returned the United States where it served as a rousing battle cry for countless pickets. This last version is from the informative album The Original Talking Union and Other Union Songs, Folkways FH 5285 (used by permission of Folkways Records).

HOLD THE FORT

1 We meet today in freedom's cause
  And raise our voices high;
  We'll join our hands in union strong
  To battle or to die--

  chorus:
      Hold the fort, for we are coming,

357

        Union men be strong.
        Side by side we battle onward,
        Victory will come.

2 Look my comrades, see the union,
    Banners waving high;
    Reinforcements now appearing
    Victory is nigh--

3 See our numbers still increasing,
    Hear the bugles blow;
    By our union we will triumph
    Over every foe--

   The Knights of Labor supported the movement for an
eight hour work day; in fact, its uncompromising position was decisive in the union's demise. The Knights
called a nation-wide strike for May 1, 1886, in support
of the eight hour issue. The strike was a failure and
both sympathetic workers and antagonistic employers knew
the union had been dealt a fatal blow. However, the
eight hour cause was not dead. A group of coal miners
achieved the long-sought goal in 1897. The song "Eight
Hour Day" was born in that struggle. From American Industrial Ballads, Folkways FH 5251 (used by permission
of Folkways Records).

EIGHT HOUR DAY

1 We're brave and gallant miner boys
    Who work in underground,
    For courage and good nature
    No finer can be found.

2 We work both late and early,
    And get but little pay
    To support our wives and children
    In free Americay.

3 If Satan took the blacklegs,
    I'm sure 'twould be no sin,
    What peace and happiness 'twould be
    For us poor workingmen.

4 Eight hours we'd have for working,
    Eight hours we'd have for play;
    Eight hours we'd have for sleeping
    In free Americay.

   In 1905 an even more radical union was founded, the
Industrial Workers of the World, or "Wobblies" as its

enemies called it. It preached revolution: the overthrow of capitalism and its replacement by a form of socialism in which the workers would direct the government. Yet its immediate goals were more practical, as one Wobbly explained: "The final aim is revolution, but for the present let's see if we can get a bed to sleep in, water enough to take a bath and decent food to eat." The IWW only survived two decades and never exceeded a membership of 150,000. But, if success could be measured by song output, it surpassed all other unions in quality and quantity. An early IWW organizer, Ralph Chaplin, composed "Solidarity Forever" which later became the theme song for the AFL-CIO. Ironically, when the song was written, the IWW and the AFL were bitter enemies. Source: The Original Talking Union and Other Union Songs, Folkways FH 5285 (used by permission of Folkways Records).

SOLIDARITY FOREVER

1 When the union's inspiration, through the workers'
    blood shall run,
There can be no power greater anywhere beneath the
    sun.
Yet what force on earth is weaker than the feeble
    strength of one?
But the union makes us strong.

chorus:
    Solidarity forever, (3X)
    For the union makes us strong.

2 It is we who plowed the prairies, built the cities
    where they trade,
Dug the mines and built the workshops, endless
    miles of railroad laid.
Now we stand, outcast and starving, mid the wonders
    we have made,
But the union makes us strong.

3 They have taken untold millions that they never
    toiled to earn,
But without our brain and muscle not a single wheel
    can turn.
We can break their haughty power, gain our freedom
    when we learn
That the union makes us strong.

4 In our hands is placed a power greater than their
    hoarded gold,

Greater than the might of atoms, magnified a
    thousandfold.
We can bring to birth a new world from the ashes of
    the old,
For the union makes us strong.

"Little red books" crammed with protest songs were
distributed at IWW meetings to fan the fires of discon-
tent as the members participated in sort of an anti-
capitalist sing-along. The author of many of these songs
was the Swedish immigrant Joe Hill (Joel Ammanuel Haag-
land). His most notable number, "The Preacher and the
Slave," was set to the tune of the Protestant hymn "In
the Sweet Bye and Bye." The text is from the best recorded source of Hill's music, The Songs of Joe Hill,
sung by Joe Glazer. Folkways FP 2039 (used by permission
of Folkways Records).

THE PREACHER AND THE SLAVE

1 Long haired preachers come out every night
  Try to tell you what's wrong and what's right.
  But when asked about something to eat,
  They will answer with voices so sweet:

  chorus:
        You will eat, bye and bye,
        In that glorious land in the sky.
        Work and pray, live on hay,
        You'll get pie in the sky when you die.

2 And the starvation army they play,
  And they sing and they clap and they pray.
  Till they get all your coin in the drum,
  Then they tell you when you're on the bum.

3 Holy rollers and jumpers come out,
  And they holler and jump and they shout.
  And when eating time comes round they say,
  "You will eat on that glorious day."

4 If you fight hard for children and wife,
  Try to get something good in this life,
  You're a sinner and bad man they tell,
  When you die you will sure go to Hell.

5 Workingmen of all countries unite,
  Together we'll stand and we'll fight.
  When the world and its wealth we have gained,
  To the grafters we'll sing this refrain:

final chorus:
> You will eat, bye and bye,
> When you've learned how to cook and to fry.
> Chop some wood--do you good,
> And you'll eat in the sweet bye and bye.

Another Joe Hill song outlived the IWW: "Casey Jones, the Union Scab," a parody of the popular ballad "Casey Jones" (see Chapter Four). From The Songs of Joe Hill, Folkways FP 2039 (used by permission of Folkways Records).

CASEY JONES, THE UNION SCAB

1 The workers on the S. P. line to strike sent out a
  call;
But Casey Jones, the engineer, he wouldn't strike
  at all.
His boiler it was leaking, and its drivers on the
  bum,
And his engine and its bearings they were all out
  of plumb.

chorus:
> Casey Jones, kept his junkpile running,
> Casey Jones was working double time;
> Casey Jones got a wooden medal
> For being good and faithful on the S. P. line.

2 The workers said to Casey, "Won't you help us win
  this strike?"
But Casey said, "Let me alone, you'd better take a
  hike."
Then someone put a bunch of railroad ties across
  the track,
And Casey hit the river with an awful crack.

chorus:
> Casey Jones hit the river bottom,
> Casey Jones broke his blooming spine.
> Casey Jones was an angeleno,
> He took a trip to heaven on the S. P. line.

3 When Casey Jones got up to heaven to the Pearly
  Gate,
He said, "I'm Casey Jones the guy that pulled the
  S. P. freight."
"You're just the man," said Peter, "our musicians
  went on strike
You can get a job a-scabbing anytime you like."

chorus:
> Casey Jones got a job in heaven,
> Casey Jones was doing mighty fine.
> Casey Jones went scabbing on the angels
> Just like he did to workers on the S. P. line.

4 The angels got together and they said it wasn't
    fair,
  For Casey Jones to go around a-scabbing everywhere.
  The Angels Union Number Twenty-Three they sure were
    there,
  And they promptly fired Casey down the Golden Stair.

chorus:
> Casey Jones went to Hell a-flying,
> Casey Jones, the Devil said, "Fine."
> Casey Jones, get busy shoveling sulphur,
> That's what you get for scabbing on the S. P.
>   line.

Joe Hill's "There Is Power In a Union" summarized
the goal of the IWW clearly and forthrightly. Members
sang it to the tune of the hymn "There Is Power In the
Blood." Text: The Songs of Joe Hill, Folkways FP 2039
(used by permission of Folkways Records).

THERE IS POWER IN A UNION

1 Would you have freedom from wage slavery?
  Then join in the grand industrial band.
  Would you from misery and hunger be free?
  Then come do your share like a man.

chorus:
> There is power, there is power
> In a band of working men
> When they stand hand in hand.
> That's a power, that's a power
> That must rule in every land--
> One industrial union grand.

2 Would you have mansions of gold in the sky
  And live in a shack, way in the back?
  Would you have wings up in heaven to fly
  And starve here with rags on your back?

3 If you've had enough of the blood of the lamb
  Then join in the grand industrial band.
  If, for a change, you would have eggs and ham,
  Then come do your share like a man.

4 If you like sluggers to beat off your head,
   Then don't organize, all unions despise.
   If you want nothing before you are dead,
   Shake hands with your boss and look wise.

5 Come, all ye workers, from every land,
   Come join the grand industrial band,
   Then we our share of this earth shall demand.
   Come on! Do your share like a man!

VII. WE SURE GOT HARD TIMES NOW

During the dark days of 1930, bluesman Barbecue
Bob recorded "We Sure Got Hard Times Now" (reissued on
Rounder 4007, <u>Hard</u> <u>Times</u>):

   You heard about a job,
   Now you is on your way. (2X)
   Twenty mens after the same job
   All in the same old day.

   Hard times, hard times,
   We sure got hard times now. (2X)
   Just think and think about it,
   We got hard times now.

Selecting a few examples of depression era songs is
difficult. There are hundreds of musical expressions
describing the emotional, spiritual and material trauma
that affected millions of Americans.

For those who wished to forget soup kitchens,
Hoovervilles, foreclosures, suicides, starving children
and economic paralysis, the 1930's offered escapist
motion pictures, books and popular music. Others preferred a realistic approach to their problems. Some
protest songs wrapped their messages in laughter and
cheerful melodies, but underneath they seethed with
tragic irony. "Beans, Bacon and Gravy," written to the
tune of "Jesse James," was one. Pete Seeger sings it on
<u>American</u> <u>Industrial</u> <u>Ballads</u>, Folkways FH 5251 (used by
permission of Folkways Records).

BEANS, BACON AND GRAVY

1 I was born long ago in 1894,
   I've seen many a panic I will own.
   I've been hungry, I've been cold,
   And now I'm growing old,
   But the worst I've seen is 1931.

chorus:
Oh, those beans, bacon and gravy
They almost drive me crazy;
I eat them till I see them in my dreams (in my
dreams).
When I wake up in the morning
And another day is dawning,
I know I'll have another mess of beans.

2 Well, we congregate each morning
At the country barn at dawning,
Everyone is happy, so it seems.
But when our day's work is done,
And we file in one by one,
And thank the Lord for the one more mess of beans.

3 We've Hooverized on butter,
And for milk we've only water,
And I haven't seen a steak in many a day.
As for pies, cakes and jellies,
We substitute sow-bellies
For which we work the country road each day.

4 If there ever comes a time
When I have more than a dime,
They will have to put me under lock and key.
For they've had me broke so long,
I can only sing this song
Of the workers and their misery.

There is a fine line between tragedy and comedy.
"White House Blues" was a political obituary for ex-
President Herbert Hoover who took a thrashing, not only
from Franklin Roosevelt in the election of 1932, but
also from country musicians. The New Lost City Ramblers
recreate the ditty on Songs of the Depression, Folkways
FH 5264 (used by permission of Folkways Records).

WHITE HOUSE BLUES

1 Look here Mr. Hoover, it's see what you done,
You went off a fishin' let the country go to ruin.
Now he's gone, I'm glad he's gone!

2 Roosevelt's in the White House, doing his best,
While old Hoover is layin' around and rest.
Now he's gone (doghide), I'm glad he's gone!

3 Pants all busted, patches all way down,
People got so ragged they couldn't go to town.
Now he's gone, I'm glad he's gone!

4 Workin' in the coal mines, twenty cents a ton,
Fourteen long hours and your work's day is done.
Now he's gone, I'm glad he's gone!

5 People all angry, they all got the blues,
Wearing patched britches and old tennis shoes.
Now he's gone (doghide), I'm glad he's gone!

6 Got up this morning, all I could see
Was corn bread and gravy just a-waitin' for me.
And now he's gone, I'm glad he's gone!

7 [repeat stanza one]

Blind Alfred Reed recorded "How Can a Poor Man
Stand Such Times and Live?" only one month following the
Wall Street crash of 1929, an indication that rural
folk, such as Reed, were experiencing hard times well
before the stock market fiasco. Reed's folk wisdom
still rings true today. The original recording was reissued on Rounder Records 1001, while the NLCR's version
is available on Songs of the Depression, Folkways FH
5264 (used by permission of Folkways Records).

HOW CAN A POOR MAN STAND SUCH TIMES AND LIVE?

1 There once was a time when everything was cheap,
But now prices nearly puts a man to sleep.
When we pay our grocery bill,
We just a-feel like a-makin' our will.

chorus:
    Tell me how can a poor man stand such times
        and live?

2 I remember when dry goods were cheap as dirt,
We could take two bits and buy a dandy shirt.
Now we pay three bucks or more,
Maybe get a shirt that another man wore.

3 Well I used to trade with a man by the name of
        Gray;
Flour was fifty cents for a twenty-four pound bag.
Now it's a dollar and a half beside,
Just like a-skinnin' off a flea for the hide.

4 Oh, the schools we have today ain't worth a cent,
But they see to it that every child is sent.
If we don't send every day,
We have a heavy fine to pay.

365

5 Prohibition's good if 'tis conducted right;
   There's no sense in shooting a man 'til he shows
      flight.
   Officers kill without a cause,
   Then complain about funny laws.

6 Most all preachers preach for gold and not for
      souls,
   That's what keeps a poor man always in a hole.
   We can hardly get our breath,
   Taxed and schooled and preached to death.

7 Oh, it's time for every man to be awake;
   We pay fifty cents a pound when we ask for steak.
   When we get our package home,
   A little wad of paper with gristle and bone.

8 Well the doctor comes around with a face all
      bright,
   And he says in a little while you'll be all right.
   All he gives is a humbug pill,
   A dose of dope and a great big bill.

The depression displaced hundreds of thousands of
people. Folk poet and philosopher Woody Guthrie wrote
songs describing the "Oakies" and their migration from
the dust bowl of the Great Plains to the "peach bowl"
of California. Tony Schwartz of the NLCR collected
"Keep Moving" from an unidentified singer with a
Guthrie-like philosophy. Source: Songs of the Depression, Folkways FH 5264 (used by permission of Folkways
Records).

KEEP MOVING

1 How can you keep on moving, unless you migrate too?
   They tell you to keep on moving, but migrate you
      must not do.
   The only reason for moving, the reason why I roam,
   Is to go to a new location, and find myself a home.

2 I can't go back to the homestead, my shack no
      longer stands;
   They said I wasn't needed, had no claim to the
      land.
   They said, you better get moving, it's the only
      thing for you.
   But how can you get moving, unless you migrate too?

3 Now if you pitch your little tent along the broad
      highway,

The Board of Sanitation says, "Sorry, you can't
stay.
Move on, move on, get moving," is their everlasting
cry.
Can't stay, can't go back, can't migrate, so where
in heck am I?

4 I can not stand the miseries that follow me as I
roam,
Unless I'm looking forward to a place I can call
home.
So I think I'll round up all the folks and see what
we can do,
Cause how can you keep moving, unless you migrate
too?

One depression song, "Dreadful Memories," offers an
insight into the folk process. Two half-sisters, Aunt
Molly Jackson and Sarah Ogun Gunning, claimed authorship. Both had been eye-witnesses to untold tragedies
in the coal fields of southeastern Kentucky in the
1930's. It was a time of strife between coal operators
and the miners who were attempting to organize. Union
miners were blacklisted and their families reduced to
starvation conditions in the company-dominated towns.
Jackson stood by helpless as thirty-seven babies died
from starvation during a particularly bitter union-
company confrontation in 1931. This incident, Jackson
later recalled, was the basis for her composing "Dreadful Memories." However, Gunning claimed that she was
the rightful author of the song and that Jackson had
learned it from her in the 1940's.

The fight over authorship is immaterial for
several reasons. (1) The sisters composed variations
modeled on the hymn "Precious Memories." (2) The songs
expose an unconscionable episode in American history.
(3) The listener is hearing the restructuring of music
by two outstanding traditionalists and this is the key
to the folk process. Both versions are printed: A is
the Jackson song from The Stories and Songs of Aunt
Molly Jackson, Folkways FH 5457 (used by permission of
Folkways Records); B is the Gunning version from Girl
of Constant Sorrow, Folk-Legacy FSA-26 (used by permission of Folk-Legacy Records, Sharon, Conn.).

A - DREADFUL MEMORIES (Jackson)

1 Dreadful memories! How they linger,
How they pain my precious soul!

Little children, sick and hungry,
Sick and hungry, weak and cold.

2 Little children, cold and hungry,
Without any food at all to eat.
They had no clothes to put on their bodies,
They had no shoes to put on their feet.

3 Dreadful memories! How they linger,
How they fill my heart with pain.
Oh, how hard I've tried to forget them,
But I find it all in vain.

4 I can't forget them little babies,
With golden hair as soft as silk.
Slowly dying from starvation,
They're parents could not give them milk.

5 I can't forget them coal miners' children
That starved to death for want of milk.
While the coal operators and their wives and their
children
Were all dressed in jewels and silk.

6 Dreadful memories! How they haunt me
As the lonely moments fly.
Oh, how them little babies suffered!
I saw them starve to death and die.

B - DREADFUL MEMORIES (Gunning)

1 Dreadful memories, how they linger,
How they ever flood my soul,
How the workers and their children
Die from hunger and from cold.

2 Hungry fathers, wearied mothers,
Living in those dreadful shacks,
Little children cold and hungry
With no clothing on their backs.

3 Dreadful gun-thugs and stool-pigeons
Always flock around our door.
What's the crime that we've committed?
Nothing, only that we're poor.

4 When I think of all the heartaches
And all the things that we've been through,
Then I wonder how much longer
And what a working man can do.

5 Really, friends, it doesn't matter
   Whether you are black or white.
   The only way you'll ever change things
   Is to fight and fight and fight.

6 We will have to join the union,
   They will help you find a way
   How to get a better living
   And for your work get better pay.

Sarah Ogun Gunning also composed a powerful protest
song that she described as autobiographical. In 1939,
Moses Asch, later director of Folkways Records, called
it the most radical number he had ever heard. Sarah
recorded it for the Library of Congress under the title
"I Hate the Capitalist System." On her Folk-Legacy
album it was titled "I Hate the Company Bosses." Text:
Girl of Constant Sorrow, Folk-Legacy FSA-26 (used by
permission of Folk-Legacy Records, Sharon, Conn.).

                I HATE THE COMPANY BOSSES

1 I hate the company bosses,
   I'll tell you the reason why.
   They cause me so much suffering
   And my dearest friends to die.

2 Oh, yes, I guess you wonder
   What they have done to me.
   I'm going to tell you, mister,
   My husband had T. B.

3 Brought on by hard work and low wages
   And not enough to eat,
   Going naked and hungry,
   No shoes on his feet.

4 I guess you'll say he's lazy
   And did not want to work.
   But I must say you're crazy,
   For work he did not shirk.

5 My husband was a coal miner,
   He worked and risked his life
   To try to support three children,
   Himself, his mother, and wife.

6 I had a blue-eyed baby,
   The darling of my heart.
   But from my little darling
   Her mother had to part.

7 These mighty company bosses,
   They dress in jewels and silk.
   But my darling blue-eyed baby,
   She starved to death for milk.

8 I had a darling mother,
   For her I often cry.
   But with them rotten conditions
   My mother had to die.

9 Well, what killed your mother?
   I heard these bosses say.
   Dead of hard work and starvation,
   My mother had to pay.

10 Well, what killed your mother?
   Oh, tell us, if you please.
   Excuse me, it was pellagra,
   That starvation disease.

11 They call this the land of plenty,
   To them I guess it's true.
   But that's to the company bosses,
   Not workers like me and you.

12 Well, what can I do about it,
   To these men of power and might?
   I tell you, company bosses,
   I'm going to fight, fight, fight.

13 What can we do about it,
   To right this dreadful wrong?
   We're all going to join the union,
   For the union makes us strong.

VIII. THE BITTER AND THE SWEET

Two songs conclude this volume: one a traditional folksong, the other a modern folk-like composition; both are personal choices. The first is an Irish anti-war song "Johnny I Hardly Knew Ye." It was based on Pat Gilmore's Civil War song "When Johnny Comes Marching Home." However, some authorities insist that it originated in Ireland much earlier. Regardless of its source, the irony is apparent--in one case a marching song for soldiers, in the other, an anti-war protest piece. The latter version was popular in the United States during the Vietnam War. Its savage commentary on the nature of war has few musical equals. Patrick Galvin sings an exceptional version on his out-of-print Riverside album Irish Street Songs.

JOHNNY I HARDLY KNEW YE

1 Where are the eyes that looked so mild?
   Haroo, haroo,
Where are the eyes that looked so mild?
   Haroo, haroo,
Oh, where are the eyes that looked so mild
   When my poor heart you first beguiled?
Oh, why did you run from me and the child?
   Johnny, I hardly knew ye.

chorus:
   With guns and drums and drums and guns,
     Haroo, haroo,
   With guns and drums and drums and guns,
     Haroo, haroo,
   With guns and drums and drums and guns,
     That enemy nearly slew you,
   Oh, me darling dear, you look so queer,
     Johnny, I hardly knew ye.

2 Where are the legs with which you run?
   Haroo, haroo,
Where are the legs with which you run?
   Haroo, haroo,
Oh, where are the legs with which you run
   When you went off to carry that gun?
Oh, by God, your dancing days are done,
   Johnny, I hardly knew ye.

3 You haven't an arm, you haven't a leg,
   Haroo, haroo,
You haven't an arm, you haven't a leg,
   Haroo, haroo,
Oh, you haven't an arm, you haven't a leg,
   Your an eyeless, boneless, chickenless egg,
You'll have to be put with a bowl to geg,
   Johnny, I hardly knew ye.

4 Oh, it's glad I am to see you home,
   Haroo, haroo,
Oh, it's glad I am to see you home,
   Haroo, haroo,
It's glad I am to see you home
   All from the island of Ceylon,
But so low in the flesh, so high in the bone,
   Johnny, I hardly knew ye.

Pete Seeger is America's singing conscience. His songs express the hopes and fears, the aspirations and failures, the good times and hard times of all of us.

371

Seeger's "Oh, Had I a Golden Thread" is an idealistic message-song tempered by the almost impossible task of locating that elusive thread and needle to "bind up this sorry world." Still, he persists. Sung on his obscure, but superb, Folkways album, The Rainbow Quest (FA 2454).

The song concludes this anthology of traditional music with the hope that its message enters the folk process and, like "The Unfortunate Rake" in Chapter One, endures for generations to come.

OH, HAD I A GOLDEN THREAD
by Pete Seeger
© Copyright 1959 by STORMKING MUSIC INC.
All Rights Reserved   Used by Permission

1 Oh, had I a golden thread
  And needle so fine,
  I'd weave a magic strand
  Of rainbow design.

2 In it I would weave the bravery
  Of women giving birth.
  And in it I would weave the innocence
  Of children over all the earth,
  Of children of our earth.

3 In it I would weave the restlessness
  Of men going ever forth
  Through heat of blistering desert sands
  And blizzards of the north,
  Through the frozen north.

4 Far over the waters
  I'd reach my magic band
  Through foreign cities
  To every single land,
  To every land.

5 Show my brothers and my sisters
  My rainbow design.
  Bind up this sorry world
  With hand and heart and mind,
  Hand and heart and mind.

6 Far over the waters
  I'd reach my magic band
  To every human being
  So they would understand,
  So they would understand.

  [repeat stanza 1]

RECORD COMPANIES

The editor has featured most of the music in this collection, and much more, on his weekly Saturday night folk music program "Folk Festival" from its inception in 1969 on WYSU-FM, 88.5 MHz., Youngstown, Ohio.

If you are not fortunate enough to have a folk music radio program or folk club in your area, then I suggest you write to the following record companies or organizations that specialize in folk music and ask them for a catalogue:

ALLIGATOR RECORDS, P. O. Box 60234, Chicago, IL 60660
ARHOOLIE, P. O. Box 9195, Berkeley, CA 94709
BIOGRAPH (HISTORICAL), P. O. Box 109, Canaan, NY 12029
COUNTRY LIFE, CPO 13222, Berea, KY 40403
COUNTY RECORDS, P. O. Box 191, Floyd, VA 24091
DELMARK RECORDS, 4243 N. Lincoln, Chicago, IL 60618
FLYING FISH, 1304 W. Schubert, Chicago, IL 60614
FOGARTY'S COVE MUSIC, R. R. #1, Hannon, Ontario, Canada
    L0R 1P0
FOLK-LEGACY RECORDS, Sharon, CT 06069
FOLKWAYS (ASCH, BROADSIDE, RBF), 43 W. 61st St., N.Y.,
    NY 10023
FRONT HALL, RD 1, Box 93, Voorheesville, NY 12186
GREEN LINNET (INNISFREE), 70 Turner Hill Rd., New
    Canaan, CT 06840
HERWIN, P. O. Box 306, Glen Cove, NY 11542
JEMF, Folklore Center, UCLA, Los Angeles, CA 90024
JUNE APPAL, P. O. Box 743, Whitesburg, KY 41858
KICKING MULE, P. O. Box 158, Alderpoint, CA 95411
LIBRARY OF CONGRESS, Archive of Folk Song, Music Divi-
    sion, Washington, DC 20540
MOUNTAIN RAILROAD, 3602 Atwood Ave., Madison, WI 53714
PHILO RECORDS, The Barn, North Ferrisburg, VT 05473
ROOSTER RECORDS, RFD 2, Bethel, VT 05032
ROUNDER RECORDS, 186 Willow Ave., Somerville, MA 02144
SUGAR HILL, P. O. Box 4040, Duke Station, Durham, NC
    27706
TAKOMA, P. O. Box 5403, Santa Monica, CA 90405
WILDEBEEST RECORDS, P. O. Box 311, Wexford, PA 15090
YAZOO, 245 Waverly Pl., N. Y., NY 10014

BIBLIOGRAPHY

This list of books which I have found useful is a
starting place for discovering song books, biographies,
collections and scholarly studies of traditional (and
some not so traditional) music.

Abrahams, Roger (ed.), Almeda Riddle: A Singer and Her
    Songs. Baton Rouge: Louisiana State University
    Press, 1970.
Ahrens, Pat, Union Grove: The First Fifty Years. Union
    Grove, N. C.: Union Grove Old Time Fiddle Conven-
    tion, 1975.
Albertson, Chris, Bessie Smith. N. Y.: Stein and Day,
    1972.
Allen, William F., Charles P. Ware, Lucy McKim Garrison,
    Slave Songs of the United States. N. Y.: Peter
    Smith, 1929 reprint.
Alloy, Evelyn, Working Women's Music. Somerville, Ma.:
    The New England Free Press, 1974.
Arnold, Bryon, Folksongs of Alabama. Birmingham: Uni-
    versity of Alabama Press, 1950.
Artis, Bob, Bluegrass. N. Y.: Hawthorn Books, 1975.
Baggelaar, Kristin and Donald Milton, Folk Music: More
    Than a Song. N.Y.: Thomas Y. Crowell Co., 1976.
Belden, Henry, Ballads and Songs Collected by the
    Missouri Folklore Society. Columbia: University
    of Missouri Press, 1955.
Bok, Gordon, Time and the Flying Snow: The Songs of
    Gordon Bok. Sharon, Conn.: Folk-Legacy Records,
    1977.
Brand, Oscar, Songs of '76. N. Y.: M. Evans and Co.,
    1972.
Bronson, Bertrand H., The Ballad As Song. Berkeley:
    University of California Press, 1969.
_____, The Singing Tradition of Child's Popular Bal-
    lads. Princeton: Princeton University Press, 1976.
_____, The Traditional Tunes of the Child Ballads, 4
    vols. Princeton: Princeton University Press, 1959-
    1972.
Broonzy, William, Big Bill Blues. N. Y.: Oak Publi-
    cations, 1955.
The Frank C. Brown Collection of North Carolina Folk-
    lore, Newman I. White et al (eds.), 7 vols.
    Durham, N.C.: Duke University Press, 1952-1964.
Burton, Thomas, Tom Ashley, Sam McGee, Bukka White: Ten-
    nessee Traditional Singers. Knoxville, University
    of Tennessee Press, 1981.
Carawan, Guy and Candie, Voices from the Mountains. N.
    Y.: Alfred A. Knopf, 1975.

Charters, Samuel, The Bluesmen. N.Y.: Oak Publications, 1967.

Chase, Richard, American Folk Tales and Songs. N.Y.: Signet Key Books, 1956.

Child, Frances James (ed.), The English and Scottish Popular Ballads, 5 vols. N.Y.: Dover Publications, 1965 reprint.

Coffin, Tristram P., The British Traditional Ballads In North America, republished and supplemented by Roger deV. Renwick. Austin: University of Texas Press, 1977.

Cohen, Anne B., Poor Pearl, Poor Girl! Austin: University of Texas Press, 1973.

Cox, John Harrington, Traditional Ballads and Folk-Songs Mainly from West Virginia. Austin: University of Texas Press, 1964.

Creighton, Helen, Maritime Folk Songs. East Lansing: Michigan State University Press, 1962.

_____, Songs and Ballads from Nova Scotia. N. Y.: Dover Publications, 1966 reprint.

Davis, Arthur Kyle, Traditional Ballads of Virginia. Charlottesville, Va.: University Press of Virginia, 1969 reprint.

Denisoff, R. Serge, Sing a Song of Social Significance. Bowling Green, O.: Bowling Green University Press, 1972.

Dunaway, David K., How Can I Keep from Singing: Pete Seeger. N. Y.: McGraw-Hill Book Company, 1981.

Dwyer, Richard and Richard Lingenfelter, Songs of the Gold Rush. Berkeley: University of California Press, 1964.

Eckstorm, Fannie Hardy and Mary Winslow Smyth, Minstrelsy of Maine: Folk-Songs and Ballads of the Woods and the Coast. Boston: Houghton Mifflin Co., 1927, reprinted 1971.

Eddy, Mary, Ballads and Songs from Ohio. Detroit: Folklore Associates, 1964 reprint.

Eliot, Marc, Death of a Rebel: Phil Ochs. Garden City, N. Y.: Anchor Books, 1979.

Epstein, Dena J., Sinful Tunes and Spirituals: Black Folk Music to the Civil War. Urbana: University of Illinois Press, 1977.

Evans, David, Tommy Johnson. London: Studio Visa, 1971.

Ferris, William, Blues from the Delta. Garden City, N. Y.: Anchor Books, 1979.

Fife, Austin E. and Alta S., Songs of the Cowboys by N. Howard ("Jack") Thorp. N.Y.: Clarkson N. Potter, Inc., 1966.

Flanders, Helen Hartness (ed.), Ancient Ballads Traditionally Sung in New England, 4 vols. Philadelphia: University of Pennsylvania Press, 1960.

Foner, Philip, American Labor Songs of the Nineteenth
    Century. Urbana: University of Illinois Press,
    1975.
Fowke, Edith and Alan Mills, Canada's Story in Song.
    Agincourt, Ontario: W. J. Gage, 1965.
Fowke, Edith and Joe Glazer, Songs of Work and Protest.
    N.Y.: Dover Publications, 1973 reprint.
Friedman, Albert B. (ed.), The Viking Book of Folk
    Ballads of the English-Speaking World. N.Y.: The
    Viking Press, 1956.
Gardner, Emelyns E. et al (eds.), Ballads and Songs of
    Southern Michigan. Detroit: Folklore Associates,
    1967.
Glassie, Henry, Edward D. Ives, John F. Szwed, Folksongs
    and Their Makers. Bowling Green, O.: Bowling Green
    University Press, 1971.
Glazer, Tom, Songs of Peace, Freedom, and Protest.
    Greenwich, Conn.: Fawcett Publications, Inc., 1970.
Godrich, J. and R. M. W. Dixon, (compl.) Blues and
    Gospel Records, 1902-1942. London: Storyville
    Publications, 1969.
Gray, Michael, The Art of Bob Dylan: Song and Dance Man.
    N. Y.: St. Martin's Press, 1981 revised.
Green, Archie, Only a Miner: Studies in Recorded Coal-
    Mining Songs. Urbana: University of Illinois Press,
    1972.
Greenway, John, American Folksongs of Protest. Philadel-
    phia, Pa.: University of Pennsylvania Press, 1953.
Groom, Bob, Blind Lemon Jefferson. England: Blues
    World, 1970.
_____, The Blues Revival. London: Studio Vista, 1971.
_____, Robert Johnson. England: Blues World, 1969.
Guralnick, Peter, Feel Like Going Home: Portraits in
    Blues and Rock 'N' Roll. N.Y.: Vintage Books,1981.
Guthrie, Woody, American Folksong. N.Y.: Oak Publica-
    tions, 1961 reprint.
_____, Bound for Glory. N.Y.: E.P. Dutton and Co.,
    Inc. 1968 edition.
_____, Alan Lomax, Pete Seeger, Hard Hitting Songs for
    Hard Hit People. N.Y.: Quick Fox, 1966.
Handy, W. C. (ed.), Blues: An Anthology. N.Y.: Macmillan
    Publishing Company, Inc., 1972 edition.
Harris, Sheldon, Blues Who's Who: A Biographical Dic-
    tionary of Blues Singers. New Rochelle, N.Y.:
    Arlington House, 1979.
Heaps, Willard, The Singing Sixties: The Spirit of Civil
    War Days. Norman, Okla.: University of Oklahoma
    Press, 1960.
Henderson, Kathy, My Song Is My Own. London: Pluto
    Press, 1979.
Hugill, Stan, Shanties and Sailors' Songs. N.Y.: Praeger

Publishers, 1969.

Ives, Burl, The Burl Ives Song Book. N.Y.: Ballantine Books, 1953.

Jackson, Bruce, Wake Up Dead Man. Cambridge: Harvard University Press, 1972.

Jackson, George P., White Spirituals in the Southern Uplands. N.Y.: Dover Publications, 1965 reprint.

Karpeles, Maud, Cecil Sharp: His Life and Work. Chicago: University of Chicago Press, 1967.

_____, (ed.), Cecil Sharp's Collection of English Folk Songs, 2 vols. N.Y.: Oxford University Press, 1974.

_____, (ed.) Folk Songs from Newfoundland. Hamden, Conn.: Shoe String Books, 1970.

Keil, Charles, Urban Blues. Chicago: University of Chicago Press, 1966.

Klein, Joe, Woody Guthrie: A Life. N.Y.: Alfred A. Knopf, 1980.

Korson, George, Coal Dust on the Fiddle. Detroit: Gale Research Company, 1965 reprint.

_____, Minstrels of the Mine Patch. Detroit: Gale Research Company, 1964 reprint.

_____, Pennsylvania Songs and Legends. Philadelphia: University of Pennsylvania Press, 1960.

Lawless, Ray M., Folksingers and Folksongs in America. N.Y.: Duell, Sloan and Pearce, 1960.

Lawrence, Vera Brodsky, Music for Patriots, Politicians, and Presidents. New York: Macmillan Publishing Co., Inc., 1975.

Laws, G. Malcolm, Jr., American Balladry from British Broadsides. Austin: University of Texas Press, 1957.

_____, Native American Balladry. Austin: University of Texas Press, 1964 revised edition.

Leach, MacEdward (ed.), The Ballad Book. N.Y.: A. S. Barnes and Company, Inc., 1955.

_____ and Tristram P. Coffin (eds.), The Critics and the Ballad. Carbondale, Ill.: Southern Illinois University Press, 1973.

Leadbitter, Mike, Blues Records, January 1943 to December 1966. N.Y.: Oak Publications, 1968.

_____, (ed.), Nothing But the Blues: An Illustrated Documentary. N. Y.: Oak Publications, 1971.

Leventhal, Harold and Marjorie Guthrie (eds.), The Woody Guthrie Songbook. N.Y.: Grosset and Dunlap, 1976.

Lloyd, A. L., Folk Song in England. N.Y.: International Publishers, 1967.

Lomax, Alan, The Folk Songs of North America. Garden City, N.Y.: Doubleday and Company, 1960.

Lomax, John and Alan, Cowboy Songs and Other Frontier Ballads. N.Y.: The Macmillan Company, 1938.

Lumer, Robert, The American Proletarian-Revolutionary Song Writer and Singer, Woodrow Wilson (Woody) Guthrie. Germany: Topos Verlag AG, 1979.

Malone, Bill, Country Music USA: A Fifty Year History. Austin: University of Texas Press, 1968.

_____, Southern Music, American Music. Lexington: University Press of Kentucky, 1979.

_____, Stars of Country Music. Urbana: University of Illinois Press, 1975.

Mitchell, George, Blow My Blues Away. Baton Rouge: Louisiana State University Press, 1971.

Niles, John Jacob, The Ballad Book of John Jacob Niles. N.Y.: Dover Publications, 1970 reprint.

Oakley, Giles, The Devil's Music: A History of the Blues. N.Y.: Harcourt Brace Jovanovich, 1976.

Oliver, Paul (ed.), Conversation with the Blues. London: Cassell, 1965.

_____, The Story of the Blues. Philadelphia: Chilton Book Company, 1969.

_____, Savannah Syncopators: African Retentions in the Blues. London: Studio Vista, 1970.

Orr, James L., Grange Melodies. N. Y.: Arno Press, 1975 reprint.

Palmer, Robert, Deep Blues. N.Y.: Viking Press, 1981.

Parades, Americo and Ellen J. Stekert (eds.), The Urban Experience and Folk Tradition. Austin: University of Texas Press, 1971.

Paris, Mike and Chris Comber, Jimmie the Kid: The Life of Jimmie Rodgers. N.Y.: DaCapo Press, 1981.

Porterfield, Noland, Jimmie Rodgers: The Life and Times of America's Blue Yodeler. Urbana: University of Illinois Press, 1981.

Price, Steven D., Take Me Home: The Rise of Country and Western Music. N.Y.: Praeger Publishers, 1974.

Rabson, Carolyn, Songbook of the American Revolution. Peake Island, Maine: Neo Press, 1974.

Randolph, Vance, Ozark Folksongs, 4 vols. Columbia, Mo.: University of Missouri Press, 1980 reprint.

Rasof, Henry, The Folk, Country, and Bluegrass Musicians' Catalogue. N.Y.: St. Martin's Press, 1982.

Rickaby, Franz, Ballads and Songs of the Shantyboys. Cambridge, Ma.: Harvard University Press, 1926.

Rinzler, Ralph, Uncle Dave Macon: A Bio-Discography. Los Angeles: John Edwards Memorial Foundation, 1970.

Ritchie, Jean, Singing Family of the Cumberlands. N.Y.: Quick Fox, 1955.

Rooney, James, Bossmen: Bill Monroe and Muddy Waters. N.Y.: Dial Press, 1971.

Rorer, Kinney, Rambling Blues: The Life and Songs of Charlie Poole. London: Old-Time Music, 1982.

Russell, Tony, _Blacks_ _Whites_ and _Blues_. N.Y. Stein and
    Day, 1970.
_____, _The_ _Carter_ _Family_. London: Old Time Music,
    1973.
Sandberg, Larry and Dick Weissman, _The_ _Folk_ _Music_
    Sourcebook. N.Y.: Alfred A. Knopf, 1976.
Sandburg, Carl, _The_ _American_ _Songbag_. N.Y.: Harcourt
    Brace Jovanovich, Inc., 1927.
Scaduto, Anthony, _Bob_ _Dylan_: An _Intimate_ _Biography_.
    N.Y.: Grosset and Dunlap, 1971.
Scarborough, Dorothy, _A_ _Song_ _Catcher_ _in_ _the_ _Southern_
    Mountains. N.Y.: AMS Press, Inc., reprint of 1937
    book.
Seeger, Pete, _The_ _Incompleat_ _Folksinger_. N.Y.: Simon
    and Schuster, 1972.
Seeger, Ruth, _American_ _Folk_ _Songs_ _for_ _Children_. Garden
    City, N. _Y_.: Doubleday and Company, 1948.
Sharp, Cecil, _English_ _Folk_ _Songs_ _from_ _the_ _Southern_
    Appalachians, 2 vols. N.Y.: Oxford University
    Press, 1974 reprint.
Shellans, Herbert, _Folksongs_ _of_ _the_ _Blue_ _Ridge_
    Mountains. N.Y.: Quick Fox, 1969.
Silber, Irwin (ed.), _Songs_ _of_ _the_ _Civil_ _War_. N.Y.:
    Columbia University Press, 1960.
_____, _Songs_ _of_ _Independence_. Harrisburg, Pa.: Stack-
    pole Books, 1973.
Sorrels, Rosalie (ed.), _What_, _Women_, and _Who_, _Myself_, I
    _Am_. San Francisco: Wooden Shoe, 1974.
Staines, Bill, _If_ _I_ _Were_ a _Word_, _Then_ _I_'d _Be_ a _Song_.
    Sharon, Conn.: Folk-Legacy Records, n.d.
Terrill, Tom E. (ed.), _Such_ _As_ _Us_: Southern _Voices_ _of_
    the _Thirties_. Chapel Hill, N.C.: University of
    North Carolina Press, 1978.
Titon, Jeff Todd, _Early_ _Downhome_ _Blues_: A _Musical_ _and_
    Cultural _Analysis_. Urbana: University of Illinois
    Press, 1977.
Townsend, Charles R., _San_ _Antonio_ _Rose_: The _Life_ _and_
    Music _of_ _Bob_ _Wills_. Urbana: University of Illinois
    Press, 1976.
Vincent, Leopold, _The_ _Alliance_ and _Labor_ _Songster_. N.Y.:
    Arno Press, 1975 reprint.
Von Schmidt, Eric and Jim Rooney, _Baby_ _Let_ _Me_ _Follow_ _You_
    Down: _The_ _Illustrated_ _Story_ _of_ _the_ _Cambridge_ _Folk_
    Years. Garden City, N.Y.: Anchor Books, 1979.
Wheeler, Mary, _Steamboatin_' _Days_: _Folk_ _Songs_ _of_ _the_
    River _Packet_ _Era_. N.Y.: Arno Press, 1969 reprint.
White, John I., _Git_ _Along_, _Little_ _Dogies_: _Songs_ _and_
    Songmakers _of_ _the_ _American_ _West_. Urbana: Univer-
    sity of Illinois Press, 1975.
White, Newman I., _American_ _Negro_ _Folk-Songs_. Hatboro,
    Pa.: Folklore Associates, 1965 reprint.

Wilgus, D. K., _Anglo-American Folksongs Scholarship
    since 1898_. New Brunswick, N.J.: Rutgers Univer-
    sity Press, 1959.
Williams, Roger M., _Sing a Sad Song: The Life of Hank
    Williams_. Urbana: University of Illinois Press,
    1980.
Wolfe, Charles K., _The Grand Old Opry: The Early
    Years, 1925-35_. London: Old Time Music, 1975.

S O N G   I N D E X

*Denotes untitled song identified by its first line or key phrase.

ABOUT THE AUTHOR

Charles W. Darling is an Associate Professor of History at Youngstown State University where he teaches courses in American social and cultural history, American economic and business history, the Vietnam War, and American folk music. Since 1969 he has hosted a weekly music program, "Folk Festival," over WYSU-FM, the University's fine arts radio station.